The Travels
of
Marco Polo

The Travels
of
Marco Polo

A modern translation by
Teresa Waugh
from the Italian by Maria Bellonci

Facts On File Publications
460 Park Avenue South
New York, N.Y. 10016

This translation first published in
1984 in Great Britain by Sidgwick and Jackson Limited.

Translation copyright © 1984 by Sidgwick and Jackson Limited.

Color illustrations copyright © 1982 by
ERI Edizioni Radio Italiana, Via Arsenale 41, 10121 Torino, Italy.

Color photography by Sergio Strizzi from the film *Marco Polo*
produced by RAI Radiotelevisione Italiana, directed by
Giuliano Montaldo, artistic script by D. Butler, V. Labella, G. Montaldo.
All rights reserved.

Line illustration picture research by Anne Horton.

Published in the United States by
Facts on File, Inc.
460 Park Avenue South
New York, NY 10016

LIBRARY OF CONGRESS CATALOGING IN PUBLICATION DATA
Bellonci, Maria.
    The travels of Marco Polo.

    Includes index.
    1. Polo, Marco. 1254-1323?   2. Travelers—Italy—
Biography.   1. Title.
G370.P9B44   1984   910'.92'4   83-25290
ISBN 0-87196-890-8

Printed in Italy by
G. Canale & Co

10 9 8 7 6 5 4 3 2 1

Contents

1254-1277

Marco Niccolo and Matteo arrive at shang-to the Mongolian summer capital

Translator's Note

Whilst in prison in Genoa during the last years of the thirteenth century Marco Polo dictated an account of his travels to a fellow prisoner, the Pisan scribe Rustichello. The original was probably written in French and various versions were then copied into Latin and many other languages. Several translations have since been made into Italian and English. This translation of Marco Polo's journeys is from the new Italian version by Maria Bellonci. I have attempted to make an easily readable modern English version, and in so doing have of necessity lost some of the antique flavour, but it should be remembered that there must be an element of 'Russian Whispers' in anything which has been translated from a translation.

In the Italian text Marco Polo is sometimes referred to in the first person and sometimes in the third. For purposes of clarity I have consistently used the third person.

Although many of the place names will be familiar to the modern reader, there are others which distinguished scholars have had difficulty in identifying. I have used various sources for the correct place names but have relied to a considerable extent on the Penguin Classics translation by R. E. Latham.

Teresa Waugh

Marco Polo in prison at Genoa

Prologue

I MARCO POLO TELLS MAESTRO RUSTICHELLO ABOUT HIS TRAVELS

To kings and emperors, lords, knights, gentlemen and to all those who wish to
know about the habits of the human race in various parts of the world this book is
offered. Read it, for in it you will find described the great and diverse wonders of
the vast countries of the East – Armenia, Persia, Tartary, India – and many other
places. This is a clear and ordered account, as told by the wise and noble
Venetian Marco Polo, of the things he saw with his own eyes and of a few things
which he did not see himself but which he was told by honest men.

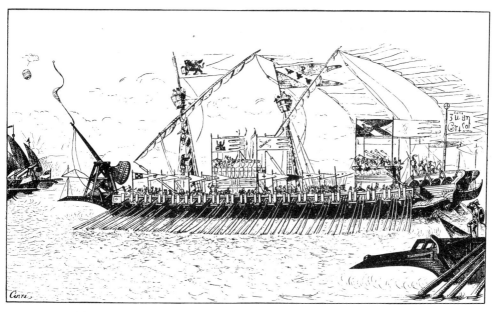

Marco Polo's galley going into action at Curzola before he was taken
prisoner

The reader must be prepared to believe everything in this book. It is all true.
And as a distinction is made between what Marco himself saw and hearsay, the

book is entirely reliable. Since God first created man, no Christian, Pagan, Tartar, Indian, or person of any other race has explored every part of the world as thoroughly as Marco Polo, nor seen so many of its wonders. He himself thought it would be wrong not to keep a record of the marvellous things he had seen and heard so that all those people who knew nothing about them could learn from this book.

Marco travelled for a good twenty-six years throughout the Orient; then, finding himself imprisoned in Genoa, he dictated this book to a fellow prisoner, Maestro Rustichello of Pisa. This was during the year 1298.

II MESSER NICCOLÒ AND MESSER MATTEO LEAVE CONSTANTINOPLE TO TRAVEL THROUGH THE WIDE WORLD

When Baldwin was Emperor of Constantinople – around the year 1250 – the Doge of Venice was represented in Constantinople by a certain Messer Ponte. Marco's father, Niccolò Polo, and Niccolò's brother, Matteo, were also there. The two brothers had come from Venice to trade with the East. With great prudence they decided, after some discussion, to cross the Black Sea with the intention of increasing their trade. They acquired a quantity of beautiful jewels and left Constantinople by sea for Sudak.

III NICCOLÒ AND MATTEO POLO LEAVE SUDAK

When they had spent some time in Sudak they decided to go further afield. They rode peacefully for a long while until they reached Barka Khan's territory. Barka Khan ruled over part of Tartary and lived at that time at Bolgara and at Sarai. He welcomed the two Venetians with great honour, obviously delighted by their visit. The two brothers sold him all the jewels they had brought from Constantinople. He was immensely pleased with the gems and paid twice their value for them, immediately sending them to different places to be splendidly set.

Niccolò and Matteo had been living in Barka's territory for a year when war broke out between Barka and Hulagu who ruled over the Levantine Tartars. The two armies attacked each other and fought a battle which resulted in great losses on both sides. Hulagu was eventually the victor.

War prevented people from travelling around freely since everyone risked being taken prisoner. In fact all retreat – the direction from which the two brothers had come – was forbidden, although it was possible to advance. So the brothers, having carefully considered the matter, decided that since they could not return to their business in Constantinople they would continue eastwards and return later to Constantinople by a different route. They prepared for their journey, left Bolgara and came to the town of Ucaca which was at the boundary of the eastern lord's territory. Beyond Ucaca they crossed the Tigris, then travelled for seventeen days through desert, where they encountered neither town nor village. They met only Tartar nomads with their tents and livestock.

IV   THE TWO BROTHERS CROSS A DESERT AND REACH THE TOWN OF BUKHARA

After having crossed the desert they came to the magnificent and great city of Bukhara. The province was also called Bukhara and was ruled over by a lord called Barak. Bukhara was the most important city in Persia. The two brothers soon realized that they could neither continue their journey nor return the way they had come so they stayed where they were for three years.

They were still in Bukhara when a messenger from Hulagu, the Lord of the Levant, passed through on his way to Kublai, the Great Khan of all the Tartars. The messenger saw Niccolò and Matteo Polo and was greatly surprised by them because he had never seen a Latin in these parts before. He said to the two brothers: 'Gentlemen, if you listen to me it will be considerably to your advantage and earn you great honour.'

The brothers replied that they were more than willing to listen.

The messenger went on to say: 'The Great Khan of the Tartars has never seen a man of Latin race and he greatly wishes to meet one. Let me take you to him. I assure you that he will be very pleased to see you and will welcome you with all honour. Also, you will be able to travel more easily and safely with me.'

V   THE TWO BROTHERS AGREE TO THE PROPOSALS OF THE GREAT KHAN'S AMBASSADOR

The two brothers listened to the messenger and willingly agreed to go with him. They travelled north-north-east for about a year until they reached the territory of the Lord of all the Tartars. During their journey they saw many marvels, all of which were seen later by Niccolò's son Marco and will eventually be fully described.

VI   THE TWO BROTHERS REACH THE GREAT KHAN'S COURT

When Messer Niccolò and Messer Matteo came to the court of the Great Khan he was pleased to see them and made them very welcome. He asked them all about their part of the world, and particularly about their emperors and whether they ruled wisely. He asked about their wars and enquired about all their affairs. He also wanted to know about the various types of government and about their kings, princes and noblemen.

VII   THE GREAT KHAN ASKS THE BROTHERS ABOUT THE CHRISTIAN RELIGION

The Great Khan asked them many questions about the Pope and the Roman Church, and about the habits of the Latin people. Niccolò and Matteo, who spoke Tartar perfectly and were well informed and intelligent men, answered truthfully, clearly and precisely.

VIII   THE GREAT KHAN NOMINATES THE TWO BROTHERS AS HIS AMBASSADORS TO THE PONTIFF OF ROME

Kublai Khan was Lord of all the Tartars in the world and ruled over all the provinces in this great stretch of land, and he was deeply interested by the clear and honest account which the two Venetians gave of the Latin people's way of life. He decided to send ambassadors to the Pope and begged the Polo brothers to take part in this mission, accompanied by one of his own barons. The brothers replied that they would be glad to act as loyal messengers. Kublai Khan then summoned one of his barons called Kogotal and told him that he was to go with the two brothers to the Apostolic See in Rome.

Kogotal replied: 'My Lord, as your loyal subject, I will do everything you ask.'

The nature of the mission was to beg the Pope to send Kublai 100 wise men, experts in the Christian religion, learned in the seven arts and articulate so that they could prove to those who believed in other religions that the idols they adored were things of the devil and that the Christian religion was greatly superior to any other. In addition, the Great Khan wanted the two brothers to bring him some of the oil from the lamp burning over Christ's sepulchre in Jerusalem. This, then, was the message sent by Kublai Khan to the Roman Pontiff.

IX   THE GREAT KHAN GIVES THE GOLDEN TABLET OF AUTHORITY TO THE BROTHERS

When the Great Khan had explained to the two brothers and to his baron how to present their mission to the Pontiff he gave them a tablet of gold. This sign of authority would ensure that the three men would be supplied with lodging and horses on their journey, as well as men to escort them from one province to another. Niccolò and Matteo then carefully prepared everything they thought they would need, took leave of the great ruler and set out on their journey.

A fourteenth-century miniature showing the Great Khan giving a golden
tablet of authority to the Polo brothers

They had ridden some way when Kogotal suddenly fell ill and was obliged to stop in a town. Niccolò and Matteo, seeing that he was in a poor way, left him and travelled on alone. Wherever they stopped they were given everything they could possibly need. They rode on, day after day, until after some three years they reached Ayas. They had suffered many delays caused by storms, heavy snow, and broad and swollen rivers.

X   THE TWO BROTHERS REACH THE CITY OF ACRE

From Ayas they headed straight for Acre which they reached in April 1269. Here they learnt that the Roman Pontiff (Clement) had died. Niccolò and Matteo therefore went to see the Legate of the Roman Church in Egypt, a wise priest of great authority called Tebaldo of Piacenza. They explained to him why the Great Khan of the Tartars had sent them to the Pontiff. The Legate listened with great amazement to the two brothers' story, concluding that the mission would have brought much good and great honour to Christendom.

'Gentlemen,' he said, 'the Pope is dead, but once a successor has been elected you will be able to take your mission to him.'

13

The two brothers agreed and replied that while awaiting the election they would go and visit their families in Venice. They then left Acre for Negropont where they boarded a ship and sailed to Venice.

In Venice, Niccolò found that his wife had died, leaving a fifteen-year-old son called Marco – the subject of this book. Niccolò and Matteo stayed in Venice for about two years, waiting for the new Pope to be elected.

XI   THE TWO BROTHERS LEAVE VENICE TO RETURN TO THE GREAT KHAN, TAKING WITH THEM NICCOLÒ'S SON MARCO

When no Pope had been elected after all this time the two brothers decided that they should return to the Great Khan. So they left Venice, taking the young Marco Polo with them, and went first to Acre to see the Church's Legate, Tebaldo of Piacenza. They talked to him at length and asked his permission to go to Jerusalem to take some of the oil from the lamp burning over Christ's sepulchre. When they returned, they went to the Legate and said: 'We can see that the election of a new Pope is continually being delayed. We would like to return to the Great Khan, for we are beginning to feel that we have waited too long.'

The Legate, who was one of the most important priests of the Church of Rome, replied: 'As soon as you want to, go back to the Great Khan.' He then prepared letters for Kublai and wrote references for Niccolò and Matteo.

XII   THE TWO BROTHERS AND THE YOUNG MARCO LEAVE ACRE

The two brothers set out from Acre carrying the letters which the Legate had written for them. They had only just reached Ayas when they learnt that the very Tebaldo of Piacenza who had welcomed them had been elected Pontiff and had taken the name 'Pope Gregory'. The brothers received the news with great joy. Shortly afterwards an envoy from the new Pope arrived in Ayas looking for Niccolò and Matteo and asked them to return to Acre. The brothers were happy to return and the King of Armenia himself had a galley fitted out for them and saw them off in great style to visit the new Pope.

XIII   THE TWO BROTHERS VISIT THE ROMAN PONTIFF

As soon as they arrived in Acre they went straight to the Pontiff and humbly prostrated themselves before him. The Pope welcomed them with honour, blessed them and fêted their arrival. He then prepared further letters for the Great Khan. Among other things, he asked that the Great Khan's brother, Abaka, Lord of the Levantine Tartars, might help Christians by making it easier for them to travel across the sea. He also sent the Great Khan many gifts, including beautiful vases and objects made of crystal. Next he nominated two Dominican friars to travel with Niccolò and Matteo. They were amongst the most knowledgeable in the country and were called Brother Niccolò of Vicenza and Brother Guglielmo of Tripolo. The Pontiff gave them letters and papers with his authority to exercise full religious powers in those far-away countries; they could, like the Pope himself, ordain priests and bishops, give or withhold absolution of sins. In the letters he explained everything he wanted the Great Khan to know.

Pope Gregory X

With the Pope's blessing all four, together with Niccolò's young son Marco, took their leave. They went straight to Ayas where they discovered that the Sultan of Egypt, Bundukdari, had invaded Armenia with a huge army, wreaking havoc throughout the country. The four messengers were in danger of being killed and the Dominican friars took fright, deciding not to continue on the journey. They handed all the Papal letters to Niccolò and Matteo and went away with the Grand Master of the Templars.

15

XIV   THE POLO BROTHERS, ACCOMPANIED BY YOUNG MARCO, REACH THE CITY OF KEMENFU WHERE THE GREAT KHAN WAS LIVING

Niccolò and Matteo and the young Marco rode on through winter and summer until they reached a very large and rich city called Kemenfu. The adventures they had on the way will all be described later. The journey took them three and a half years. Snow, rain, flooded rivers and fierce winds impeded their passage, and in winter they could travel only slowly. When the Great Khan heard that the Venetians were on their way he sent messengers to meet them – a journey of some forty days – and they were honoured and given everything they needed.

XV   THE TWO BROTHERS AND MARCO GO TO THE COURT OF THE GREAT KHAN

When Niccolò, Matteo and Marco reached Kemenfu they went to the Royal Palace where they found the Great Khan surrounded by a large assembly of his barons. They knelt down before him and greeted him with the greatest possible reverence. The Great Khan asked them to rise and welcomed them with rejoicing and honour. He asked about their health and how their journey and mission had been. The two brothers replied that all was well since they found the Khan flourishing and in good health. Then they handed him the papers and letters from the Pope, with which the Khan was greatly satisfied. Finally they presented him with the holy oil from the lamp at Jerusalem, which he received with much joy. At a certain point he noticed the young Marco and asked who the boy was.

'My Lord,' replied Niccolò, 'he is my son and your servant.'

'You are welcome,' said the Great Khan.

In short, the delight of the Great Khan and his court at the arrival of the two Venetians was incredible. They were honoured with magnificent feasts, all their needs were seen to. They remained at court and were given precedence over the other barons.

XVI   THE GREAT KHAN SENDS MARCO AS HIS AMBASSADOR

It so happened that Niccolò's son Marco adapted himself very quickly to Tartar customs. He learnt their language and their writing. Within a short time of his arrival at the Great Khan's court he knew four languages and the alphabet and writing of each. The young man proved himself wise and thoughtful and the Great Khan valued him for his goodness and worth. Precisely because he was so wise the Great Khan sent him on an important affair of state to a city called Kara-jang, which meant a journey of six months. The youth carried out the mission in the best possible way. Moreover he had observed a particular characteristic of the Khan. When messengers returned from different parts of the world and related the results of their missions the Khan called them foolish and ignorant if they could tell him nothing about the countries they had visited, because in fact he was more interested in the customs of those countries than in the missions. Knowing this, the young man paid attention to new and curious things so that he could report everything to the Great Khan. He also collected for himself many unusual objects.

XVII MARCO RETURNS FROM HIS FIRST MISSION WHICH HE RECOUNTS TO THE GREAT KHAN

As soon as he returned from his mission Marco presented himself to the Great Khan and told him the outcome of the affair; then he spoke of all the new and unusual things which he had seen on his journey. So interesting was his story that the Great Khan and everyone who heard it said to each other in their amazement, 'If this young man lives, he will certainly become someone of great knowledge and worth.'

The young Marco was accorded the title of Messer Marco Polo, by which he was known from this time on. Indeed, he well deserved the title by virtue of his great wisdom and excellent behaviour.

Marco stayed at the court of the Great Khan for some seventeen years during which time he was sent on many missions. The Great Khan, delighted by the news Marco brought back from every place he visited and pleased by his ability in every sort of dealing, entrusted him with all the most important missions. Marco carried them out in an exemplary fashion and always returned with interesting news and unusual objects. His methods greatly pleased the Khan, who grew very fond of him, holding him in much respect and keeping him always at his side, which aroused considerable jealousy among the barons at court.

This, then, is why Marco Polo, more than any other man, knew those parts of the world, their geography and the habits of their people. No one explored those far-off countries as thoroughly as he did, nor observed things of interest with a finer intelligence.

XVIII NICCOLÒ, MATTEO AND MARCO TAKE LEAVE OF THE GREAT KHAN

Having spent so many years at the Great Khan's court, Niccolò, Matteo and Marco decided to return to their own country. They had frequently begged the

The world as perceived by Marco Polo

Khan's permission to leave, but he loved them so much and was so happy to have them with him that for nothing in the world would he let them go.

Then it so happened that Queen Bulagan, the wife of Arghun, Lord of the Levant, died. The Queen left a will to the effect that no woman who was not of her lineage could marry Arghun and sit on her throne. Arghun sent three barons, Ulatai, Abushka and Koja, with a large retinue to the Great Khan, begging the Khan to send him a lady of the same lineage as Queen Bulagan. The Great Khan welcomed the three barons with much festivity and then summoned a lady called Kokachin. She was of the same lineage as Bulagan, seventeen years old, very beautiful and charming. The Khan told the barons that this was the right lady and they agreed enthusiastically.

Meanwhile, Marco had just returned from India, having crossed unknown seas and with much to tell about that vast country. When the three barons saw the wise Latins, Niccolò, Matteo and Marco, they asked the Great Khan as a favour to allow them to travel by sea with the three. As has been said, the Great Khan loved the Polo family and so it was only with reluctance that he allowed them to accompany the three barons and the lady.

XIX   THE POLOS TAKE THEIR LEAVE

As the time drew near for their departure, the Great Khan summoned Niccolò, Matteo and Marco to his presence and gave them the tablets of authority which would allow them to pass without hindrance through his provinces and be provided with food and an escort. He entrusted them with missions for the Pope, the King of France, and the King of Spain and other Christian kings. He then had fourteen ships fitted out: each one had four masts, and many of them had twelve sails. There is much more which could be said but it would take too long, although it must be mentioned that the crew of four or five of those ships numbered 250 or 260 sailors.

As soon as the ships were ready, the three barons, the lady, the Polo brothers and young Marco took their leave of the Great Khan and, with a large retinue, went on board. The Great Khan supplied them with two years' worth of provisions. They put to sea and sailed for three long months until they came to a southern island called Java. This island, as we shall see, was full of wonderful sights. They left Java and sailed on for at least eighteen months before reaching their destination. All the time they came across marvellous things of which this book will tell.

It should be said that more than 600 people, excluding sailors, had boarded the ships on this expedition, but only eighteen survived. Of the three envoys, only Koja was saved, and out of 100 women, only the princess remained alive.

An ancient Chinese ship

They arrived at their destination only to learn that Arghun was dead. He had been succeeded by the noble Kaikhatu who took the Princess Kokachin into his protection. He received the ambassadors and then ordered that the lady be given to Arghun's son, Ghazan, who was on the borders of Persia at the time with an army of 60,000 men, defending certain passes against enemy raids.

When Niccolò, Matteo and Marco had delivered the lady to her destination and presented the Great Khan's letters, they took their leave and prepared to travel on. Kaikhatu gave them gold tablets of authority, each of which was a cubit long and five fingers wide and weighed three or four pounds. Two of the four tablets bore a gerfalcon, one bore a lion and the other was plain. These tablets signified that the three messengers should be treated as Kaikhatu himself would be and supplied with food, horses, escorts and protection. On more than one occasion the travellers were given an escort of up to 200 men and horses, according to their needs, to escort them safely from one province to another. This was necessary since Kaikhatu was not the lawful sovereign and the people were liable to be hostile, which they would not have been under their rightful ruler.

There is another point worth mentioning. The Great Khan had such faith in the three messengers and such affection for them that not only had he entrusted Princess Kokachin to them but the daughter of the King of Manzi as well, who was also to be taken to Arghun, the Lord of the Levant. This they did, travelling, as has been said, by sea with a large retinue and at great expense. The three messengers watched over the two ladies as they would have over their own daughters, and the young and beautiful ladies looked on the Venetians as their fathers and obeyed them. Kokachin, who is now married to the present ruler Ghazan, was so fond of the three messengers that she would have done anything for them and wept bitterly when she saw them leave to return to their own country.

It was a great honour for the envoys that they should be entrusted with the care of conducting two such grand princesses to their lord in so distant a country. But enough of that.

The reader will hear how, after the three messengers left Kaikhatu's court, they went to Trebizond, from Trebizond to Constantinople, from Constantinople to Negropont, and from there to Venice which they reached in 1295.

That is the end of the Prologue and now the book will begin.

The Piazzetta in Venice in Marco Polo's day

I

The Middle East

XX LESSER ARMENIA

There are two Armenias, the Greater and the Lesser. The King of Lesser Armenia rules the country justly under the suzerainty of the Tartars. There are many towns and cities and the land is rich; it is also a country where all kinds of birds and animals are hunted. But the unhealthy climate is harmful to the inhabitants. The nobility, once a breed of valiant warriors, has degenerated into a race of sickly weaklings whose only prowess lies in their capacity for drinking. The rich trading town of Ayas is built on the coast, and to it are brought not only all the spices and silks from the interior, but many other precious goods, all of which attract merchants from Venice, Genoa and every other country. Anyone, merchant or otherwise, wishing to travel into the interior sets out from this city. Lesser Armenia is bordered on the south by the Promised Land under Saracen rule; to the north are the Turkish lands known as Karaman; to the east and north-east lies Turkey, with Kaisarieh, Sivas and many other towns ruled by the Tartars; to the west is the sea which divides that part of the world from Christendom.

Let us now turn to Turkey.

XXI TURKEY

In Turkey there are three different races. There are the Turkomans who worship Mohammed and who are faithful to his laws. These are primitive people who speak a rough and ready language and who live in the mountains or in the plains where livestock graze off rich pastureland. Many fine horses and sturdy mules are to be found here.

Then there are the Armenians and the Greeks who live together in the cities making a livelihood from trade and crafts. The finest carpets in the world are made here; crimson silk and silks in other rich and delicate colours are woven here, and many other precious objects are produced. The best-known cities are Konya, Kaisarieh and Sivas, but there are many more towns and villages which it

22

would take too long to list. They are subject to the Tartar who sends noblemen to govern them.

From Turkey let us turn to Greater Armenia.

XXII   GREATER ARMENIA

Greater Armenia covers a vast area. The first city one reaches is Erzincan where the best buckram in the world is worked and where the best spas are to be found. The Armenians are ruled by the Tartars. The country abounds in castles and cities, the most beautiful city being the archbishopric of Erzincan. Other important cities include Erzerum, where there is a very rich silver mine, and Ercis. It is a very large province and during the summer months the armies of the Levantine Tartars arrive with their livestock for the grazing. They leave in winter because the animals could not survive the cold and the enormous amount of snow and they move to warmer regions where they find plenty of grass and rich pastureland.

In the middle of Greater Armenia there is a very high mountain called the Mountain of the Ark on which it is said Noah's ark came to rest. It is so big that it would take more than two days to travel round it and the peak is always covered in snow so that no one can attempt to climb it. But because the melted snow flows so abundantly down the hillside the land at the bottom is particularly fertile and livestock from all around is brought here in the summer.

To the south of Greater Armenia lies the kingdom of Mosul inhabited by Christians, Nestorians and Jacobites, of whom more will be said later. To the north the country borders on Georgia of which more will also be said later. Near the Georgian boundary there is a spring of oil which flows so copiously that 100 ships at a time can be laden with it. It is not edible oil, but is used to burn and to grease camels as a protection against mange and dandruff. People come a long way for this oil and it is the only oil in the region which can be burnt.

Now we must turn from Greater Armenia to Georgia.

XXIII   THE GEORGIANS, THEIR KING AND OTHER MATTERS

The King of the Georgians is always called David Malik – or King David. He is subject to the Tartars, and it used to be said that the kings of that country were born with the mark of an eagle on their right shoulder. They are handsome, valiant people, excellent archers and strong in battle. They are Christians of the Greek Orthodox persuasion who wear their hair cut short like monks.

This is the region which, because of its narrow and dangerous paths, Alexander the Great was unable to cross on his eastward march. On one side is the sea and on the other a range of impassable mountains; the extremely narrow path winds on for four leagues in such a way that a mere handful of men can prevent anyone from advancing. For this reason not even Alexander the Great could make his way through. In this place, now known as the Iron Gates, Alexander had fortifications and a tower built to repel attacks. The Book of Alexander relates how he trapped the Tartars between two mountains on this spot. In fact, they were not Tartars – Tartars had not by then reached these parts – but a mixed race of people known as Comanians.

There are a great many towns in the region and the people depend on trade for their livelihood. There is an abundance of silk which is woven with gold thread to make the most beautiful material imaginable. Furthermore, the finest goshawks in the world are to be found here; in fact the land is rich in everything. The countryside is very mountainous and the impassable mountain routes make it quite impossible for the Tartars to subject it entirely to their rule. Then there is the monastery known as St Leonard's where a miracle takes place every year. Next to the church is a wide lake formed by the water which has flowed down the mountainside. No fish are to be found in that water, except during Lent; from the first day of Lent the lake begins to be filled with a multitude of fish which remain there until Holy Saturday. So for forty days there is always a good catch, whereas not one fish is to be found there at any other time.

The sea beneath the mountains is called the Ghelan Sea. It has a circumference of about 2,800 miles and is at least twelve days' walking distance from any other sea. It is entirely surrounded by mountains, and many rivers, including the Euphrates, the Tigris and the Gihon, flow into it. Recently Genoese traders have begun to cross it in their boats to bring back the silk known as *ghilan*. There is also in this province a very fine and beautiful city called Tiflis which is surrounded by a considerable number of dependent towns and castles. The inhabitants are mostly Christians, Armenians and Georgians, although there are also some Saracens and Jews.

XXIV THE KINGDOM OF MOSUL

Mosul is a vast kingdom inhabited by various races of men, as we shall see. There are Arabs who worship Mohammed and there is a race of Christians who do not adhere to the teachings of the Church of Rome and who, as a result, fall into considerable error. They are Nestorians and Jacobites; they have a patriarch whom they call Catholicus who nominates archbishops, bishops, abbots and every sort of priest, just as the Pope does. It should be borne in mind that all Christians in these parts are Nestorians and Jacobites.

In these parts material known as *mosulin* is woven from silk and gold thread.

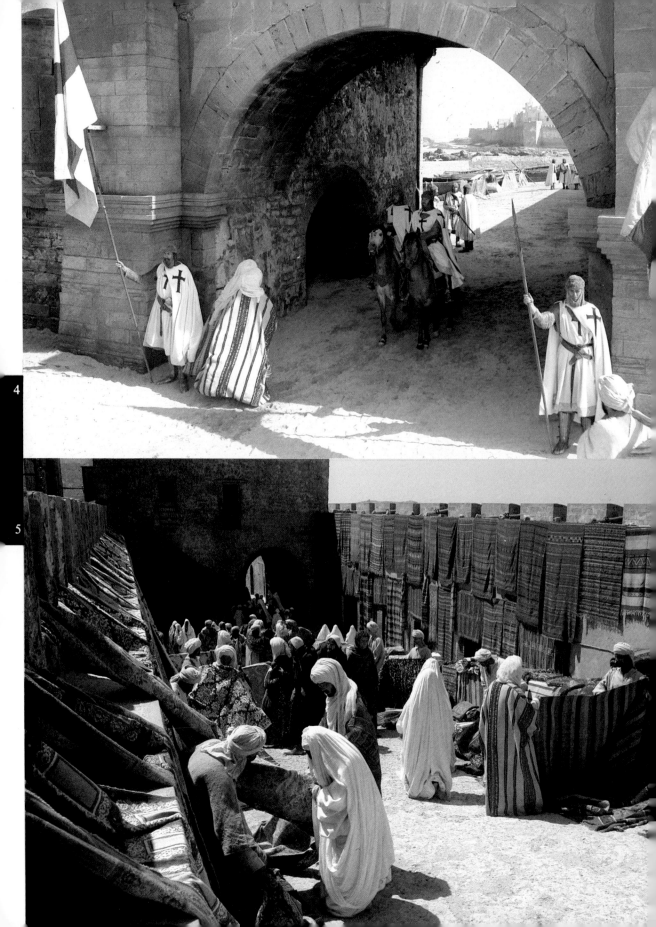

There are, too, some rich merchants who deal in huge quantities of the rarest spices and who are also called *mosulins*.

In the mountains in the interior of this kingdom lives yet another race – the Kurds, some of whom are Christian Nestorians and Jacobites and some of whom are followers of Mohammed. They are a warlike and ferocious people who frequently attack and rob the merchants.

Let us now leave the kingdom of Mosul and speak of the great city of Baghdad.

XXV   THE GREAT CITY OF BAGHDAD

Baghdad is a huge city where the Caliph of all the Saracens lives, just as the head of the Christian world lives in Rome. It is built on a large river which flows into the Indian Sea, and up and down which traders travel with their goods. It takes some eighteen days to reach the sea by river and merchants on their way to India sail down to the city of Kais where they come into the open sea. On the river, between Baghdad and Kais, is another city called Basra, in the woods around which the best date palms in the world can be found. In Baghdad itself a great variety of materials are worked – cloth of gold, silk, damask, brocade and cramoisy, embroidered with many different designs of animals. Most of the pearls imported from India into Christendom are pierced in Baghdad, and the city is a centre for the study of the laws of Mohammed, of necromancy, physics, geomancy and physiognomy. It is the most important and largest city in that part of the world.

It must be explained how it was discovered that the Caliph of Baghdad owned the greatest collection of gold, silver and precious objects ever to belong to one man.

In the early days of their power, the Tartar lords consisted of four brothers; the eldest, Mongu, was the Great Khan. They had already subjected Cathay to their rule, but this was not enough. They planned to conquer the world. So they divided it into four parts: one of them was to subjugate the Orient, another the south and the two others were to divide the rest. In about 1255, Hulagu, one of the four brothers, raised an enormous army and came to conquer Baghdad. It was a tremendous undertaking because there were in Baghdad over 100,000 cavalrymen, not to mention the infantry. Once he had taken the city, Hulagu discovered that the Caliph owned a tower full of gold, silver and precious objects such as had never been seen in one place. When Hulagu saw so much treasure, he was amazed and summoned the Caliph to his presence.

He asked the Caliph: 'Why have you amassed so much treasure? What were you planning to do with it? Didn't you realize that I was your enemy and that I would attack you with a large army in order to take your throne? And if so, why didn't you use your treasure to enlist more soldiers and to defend your city?'

The Caliph had no answer, so Hulagu went on to say: 'Since you are so fond of your treasure, I will make you eat it.' He then had the Caliph locked up in the tower and ordered that under no circumstances should he be given anything to eat or drink.

'You may eat your treasure to your heart's content since you like it so much,' Hulagu told the Caliph, 'and remember, you will never have anything else to eat again.'

The Caliph died in the tower after four days; he was the last of the Caliphs.

There is much more that could be said about the people of Baghdad, their affairs and their way of life, but it would take too long to tell. However, before turning to Tabriz, the story of the great miracle at least must be told.

XXVI THE GREAT MIRACLE OF THE MOUNTAIN

The following miracle occurred in Baghdad and Mosul around the year 1225. The Caliph of the time hated Christians so much that day and night he could think of nothing but how to make them become Saracens, or, if they refused, of killing them. He discussed the matter every day with his religious leaders who themselves hated Christians, for, as is well known, Saracens are the fiercest enemies of Christians. In discussion with his advisers, the Caliph formulated the following plan. It was written in one of the Gospels that if a Christian had as much faith as a grain of mustard, he could, by praying to his god, move mountains. When the Caliph and his men discovered this they were overjoyed because they thought they had found either a way of making Christians become Saracens or an excuse to murder them all. Then the Caliph summoned together all the Nestorians and Jacobites who were in the city and showed them the Gospel, asking them if it was true. The Christians replied that it was.

'So,' the Caliph said, 'you claim that if a Christian has as much faith as a grain of mustard, he can, by praying to his god, move mountains?'

The Christians answered, 'Certainly.'

'This, then, is what I propose,' the Caliph told them. 'There are so many of you Christians that at least one man among you must have a little faith. You must either move that mountain,' and he pointed to a mountain near the city, 'or you will all die a dreadful death. If you cannot move the mountain it will mean that you have no faith and you will die; either that or you will convert to the true religion which the Prophet Mohammed has taught us, and by the true faith save yourselves. I give you ten days to do this, and if after that time you have not done what I ask, I will have you killed.'

26

XXVII   THE GREAT FEAR INSPIRED IN THE CHRISTIANS BY THE CALIPH'S THREATS

When they heard what the Caliph had to say, the Christians were terrified and suffered considerable anguish. Nevertheless, they had faith that the Creator would help them in the hour of their need. So the bishops, archbishops and many priests in Baghdad met together to discuss the matter. The only solution was to pray that the Lord in His mercy would help them in their danger and save them from the cruel death with which the Caliph threatened them. The Christians prayed day and night, devoutly beseeching the Saviour, the Lord of heaven and earth, to come to their aid. All the Christians, men, women and children, prayed for eight days and eight nights. While they were praying, an angel, a messenger of God, appeared to one particularly saintly bishop. The angel said to the bishop, 'Go to that cross-eyed shoemaker and tell him to pray for the mountain to be moved, and then the mountain will immediately move.'

The shoemaker was an honest man who lived a chaste life. He attended mass every day and shared his bread with the poor. No one led a more religious life than he and there was one particular reason why his saintliness and faith were known to everyone.

He knew from the Gospel that if the eye offends, it must be plucked out to prevent further occasion for sin. One day a very beautiful woman came to this man's shop to buy a pair of shoes. The shoemaker asked her to show him her leg and her foot so that he could tell which shoes would suit her. It would have been hard to find a more elegant pair of feet or finer legs, and when this good and chaste man saw them he was overcome with temptation and looked at them with pleasure. Suddenly he asked the woman to leave the shop and refused to sell her the shoes. When she had gone he berated himself, saying, 'False and treacherous man that I am, what am I doing thinking these lustful thoughts? I must take vengeance on my eyes which have shocked me so.'

Without hesitation he picked up a little awl and sharpened it carefully before thrusting it into one of his eyes so that the eye burst open inside his head and he could no longer see with it. So, in effect, the shoemaker plucked out his eye, proving in this way that he was a really virtuous and saintly man.

XXVIII   THE DIVINE APPARITION

The angel reappeared several times to the bishop and repeated that the shoemaker's prayers would move the mountain. The bishop told the other Christians about his recurrent vision and they decided to summon the shoemaker.

When he came he knew that they needed his prayers to work a miracle. But when he heard what the bishop and the Christians had to say he replied that he did not feel he was good enough to have been chosen by God to move the mountain. The Christians begged him to pray for them and eventually he agreed.

XXIX   THE SHOEMAKER'S PRAYERS MOVE THE MOUNTAIN

On the tenth day all the Christians, large and small, men and women, rose early and went to sing mass. When they had finished singing and the mass was over, they lined up behind the Cross of the Saviour and began to walk towards the plain out of which rose the mountain. On reaching the plain – there were more than 100,000 of them – they spread themselves out around the Cross. Certain that the mountain would not be moved, the Caliph and large numbers of Saracens had also come – to kill the Christians. Although they were very frightened, the Christians of all ages still put their trust in their Maker. When all the Christians and Saracens were gathered in the plain, the shoemaker knelt in front of the Cross, lifted his arms to heaven and fervently prayed to the Lord to make the mountain move so that all the Christians there would not be cruelly put to death. When he had finished his prayer the mountain began to move, first to tremble and then to advance.

When the Caliph and the Saracens saw what was happening they were so astonished that many of them were converted to Christianity. The Caliph himself was converted, but secretly, and it was not until his death that a cross was found hung round his neck. Because of this he was not buried in the tomb with the other caliphs, but in a separate place. That, then, is how the miracle came about.

XXX   TABRIZ

Tabriz is a large city built in the district known as Iraq where there are also many other cities. But Tabriz is by far the grandest of these cities. It is surrounded by beautiful gardens full of flowers and every kind of fruit. Its inhabitants live by trade and craft, making much cloth of gold and valuable silk. The city is particularly well situated: merchandise is brought there from India, Baghdad, Mosul and Hormuz and many other places, and large numbers of Latin traders come there to buy all these riches. Here, merchants who have travelled a long way can make important deals.

The citizens of Tabriz are not very well considered. They are of mixed races including Armenians, Nestorians, Jacobites, Georgians, Persians as well as native Mohammedans. The Saracens there are particularly wicked and treacherous. The law of the Prophet Mohammed has taught them that they may maltreat as they please men of other religions; they may assault and rob them with impunity, and if it were not for the supervision and authority of the government they would do a great deal of evil. Saracens the world over seem to behave in this way.

From Tabriz we go on to Persia.

XXXI   THE GREAT PROVINCE OF PERSIA

Persia is an enormous territory which in antiquity was a noble country of great importance, but now it has been ruined and ravaged by the Tartars. Saveh, the city from which the three kings set out to worship the infant Christ, is in Persia and the three fine, great tombs of the kings are still to be seen there. Over each of these tombs has been constructed a square building surmounted by a very finely-carved dome. The tombs are close to one another and Balthasar, Caspar and Melchior, the three embalmed kings, can be seen with their hair and their beards. Marco Polo asked many people about the three Magi but no one knew anything about them except that they were three kings who had been buried there for a long time. Eventually he was able to discover more.

Three days' walk from Saveh he came to a town called Kala Atashparastan which means castle of fire-worshippers. The name was justified since the inhabitants of this place did indeed worship fire. Their explanation for this was that a long time ago three kings from the district had gone to visit a newly-born prophet, taking with them gold, frankincense and myrrh in order to discover if the prophet were God, a king or a sage. They thought that if he accepted the gold he would be a king, if he took the incense he would be God and if he took the myrrh he would be a sage.

When they reached the place where the baby had only recently been born, the youngest of the three kings went in to see him alone. He found that the baby looked like himself, appearing to be the same age and to have the same features. He came out amazed. The second youngest king then went to see the baby and he also had the impression that he was seeing someone of his own age with his own physical appearance. He, too, was astounded. Then the third and oldest king went in and the same thing happened to him as to the other two. He came out deep in thought. Finding themselves together again, the three kings told each other what they had seen and were greatly surprised. They decided to go back to the baby together. When they were all in front of the child they found that he had the appearance of a thirteen-day-old baby. They worshipped him and offered him the gold, frankincense and myrrh. He accepted the three gifts and then gave them a closed casket. The three kings left to return to their own country.

XXXII   THE THREE MAGI'S STORY

When they had been riding for several days the kings decided that they wanted to see what the child had given them. They opened the casket and found a stone inside it. They were very surprised by this gift and discussed it for a long time because they could not understand its significance. When the baby had accepted all three offerings, the wise men had decided that the child was at once God, king and sage. The child, knowing that faith had been born in the Magi, had given them the stone as a sign that they should be as firm as a rock in the faith which they had glimpsed. But the kings were unable to understand why they had been given the stone so they threw it in a well. But as soon as they had done so a burning flame from heaven struck the well. The three men were dumbfounded by this omen and regretted having flung away the stone for they realized that this had been a miraculous sign. So they took some of the fire which had been kindled and put it in a rich and beautiful church where it has been burning perpetually ever since, and where it is worshipped as a god. Burnt offerings to the divinity are placed on this fire and should the flame ever go out it is relit from fires belonging to people of the same religion. It can never be relit in any other way, although a journey of ten days may be needed to find the same fire. So this was how the cult of the fire-worshippers originated – and it has no small number of followers. This story was told directly to Marco Polo by the inhabitants of Kala Atashparastan and is the absolute truth. As for the three kings, one came from Saveh, one from Hawah, and the third from Kashan.

Now it is time to say more about the many other Persian cities and their customs.

XXXIII   THE EIGHT KINGDOMS OF PERSIA

The great area called Persia contains eight kingdoms whose names are as follows: the first one to be reached, coming from Tabriz, is Kasvin; then, to the south, is Kurdistan; the third and the fourth are Luristan and Shulistan; the fifth is Isfahan; the sixth Shiraz; the seventh is Shabankara; and the eighth and last kingdom of Persia is Tun and Kain. All these kingdoms lie to the south of Kasvin with the exception of Tun and Kain which is nearer to the Solitary Tree.

There is a magnificent breed of precious horses in these parts. They can cost as much as 200 pounds of *touraine** each; in fact most of them cost that much. There are also the finest donkeys in the world which, because they are so sturdy and swift, are worth around thirty silver marks each. They eat very little and can

---

Livre tournois, 1lb being equivalent to ¼lb of sterling.

travel a long way in one day – further, in fact, than any horse or mule. Traders travelling in those parts have to cross vast sandy and arid deserts where nothing grows which could possibly be used to feed animals. The wells are far apart and on the long journeys from one to the other horses collapse from exhaustion. Camels are also used because they can carry huge loads and do not eat much, but they are slower than donkeys. The peoples of these kingdoms take their horses down to Kais and Hormuz, two towns on the Indian Sea, where merchants are prepared to pay a high price for them.

These kingdoms are inhabited by cruel and murderous people; they frequently kill each other and but for their fear of the Levantine Tartar they would commit every sort of crime against travelling tradesmen. But the laws are not enough to protect the merchants from every assault and robbery, and unless they defend themselves with cunning and arms they may be cruelly killed and wounded. Needless to say, these people are followers of the Prophet Mohammed.

There are a great many traders and artisans earning their living in the cities. They make every kind of cloth of gold and their fields produce rich crops of cotton. They also grow cereals, barley, millet, panic grass, all sorts of fodder and a variety of fruits. One may think that the Saracens drink no wine since their religion forbids it. But they interpret their religion in their own way: the wine only has to come to the boil for a few minutes, reduce a little bit and become sweeter, and they can drink it without breaking their law. They no longer call it wine. The name is boiled away with the taste.

Let us now turn from these kingdoms to the great city of Yazd.

XXXIV   YAZD

Yazd is another beautiful great trading city of Persia. The silk woven there is also called Yazd and is much in demand by merchants who make a lot of money by taking it all over the world. The inhabitants worship Mohammed.

Anyone wishing to travel beyond these regions must ride for seven days across an endless plain where there are only three villages in which to stay. But there are also, at frequent intervals, delightful little palm groves to be ridden through, all full of game – grouse and partridges, which are a great pleasure to travelling merchants, are to be found in those pleasant places. And there are beautiful wild donkeys. A journey of seven days takes the traveller to Kerman.

XXXV   THE KINGDOM OF KERMAN

The kingdom of Kerman is also part of Persia and used to be ruled by a hereditary dynasty, but since the Tartar conquest, power is no longer handed down from father to son: overlords are chosen by the Tartars and sent to govern the kingdom. In Kerman large quantities of stones called turquoises are excavated from the rocky mountains.

There are also deposits of steel and *ondanique**, and the finest cavalry equipment is made here – saddles, spurs, bits, swords, bows, quivers and any other piece of armour which might be needed.

Women and girls show great imagination in embroidering silks of every colour with birds and animals and other designs. For the noblemen they make enchantingly beautiful curtains, as well as bedcovers, cushions and pillows, all embroidered with great delicacy.

Falcons, some of the strongest flyers in the world, nest in the mountains here; they are a little smaller than peregrine falcons and have red breasts and red on the inside of their legs. They fly so fast that no bird in the world can escape from them.

Beyond the city of Kerman lies a plain with many more cities, towns and dwellings. It takes seven days to ride across this plain. It is a very pleasant ride, through countryside filled with game, especially partridges. After seven days the traveller will come to the foot of a very high mountain and here the path begins to wind downhill; he will travel on downwards between gardens and orchards for two whole days. Once this place was densely populated, but this is no longer the case; there are now only a few herdsmen with their flocks. The whole of this area is so cold in winter that it is hard to survive even with many clothes and furs.

An experiment which took place in the kingdom of Kerman is worth mentioning. The people there are honourable, peaceful and simple, and they help each other. On one occasion the King of Kerman, in consultation with his advisers, announced: 'There is one thing which has come to my notice and which I fail to understand: whereas the inhabitants of the Persian kingdoms which surround us are wicked and bloodthirsty and are forever killing each other, our people, who are only next door, do not squabble among themselves.'

His advisers replied that it must have something to do with the soil. The King then sent some envoys to Persia – in fact to Isfahan where, as has already been said, the people excel in all the worst qualities – asking them to bring back seven shipments of earth. When the earth arrived, he ordered it to be spread on the floor of several rooms and had it covered with carpets. A great banquet was to take place in these very rooms and as soon as the food was handed around, the guests began to insult and threaten each other and even to kill each other. So the King was convinced that the difference between his people and others really was caused by the soil in their countries.

*High-grade Indian steel.

XXXVI The City of Kamadin

After this downhill journey of two days the traveller reaches a vast plain. The city of Kamadin stands just on the edge of the plain. It was once a rich and powerful city, but its importance has been greatly diminished since it has been sacked several times by the Tartars. The plain on which this city is built is extremely hot. The region is called Rudbar and it produces dates, passion fruit, pistachios and other fruits which cannot be grown in cold climates. There is wheat and cereal and a large population of turtle doves who thrive on the variety of berries growing there. The quantity of doves is due to the fact that the Saracens do not like to eat them. There are also partridges known as francolin partridges which are unlike partridges anywhere else, being black and white with red beaks and claws. The other animals also are unusual; the oxen, for instance, are very large, as white as snow and suitably short-haired for the hot climate. Their horns are stumpy, thick and blunted, and between their shoulders they have a kind of rounded lump nearly two spans high. They seem the most pleasing creatures in the world. They kneel down like camels to be laden, and when they stand up they are well able to bear their load as they are very strong. There are also rams as big as donkeys with thick, fat tails which must weigh at least thirty pounds; they are very fine and fat and good to eat.

Many of the towns and cities in this plain are surrounded by high walls to protect them from bands of marauding brigands called the Karaunas, which means half-breed because their mothers are Indian and their fathers Tartar. When these thieves want to ransack a village they work a diabolical spell – they darken the day so that two people standing close together can barely see each other. This cloak of darkness can cover a distance of seven days' walking, and as the Karaunas know the country well they ride along side by side in the dark – sometimes as many as 10,000 of them – covering the whole area they want to sack. Everything they see they take – men, objects and animals. They kill the old and carry the young away to sell as slaves.

Their king is called Nigudar. Once he went with 10,000 men to the court of his uncle, Chaghatai, the Great Khan's brother. He wanted to stay there because his uncle was a very powerful man, but while he was there he committed the following very dishonest deed: he left the court of his uncle, who was in Armenia at the time, and with his 10,000 cruel and lawless men he crossed Badakhshan, Pashai and the province of Kashmir where, because of the treacherous paths, he lost many men and animals. Then he came to a part of India known as Dilivar where he took possession of the town of the same name and usurped the King, a rich and powerful man called Asidin Sultan. Nigudar, afraid of no one, settled in with his army and began to wage war on the Tartars whose lands bordered on his kingdom. His men, who were Tartars and white, mixed with the dark-skinned Indian women and the children born to them were called 'Karaunas', which means mixed. And they are the brigands who, having learnt in Dilivar diabolical ways of making darkness fall, scour the plains of Rudbar and other countries. The Karaunas use their magic darkness to plunder at will, kidnapping men and selling those who are unable to pay ransom.

Marco Polo himself was nearly captured in this way, but he managed to escape and take refuge in a castle called Kamasal. Some of his companions were caught, however, and were sold as slaves; and some were even killed.

XXXVII THE GREAT DESCENT

The plain which has been mentioned earlier stretches for another five days' journey to the south and then reaches a twenty-mile descent where the worst and most dangerous paths are overrun by brigands. At the bottom of this descent there is another plain called the plain of Hormuz which takes two days to cross. Here are fresh streams, date palms and other fruits, parrots, francolin partridges and many other birds unknown to us.

After a two-day journey the traveller reaches the Ocean, and on the coast is the city of Hormuz with its fine port. This is where the Indian merchants land after crossing the sea in ships laden with every type of spice, all sorts of precious stones, pearls, cloth of gold, elephants' tusks and a variety of other merchandise. They sell their goods to other traders in the city who export them all over the world. Hormuz is an extremely busy city with many other cities and towns dependent on it, and the capital of a kingdom. The King is called Ruemedan Ahmad. Because of the intense heat the country is very unhealthy. When a foreign trader dies, the King confiscates all his belongings.

A very delicious and highly-spiced date wine is made here which acts as a strong purgative when drunk by anyone unused to it. Apart from that it is good for people and makes them fatter. The natives of Hormuz do not eat the same food as we do (wheat bread and meat) because it would make them ill, so for the sake of their health they eat dates and salted fish, like tunny; they also eat a lot of onions. This kind of diet suits their climate.

The ships are very badly built and often sink because instead of being nailed together with iron nails the planks are sewn together with thread made from coconut husks. The husks are soaked until they become like very strong horsehair which will not rot in salt water. The ships are all open and each one has a mast, a sail and a rudder. Since they have no iron anchors, they use wooden pegs and various other instruments. It is very dangerous to sail in those ships; they are often sunk by the many storms in the Indian Sea.

The people are dark-skinned and worship Mohammed. In the summer everyone leaves the city or they would die of the heat. They go away to their gardens where there are many streams, and beside the rivers they build shelters made of rushes, one side of which stands on the bank while the other is supported in the water by stakes, with a roof of leaves as protection from the sun. Even so, they are not safe under certain circumstances. Quite often during the summer a sandstorm is whipped up from the surrounding plains by a wind so hot that it would kill anyone who was not warned in time to rush to the river and immerse himself in water up to the neck. In that way the people can save themselves.

Marco Polo, who happened to be in those parts during the hot weather, gave the following account of an event that took place while he was there. The Lord of Hormuz had not paid the tribute due to the King of Kerman and the King decided to claim it at a time when the people of Hormuz were living in the hinterland, a long way from the city. The King mustered an army of 1,600 cavalry and 5,000 infantry which he sent across the Rudbar plain to take the people by surprise. It so happened that because the soldiers were badly led they did not reach their destination before nightfall, but lay down to sleep in a wood a long way from Hormuz.

In the morning they started to move but the hot wind was blowing so that they were all suffocated and no one was left to take the news back to their King. When the men of Hormuz heard what had happened they went to bury the bodies to prevent the air from becoming infected, but when they picked them up by the arms to put them in the graves they discovered that they had been cooked by the great heat and the arms came away from the bodies. They had to dig the graves very close to the dead so that they could push them in.

In these parts the wheat and fodder are sown in November and harvested in March; so are all other crops, as everything ripens in March. By April there is nothing green to be seen in the whole country except for the date palms which last until May. The heat dries everything up.

With regard to the ships, it must be added that they are not tarred but greased with fish oil to prevent the wood from rotting.

Anyone who dies is greatly mourned – both men and women. Widows weep for their husbands for at least four years after their death, wailing in a high-pitched voice once a day. All the neighbours and relations gather round and lament the deceased with much howling and crying; and since there are a lot of deaths there is no end to the lamentations. There are women in this country who are so good at crying that for a price they will cry for any length of time beside anyone's grave.

Enough of Hormuz. India will be dealt with later; we will now turn north and follow another route back to Kerman because there are some places in the north which can only be reached from that city. It will be remembered that Ruemedan Ahmad is a vassal of the King of Kerman. The journey back from Hormuz to Kerman is across a beautiful and richly fertile plain where there are also many hot-water springs. There are a lot of inexpensive partridges and masses of dates and fruit. But the wheat bread in these parts is so sour that those who are unused to it find it uneatable. This is because the water there has a bitter taste. The water from the springs is very hot and good for many illnesses, especially skin infections.

Now the more northern countries will be described.

XXXVIII   A POOR AND WILD COUNTRY

Seven days' journey northwards on bad roads will take the traveller out of Kerman. For three days there is very little water and what there is tastes brackish. It is as green as grass and too bitter to be drunk; one single drop is enough to cause more than ten bowel movements, and one grain of salt from that water has the same effect. Travellers must carry their drinking water with them; only the hard-working animals drink this green water so as not to die of thirst and it has the same burning effect on their stomachs. For these first three days there is no sign of a human habitation, nothing but arid desert; there are not even any animals, for the simple reason that there is nothing there for them to eat. On the fourth day the traveller comes to a river of fresh water. It runs underground but in some places there are deep caverns worn away by the running water where the river is visible before it plunges back underground. There is a lot of water, and men who are worn out by the rough desert journey can rest beside it with their animals and revive themselves. The last three days of the journey are across more desert until finally the city of Kuh-banan is reached.

XXXIX   KUH-BANAN, A LARGE AND NOBLE CITY

Kuh-banan is a large city where Mohammed is worshipped. There is much iron, steel and *ondanique* and they make big, very shiny steel mirrors here as well as producing *tutty** which is good for the eyes, and *spodium*. They do this by piling earth particularly suited to the purpose in a very hot furnace on top of which is a kind of iron grid. The smoke and humidity escaping from the earth are collected on the grid and consist of *tutty*. The residue is *spodium*.

Now we must leave this city.

*Zinc oxide.

XL ANOTHER DESERT

After Kuh-banan there is another journey of eight days across a completely arid desert devoid of fruit and trees and where the water is as bitter and bad as that which has already been described. The traveller must take all food and drink, except water for the animals, with him, although even the animals are reluctant to drink the bad water.

After a journey of eight days the province of Tun and Kain with its many cities and castles is reached. This country lies along the borders of northern Persia. Here there is an endless plain out of which rises the Solitary Tree, known to Christians as the Dry Tree. This tree is huge and sturdy with leaves that are green on one side and white on the other. It produces husks like chestnut husks, but there is nothing inside them. The wood is tough and yellowish like boxwood. It is the only tree within a hundred-mile radius except in one direction where there are some trees ten miles away. And this, according to the people in those parts, is where the battle between Alexander and Darius took place.

The Solitary Tree

The cities and towns are filled with plenty of good and beautiful things because the climate is temperate throughout the region. The people worship Mohammed. The men are very fine to look at, and as for the women, they are magnificent.

Now we will turn to the region of Mulehet where the Old Man of the Mountain used to live.

37

XLI   THE OLD MAN OF THE MOUNTAIN

Mulehet, the name given to heretical Saracens, is also the name of the famous place where the Old Man of the Mountain used to live. This is the story of the Old Man just as it was told to Marco Polo by many people.

According to legend, the Old Man was called Alaodin. He had had made, in a valley between two mountains, the biggest and most beautiful garden imaginable. Every kind of wonderful fruit grew there. There were glorious houses and palaces decorated with gold and paintings of the most magnificent things in the world. Fresh water, wine, milk and honey flowed in streams. The loveliest girls versed in the arts of caressing and flattering men played every musical instrument, danced and sang better than any other women. The Old Man had persuaded his men that this was Paradise. The Prophet Mohammed had taught that those who went to Paradise would find as many beautiful women as they wanted, rivers of wine, milk, honey and fresh water. So the Old Man of the Mountain had had his garden built like Mohammed's Paradise and the Saracens really believed it was Paradise.

However, only men who were to become murderers could go into the garden. There was just one entrance, guarded by a fort able to withstand any attack. The Old Man kept at his court all the boys between the ages of twelve and twenty who showed any aptitude for battle. All these boys had heard tell that Mohammed's promised land was like this garden and they firmly believed in it.

The Old Man made these boys go into the garden in groups of four, ten, or sometimes twenty. First he had drinks prepared for them which sent them straight to sleep, then he had them carried into the garden, where they woke up. When they awoke and saw the wonderful things around them they thought they were in Paradise. Women and girls with whom they could take their pleasure at will played and sang to them. The boys had everything they wanted and for nothing in the world would they have left this paradise.

XLII   THE OLD MAN TRAINS HIS ASSASSINS

The Old Man's court was rich, splendid and sumptuous and he made the simple mountain people believe that he was a prophet.

When he wanted to have someone killed, he ordered the sleeping draught to be given to some of the boys in the garden and when they were asleep he had them brought to his castle. When they awoke to find themselves in the palace they were surprised and highly displeased. They went to the Old Man and, believing him to be a great prophet, knelt at his feet. When the Old Man asked where they had come from they replied, 'From Paradise', and assured him that the paradise promised to their forefathers by Mohammed really existed, telling the Old Man of all the delights to be found there. The other boys who had not been there longed to go and would willingly have died, indeed were eager to do so as soon as possible. So when the Old Man wanted an important person killed he put his assassins to the test to find out which of them was the boldest. He sent a fairly large group of them to a nearby province and told them to kill a man. When they had done so they came back to court – that is to say, those who were not captured and put to death. Those who returned, having accomplished the mission, were warmly welcomed by the Old Man. He knew perfectly well which of them had been the bravest because he sent spies to report back to him.

XLIII   THE ASSASSINS AND THE END OF THE OLD MAN

In this way the Old Man knew whom to trust when he wanted someone killed. He could send the boys wherever he wanted by telling them that he was making sure that they went quickly to Paradise. If they died carrying out their mission they would go straight there. The idea of going to Paradise made the assassins very happy, so they went off and did whatever they were asked, unafraid of death. Many kings and barons paid tribute to the Old Man and cultivated his friendship for fear of being murdered. The Old Man was aided in this by the fact that the kings were always quarrelling amongst themselves and were not united under one power.

So much for the way of life of the Old Man of the Mountain and his assassins. Now we come to his death. But first there is one other thing: this Old Man had nominated two other Old Men of the Mountain to serve under him; they behaved exactly as he did. He sent one of them to a place near Damascus and the other to Kurdistan.

In about 1262, Hulagu, the Lord of the Levantine Tartars, having heard of the Old Man's horrible ways, decided to destroy him. Hulagu chose a few of his barons and sent them with a large army to attack the Old Man's fortified castle. It seemed impossible to capture and would certainly never have been taken if the people inside had been able to get food. The siege lasted three years, by the end of which time there was nothing left to eat. The Old Man of the Mountain, Alaodin, was captured and put to death with all his men, and the castle and the garden of paradise were demolished. So that ended the evil rule of the Old Man of the Mountain and his assassins.

The time has now come to turn to other matters.

II

The Road to Cathay

XLIV   THE CITY OF SHIBARGHAN

On leaving the Old Man's castle the traveller rides through a beautiful plain with agreeable valleys and gentle, fertile hills; the pastureland is good and the fruit plentiful, which is why the army is stationed there in the summer. This countryside takes six days to cross and the inhabitants are Mohammedans. At intervals there are fifty- or sixty-mile stretches of desert with no water at all, so the traveller must take his own. The animals drink when they have crossed the desert and reach places where there is plenty of water.

After riding for six days the traveller comes to the town of Shibarghan where an abundance of everything is to be found. The best melons in the world are eaten there, prepared in the following way: they are cut into strips and put in the sun to dry until they become sweeter than honey. They are sold in large quantities in the neighbouring territories. There are also a great many wild animals and birds in this region. But now for Balkh.

XLV   THE GREAT AND NOBLE CITY OF BALKH

Balkh is a large and magnificent city. In the past it was even larger and more important but it has been sacked and plundered by the Tartars. There used to be many marble palaces and beautiful houses but they are all in ruins now. If the inhabitants are to be believed, it was here that Alexander married Darius's daughter. The people worship Mohammed and the city stands at the north-east frontier of Persia at the limits of the Lord of the Levantine Tartars' domain.

Next we come to a place called Talikhan which is a good twelve days' ride from Balkh across uninhabited lands, the people having fled to the mountains for fear of the enemy who ravaged the countryside. There is plenty of water, a considerable amount of game and also a lot of lions. During the whole twelve days' ride there is nothing to be found to eat so the traveller would be advised to take food for himself and for his animals.

40

XLVI THE SALT MOUNTAINS

At the end of this journey there is a town called Talikhan where there is a very big grain market. It is situated in magnificent surroundings: to the south rises a range of majestic salt mountains and other mountains which are rich with almonds and pistachios – both valuable commodities. People travel for thirty days from every direction for the salt, which is the best to be found. It is so hard that it has to be hacked up with iron picks, but there is so much of it that the whole world could be supplied forever.

From Talikhan a three days' ride takes the traveller through more beautiful and well-populated countryside where fruit, cereals and vines grow. The people here, who are evil and bloodthirsty, worship Mohammed. They drink a lot and often, and they are delighted to do so because they make excellent boiled wine. They wear nothing on their heads but a cord some ten spans in length which they wrap round and round. They are very good huntsmen and their clothing and shoes are made from the cured skins of the animals they have caught. Everyone knows how to cure skins.

Three days further on is a city called Ishkasham which stands on a fairly wide river and which is in the domain of a lord who rules over a number of other cities and castles spread among the mountains. There is a large number of porcupines which, when the huntsmen send their dogs after them, roll themselves up into small balls and hurl themselves at the dogs, wounding them with their quills. The region, which is also called Ishkasham, is really large and the people speak their own language. The peasants with livestock live in agreeable dwellings cut into the mountains. This is possible because the mountains are made of earth and not of rock.

On leaving Ishkasham the traveller will find no food or water or human habitation for three days. There is enough grass for the horses, but he must carry his own provisions with him. After three days he will come to the province of Badakhshan.

XLVII THE GREAT KINGDOM OF BADAKHSHAN

Mohammed is worshipped in the province of Badakhshan and a language unlike any other is spoken there. It is ruled by an hereditary dynasty descended from Alexander and Darius's daughter. Every man who inherits the throne is called Zulkarnein, which means Alexander, after Alexander the Great.

Beautiful and valuable rubies are mined, like silver, from deep in the mountains. They are mainly found in the mountain called Sighinan. Only the King has the right to mine the rubies. Anyone caught stealing them is immediately put to death, and anyone trying to take the stones out of the kingdom

41

without authority risks losing his life and possessions. This is because the rubies are extremely valuable and if people were allowed to export them their value would soon be lowered. The King uses the rubies as gifts or tributes to other kings, princes or great lords. He also exchanges them for gold and silver.

In the same province, but in another mountain, the most precious and the bluest possible sapphires are mined. They are dug out in the same way as the rubies. In yet more mountains there are large deposits of silver, copper and lead.

This region is very cold. It is also worth noting that fine horses are bred here. They are very swift and are left unshod, even those which are used in the mountains. They can gallop over land where no other horses would go. There used to be horses here descended from Alexander's horse, Bucephalus, which were all born with a small white horn on their heads like their ancestor. The breed belonged to the King's uncle, and the King, who was jealous, had him killed. Thereupon the uncle's widow ordered all the horses to be put to death to avenge her husband's murder, and so the race died out.

Swift-flying saker falcons and lanner falcons come from these mountains; the countryside is thick with birds and animals of every sort. The best wheat is grown here, and barley without husks; and although they have no olive oil, there is sesame oil and nut oil.

This is a kingdom of narrow valleys and great strongholds which protect it from invasions. All the cities and castles are situated on mountains and are impossible to capture. These mountains are extremely high and it takes a whole day to climb up them, but on the top are huge grassy plateaus with rich vegetation and an abundance of fresh spring water which tumbles down the cliffs. These springs are filled with grayling and other delicately flavoured fish. The pure air of the plateaus is so salubrious that anyone from the city or valleys below who is sick only has to spend two or three days in the mountains to recover. Marco Polo proved this for himself, for when he was ill in these parts he was advised to go into the mountains and was cured.

The men of Badakhshan are excellent archers and huntsmen. Because of the scarcity of cloth they are usually dressed in skins, but the noble women wear trousers made from as much as 100 ells of cotton. This is to make their bottoms seem plump because men in those parts like fat women.

XLVIII PASHAI

Ten days' journey south of Badakhshan is the province of Pashai. The people there are idolatrous and speak their own language. Their skins are dark and they are experts in all forms of black magic and witchcraft. The men wear gold and silver earrings with precious stones. They are very cunning, and, by their standards, courageous. They eat meat and rice. The country is very hot. But let us move on to the province of Kashmir seven days' journey away.

XLIX KASHMIR

The people of Kashmir are also idolatrous and have a language of their own. They are so versed in witchcraft and the occult that they can make their idols speak. They are able, by their spells, to change the weather and to make night fall. The things they accomplish by magic are unbelievable to anyone who has not been there. Kashmir is the centre of idolatry. From it the Indian Sea can be reached.

The people are dark-skinned and slim, and the women are as beautiful as it is possible for dark-skinned women to be. They eat meat, milk and rice. The climate is neither too hot nor too cold and there are many cities, castles, wooded plains, deserts, and mountain passes which protect them from enemies.

It is an independent country with its own rulers, who uphold the laws.

There are certain hermits here who fast rigorously, live a chaste life and strive in every way to abide by the rules of their religion. They are regarded by the people as saints and they live to a great age in the strictest abstinence, all for the love of their idols. There are also a large number of monasteries and abbeys belonging to that religion, where the monks live by the strictest rules and are tonsured like Dominicans and Franciscan friars. The men in these lands neither kill animals nor shed blood, but there are Saracens among them who kill animals to eat.

It is worth noting that coral from our countries sells better there than anywhere else.

A journey of twelve days towards the south would take the traveller to the land where pepper grows, the land of the Brahmins, but this is India and we shall come to it later. First we must go back to the province of Badakhshan in order to continue on our route.

L THE BADAKHSHAN RIVER

From Badakhshan the traveller follows a wide river to the north-east for twelve days. The surrounding countryside belongs to the King of Badakhshan's brother and there are a good number of dwellings and towns. The inhabitants are a war-like people, worshippers of Mohammed. At the end of twelve days the traveller comes to a small country which takes only three days to cross, called Wakhan and populated by Mohammedans who speak their own language. They are a brave race, governed by a man they call 'Nona', which is roughly the equivalent of 'count', who is the vassal of the King of Badakhshan. The country is full of wild animals and game of every kind.

43

From here the road to the north-east leads through mountains for three days. They are so high that they are thought to be the highest in the world. Up in the mountains there is a plateau with a large lake from which a beautiful river springs. The pastures are so rich that a thin animal will grow fat there in ten days. There is a considerable amount of wildlife, including exceptionally large rams with horns at least six spans long. The shepherds make these horns into big ladles and also fencing to enclose the animals at night. Packs of wolves which eat the sheep roam these mountains. The bones and horns they leave littered around are piled alongside the path to direct travellers through the snow.

It takes twelve days to cross this plain, which is called Pamir, and throughout it there are neither dwellings nor lodgings so the traveller must take everything he needs. Because of the rarified mountain air and the intense cold there are no birds so high up, and even fires burn badly. A further forty days' travel in the same direction takes the traveller on through mountains and valleys and across rivers and deserts where there are no houses and nothing grows. The country is called Belor and its inhabitants live up in the mountains. They are a wild, evil and idolatrous people who live on game and dress in animal skins.

LI   THE KINGDOM OF KASHGAR

Kashgar, once an independent kingdom, is now ruled by the Great Khan. The people worship Mohammed and live in towns and cities of which the most important is Kashgar to the north-east. They depend for their livelihood on trade and craft. There are beautiful gardens and vineyards and fine smallholdings. Cotton, flax and hemp are all grown, and large numbers of merchants take their goods all over the world from here. But they are a wretched and mean people who eat and drink badly. Some Nestorians who have their own church and their own religious laws live here. The language is particular to the country, which it takes five days to cross.

Now we will turn to Samarkand.

LII   SAMARKAND

Samarkand is a very large and noble city with a population of Christians and Saracens, ruled over by the Great Khan's nephew who is not on very good terms with his uncle against whom he frequently rebels.

A strange thing happened in this city. Not long ago, Chaghatai, the Great Khan's brother, converted to Christianity. He ruled over this country and others besides. When the Christians in Samarkand heard that their ruler had converted, they were so overjoyed that they built a big church dedicated to St John the Baptist. They then took possession of a large and beautiful stone belonging to the

Saracens, which they used as the base of a column supporting the roof in the middle of the church. When Chaghatai died, the Saracens, who were very angry with the Christians about the stone, decided to take it back by force. They were in a good position to do so since they outnumbered the Christians ten to one. Some of the more important Saracen leaders went to the church and announced their intention. The Christians replied that if they removed the stone the church would collapse, and they offered to pay whatever sum the Saracens demanded. The Saracens answered that all they wanted was their stone and, whatever happened, they would take it. The Great Khan's nephew, who now ruled the city, ordered the Christians to return the stone within two days. This worried and saddened the Christians, who did not know what to do. In tears and humility they addressed themselves to St John and then the miracle happened.

On the morning of the day fixed for the return of the stone, the column lifted itself up by the grace of God, leaving a gap of some three spans between it and the stone. It has remained suspended like this from that morning until the present day. This has always been regarded as one of the world's greatest miracles.

Now we will move on to Yarkand.

LIII   YARKAND

It only takes five days to cross the province of Yarkand. The population is partly Saracen and partly Nestorian Christian and the province is ruled by the Great Khan's nephew. Little is grown in these parts and there is no cotton at all. Most of the inhabitants have one very large foot and one normal one; they also tend to have a goitre, apparently because of the water they drink.

Since there is nothing of interest in this place, we will move on to Khotan.

LIV   KHOTAN

Khotan is a province to the north-east which extends for a distance of eight days' journey. It is subject to the Great Khan and the people worship Mohammed. There are castles and cities, of which Khotan is the most beautiful. The country is rich in everything, especially cotton; there are a lot of vineyards and smallholdings producing flax, hemp and grain. The people are peace-loving and live by trade and craft.

LV   PEM

It takes five days to cross Pem, a province to the north-east. The inhabitants are Mohammedans and subjects of the Great Khan. The finest city in the kingdom is

45

Pem. Large numbers of jaspers and chalcedonies are to be found in the rivers. There is much of everything, especially cotton, and the people live by trade and craft. They have one strange habit whereby if a husband goes away for more than twenty days his wife takes another husband. But the men, too, can have a wife wherever they go. The whole stretch of land from Kashgar to these regions is part of Turkestan.

Let us now turn to the province of Charchan.

LVI CHARCHAN

To the north-east of Turkestan is the province of Charchan, which was beautiful and fertile before it was plundered by the Tartars. Of all the castles and towns, the city of Charchan is the most important. Many high-quality jaspers and chalcedonies are found in the rivers and taken to be sold in Cathay. The whole province, stretching as far as Pem, is a sandy desert. The water can be bad and sour, although some of it is sweet and clear. If enemy armies appear on the frontiers, the inhabitants flee with their women, children and animals, travelling for two or three days across the desert to places with water where they can settle. No one can tell where they have gone because the wind covers their tracks with sand, so they can always escape from their enemies. They hide their harvested crops far from their homes in caves in the sand because they are afraid of raiding soldiers. They carry what they need back to their homes each month. Even when friendly armies cross their territory they put their animals in a safe place to prevent them from being commandeered, as soldiers never pay for what they take.

There is nothing more to say about Charchan except that on leaving it the traveller must spend five days travelling across continuous sand where the water is mostly bad.

LVII THE CITY OF LOP

Lop is a large city, situated on the edge of the Great Desert, which is also called Lop. It lies to the north-east, belongs to the Great Khan and is populated by Mohammedans.

Travellers preparing to cross the Great Desert with their camels rest in this city for a week before beginning the journey. It is said that it would take a year to cross the whole desert, and a month in the narrowest parts. It consists of mountains, sand and valleys, and there is nothing to eat. After travelling for a day and a night drinking water can be found in the winter, but only enough for between fifty and one hundred men with their animals. Then there is no more water for another day and night, and so on right across the desert. There are about twenty-eight watering places all told and the water is good in all but two or three. There are no wild animals or birds because there is nothing for them to eat.

A strange thing can happen in the desert. If someone riding through the night falls asleep or for any reason lags behind his fellows and tries to catch up with them he will suddenly hear spirits, calling him by name, as if they were his companions. Often, tricked by the voices, he will stray from the right path and be hopelessly lost in the desert. Many travellers have died or disappeared in this way. Sometimes, when crossing the desert, men have seen an army advancing on them and for fear of being attacked and robbed they have run away and left the main track. They have then been unable to find it again and so have died miserably of hunger. The desert spirits can do amazing and incredible things. Even in the daytime their voices can sometimes be heard, or there is a clash of arms, a roll of drums or the sound of different musical instruments. For these reasons, travellers go in large numbers and stay close to one another. They also hang bells around their animals' necks so they can be heard if they stray from the path.

Marco Polo's Great Desert, known today as the Gobi Desert

These then are the difficulties to be found in the desert; but enough of that. Let us move on to the lands beyond the desert.

LVIII   THE PROVINCE OF TANGUT

After thirty days in the desert the traveller comes to a town called Sa-chan which belongs to the Great Khan. It is in the province of Tangut. Apart from a few Nestorians and Saracens, the people are idolaters. The idolaters have their own language. The city is situated to the north-east and the people are not traders but make a good living from their corn and cereal harvests.

There are monasteries and abbeys filled with different idols to which many sacrifices are reverently made. Fathers of male children fatten a ram in honour of the idols and on the first day of the year – or on the idol's feast day – fathers and sons, large and small, pay their respects to the god and then cook the rams which they lay before the idols, leaving them there while they pray for the sons to grow into healthy men. They believe that the idol meanwhile absorbs the substance of the meat. When they have finished praying they take away the meat and summon their relations to a devotional feast. They give the head, feet, entrails, fleece and part of the meat to their priests, and when they have finished eating, they carefully collect all the bones and put them in a tomb.

It is worth knowing that all the idolaters in the world burn their dead. And when they carry them from their homes to be cremated, the relatives stop along the way at small wooden houses hung with silk and cloth of gold where the men present the dead with quantities of wine and food. They do this because they believe that the soul of the departed will then be welcomed into the next world in the same way. At the funeral pyre figures of men, horses and rams, all cut out of paper, and paper coins the size of Byzantine ones, are burnt with the body because it is thought that the dead man will then have the equivalent number of slaves, animals, rams and money in the afterlife. All the musical instruments of the country are played for the deceased.

Also, when one of these idolaters dies, the relations summon an astrologer to whom they tell the date and hour of the dead person's birth. With reference to the stars under which the deceased was born, the astrologer then calculates, by diabolical means, when the body should be burned. Sometimes there is a delay of a week, a month, or even six months, during which time the relatives keep the body at their house, because they would never dare to burn it before the time appointed by the astrologer.

The faithful believe that the deceased can only leave home under the influence of a favourable planet, otherwise it will take its vengeance on the living. Until the day of cremation arrives, the body is kept in a coffin made of planks which are a span thick and joined together with pitch and lime. The coffin is brightly painted and covered with cloths soaked in camphor and other substances to prevent bad smells. So long as the body remains at home the relations prepare food and drink as they would for a living person and leave it beside the coffin for as long as it would take to be eaten so that the departed soul can take sustenance from it.

Occasionally the astrologer decides that the stars have a bad influence over a certain door. Then another exit must be used, or, failing that, a hole has to be broken in the wall for the dead body to pass through. Idolaters the world over behave like this.

LIX THE PROVINCE OF KAMUL

The province of Kamul was formerly a kingdom. It is quite well populated and the principal town is Kamul. The region is situated between two deserts, on one side the Great Desert and on the other a smaller desert which can be crossed in three days. The people are idolaters and have a language of their own. They live off the fertile land and sell their produce to travellers. They are a cheerful, pleasure-loving people who care only for music, singing and dancing, and for the pleasures of the flesh.

If a stranger seeks lodging in these parts, he is made very welcome. His host orders his wife to fête the guest and to obey him in everything. The husband then goes away for two or three days leaving the wife and the stranger to share a bed and enjoy themselves together. The wives of all the men in the region do this, and the husbands are not ashamed of it. Their women are beautiful and sensual.

During the reign of Mongu Khan, Lord of the Tartars, the inhabitants of Kamul were denounced for lending their wives to foreigners. Mongu Khan forbade the practice under pain of severe punishment, and ordered inns to be built for foreign travellers. The people of Kamul were very disappointed but they obeyed the King for three years. Then they noticed that their harvests were falling off and many misfortunes were coming their way so they gathered together and decided to send Mongu Khan a magnificent present, begging him to allow their women to behave according to the custom of their forebears who believed that in exchange for their hospitality to strangers the idols would bless them and grant them rich harvests. Mongu Khan replied: 'If your dishonour pleases you, let it continue.' So the people reverted to their old habits and continue in them to this day.

Let us leave Kamul for another town to the north-west which also belongs to the Great Khan.

LX THE PROVINCE OF GHINGHINTALAS

It takes sixteen days to cross the province of Ghinghintalas, which lies to the north-east, on the edge of the Small Desert. Three types of people live there – idolaters, Mohammedans and Nestorians. On the northern border of this country is a high mountain with excellent deposits of steel and *ondanique**. There is also a deposit of salamander. Salamander is not, as some maintain, an animal. Everyone knows that all animals are made up of the four elements and cannot live in fire, but since no one was certain what a salamander was, it was said to be an animal, which it is not.** Marco Polo once had a very learned Turkish friend called Zurficar who, on the orders of the Great Khan, lived in the area for three years, extracting salamander, steel and *ondanique* among other things, because the Great Khan used to send a representative to rule the province and to supervise the mining for a period of three years. Marco Polo's friend explained everything and he was also able to see for himself.

When the salamander is extracted from the mountain and crumbled, the small pieces stick together and form threads like wool. After it has been extracted and dried, it is pounded in large copper mortars. Next it is washed and the residue of earth thrown away. The thread is then carefully woven into cloths. These cloths are not very white but when they are put in a fire and left there for a little while they become as white as snow. And whenever they are dirty they only have to be put back in the fire for a moment or two to become clean.

This is the truth about salamander. Anything else is a fable or a lie. There is one of these cloths in Rome. Niccolò and Matteo Polo took it as a gift from the Great Khan to the Pope to wrap around Christ's sudarium. On this cloth was written in gold: *Tu es Petrus et super hanc petram edificabo ecclesiam meam*.

LXI   THE PROVINCE OF SU-CHAU

A ten-day journey from here to the north-east takes the traveller through sparsely inhabited countryside with nothing worth mentioning until he reaches the province of Su-chau with its many castles and cities. The biggest town is Su-chau, inhabited by idolaters and Christians, all subjects of the Great Khan. This province and the three described above are all part of the major province of Tangut. Excellent rhubarb grows in the mountains, which merchants take all over the world. The people live off the land and do not concern themselves with trade. The province is healthy and the people brown-skinned. Now for Kan-chau.

LXII   THE CITY OF KAN-CHAU

Kan-chau is a huge and noble city, the capital of Tangut. The inhabitants are, for the most part, idolaters but there are Mohammedans and also some Christians

---

Ondanique: high-grade Indian steel.
**It is asbestos.

50

who have built three large and ornate churches in the town. There are a considerable number of idolatrous abbeys and monasteries with quantities of huge idols, some of which are ten paces long, well carved in wood, clay or stone, and decorated with gold. Gigantic statues are laid out on the ground, surrounded by small idols in devotional positions.

The time has come to say more about the customs of idolaters.

Their priests lead more honest lives than others. They avoid lechery although it is not considered a grave sin. They believe that it is not wrong to sleep with a woman at her suggestion, but it is sinful for the man to make a proposition. A man who is known to have sinned against a woman is condemned to death. Time is divided into lunar months and for five days in some lunar months no one may kill a bird or an animal, nor may they eat meat. During those five days the people are more virtuous than at other times.

A man may have up to thirty wives, the number depending on his wealth, and each will receive from her husband a dowry of animals, slaves and money according to his means. But the first wife is held in higher esteem than the others. If a wife displeases her husband, he may discard her at will. A man may marry his cousins and even his father's wife, but not his mother. Living as they do, like beasts, many things which we regard as wrong do not seem sinful to them.

Enough of idolaters. Before moving on, however, it is worth noting that Niccolò, Matteo and Marco Polo spent a year in this town attending to their business. Now we will travel sixty days to the north.

LXIII   THE CITY OF ETZINA

To the north, on the edge of a sandy desert twelve days from Kan-chau, stands the city of Etzina. It is also part of the province of Tangut. The people are idolaters and they own large numbers of livestock, including camels. Lanner and saker falcons nest here. The people live off the land and not by trading.

The traveller must stock up here with forty days' provisions before crossing the interminable desert where there is no sign of human habitation. No one lives in these parts, except in the mountains and valleys during the summer, but there are pine groves with wild animals like donkeys, and clear streams full of fish. After going north for forty days, the traveller reaches another province.

LXIV   KARAKORUM AND THE TARTARS

The city of Karakorum has a circumference of three miles and is built of wood and earth because of the lack of stone in those parts. Only a little way out of the city is a large town with a beautiful palace in which the ruler of the city lives. This was the first place where the Tartars settled when they began to leave their own country.

The time has come to explain more about the Tartars, their expansion and the growth of their power.

The Tartars originally came from the north, around Chorcha and Bargh, where there are vast plains without cities or castles, but with rich pastureland and wide rivers. The people had no overlord but paid tribute to a king whom they called Ung Khan, which means 'Great Lord'. This lord was Prester John who is now famous throughout the world. The Tartars' tribute to him consisted of one in ten of their animals. As the population increased, Prester John began to feel threatened by them and decided that they should be spread around the world and he gave some of his barons the task of dispersing them. The Tartars were very angry when they heard about this and at once moved northwards, out of Prester John's reach. They travelled with such speed that Prester John was unable to catch up with them. They revolted against him for some time, refusing to pay him tribute.

LXV   GENGHIS KHAN, THE FIRST KING OF THE TARTARS

Around 1187 the Tartars elected their own king, a wise man, clever politician and valiant soldier called Genghis Khan. When he was elected, Tartars from everywhere came to acknowledge him as their ruler. He was a good and noble king.

An incredible number of Tartars followed him and Ghengis Khan, seeing so many courageous men, equipped them with bows and other arms and set out to conquer new countries. In a short time he had defeated more than eight provinces. He neither harmed the inhabitants nor ravaged their countries; he formed alliances with them and took them with him to conquer other countries. In this way he came to rule over many provinces, for people were glad to follow him because he was just and good.

When Ghengis Khan had united enough men to populate the whole earth, he announced that he intended to conquer most of the world, and in about 1200 he sent envoys to Prester John asking for his daughter's hand in marriage. Prester John was deeply offended by the request and replied: 'Ghengis Khan should be ashamed to ask for my daughter's hand. He should remember that he is my subject and my servant. Go and tell him that I would rather burn my daughter than allow her to marry him. Tell him also that he deserves to die as a traitor.'

Then he ordered the messengers to go away and never to return. So they left him and after a long journey returned to Genghis Khan and told him exactly what Prester John had said.

52

LXVI   GENGHIS KHAN PREPARES HIS ARMY

When Genghis Khan heard Prester John's offensive message he was very angry, for he was far too great a ruler to stand for such effrontery. At first he was struck dumb, then he shouted for everyone to hear that if Prester John's insult were not repaid a hundredfold, he would no longer remain king. As for Prester John, he would soon learn the degree of Genghis Khan's servitude.

He mobilized his army and prepared for war in an unprecedented fashion. He sent a warning to Prester John to be ready to defend himself since his entire army was about to attack. Prester John merely laughed when he heard that Genghis Khan was coming and showed not the slightest concern. He was sure that the enemy would be badly armed. Nevertheless he secretly intended to do everything possible to capture Genghis Khan and put him cruelly to death. He mobilized men from far and near and collected one of the largest armies imaginable. Both sides were now prepared. Genghis Khan and his army encamped on the vast and beautiful plain of Tenduc which belonged to Prester John. There were more men than could be counted. When Genghis Khan heard that Prester John had decided to march on him he was pleased because the open plain was a suitable place for a great battle, and he waited there impatiently.

Let us leave Genghis Khan's army for a moment and turn to Prester John's.

LXVII   PRESTER JOHN AGAINST GENGHIS KHAN

It is said that when Prester John heard that Genghis Khan's army was advancing on him, he roused his own men and went to meet the enemy on the plain of Tenduc, pitching camp twenty miles from his opponent's. Then the soldiers on both sides rested so as to be full of energy for the battle.

While the two armies were arrayed confronting each other, Genghis Khan summoned both Christian and Saracen astrologers and asked them who was going to win. The Saracens were unable to give an answer but the Christians demonstrated the outcome. In front of the Great Khan they split a green stick in half lengthwise, and put one half on one side and the other opposite it. They called one half Genghis Khan and the other Prester John. Then they said to Genghis Khan: 'Look at these sticks, one of which bears your name, and one the name of your enemy. When we have worked our spells, the stick which climbs on to the other will be the winner.'

Genghis Khan said that he had no time to waste and asked the astrologers to carry out their experiment at once. The Christian astrologers then read some psalms and worked their spells. Suddenly, without anyone touching it, the stick called Genghis Khan moved towards the other and climbed on top of it. Everyone

53

present witnessed this amazing sight and Genghis Khan was delighted. Later, when it was clear that the Christians had been truthful, he honoured them and thereafter always respected them for their sincerity and ability as prophets.

LXVIII THE GREAT BATTLE

After resting for two days the two armies attacked each other in the mightiest battle ever seen. There were heavy losses on both sides but eventually Genghis Khan won. Prester John was killed in the confrontation and Genghis Khan went on to conquer all Prester John's lands. After the great battle Genghis Khan lived another six years and took more provinces. But, at the end of the sixth year, he was wounded in the knee by an arrow while attacking a town called Ho-chau, and subsequently died. This was a great loss because he was a wise and courageous man.

The death of Genghis Khan, from a miniature in the *Livres des Merveilles*

Having dealt with how the Tartars elected their first king, Genghis Khan, and how they beat Prester John in battle, let us turn to their way of life.

LXIX The Khans who Ruled after Genghis Khan

Genghis Khan was succeeded in turn by Knyuk Khan, Batu Khan, Oktai Khan and Mongu Khan. The present ruler, Kublai Khan, is the sixth – the greatest and most powerful of them all. The combined power of the first five Khans was, as we shall see, inferior to the power of Kublai Khan alone.

All the Khans of Genghis Khan's lineage are buried on a mountain called Altai. These Tartar lords are brought there even if they die a hundred days' journey away. When the body of a Great Khan is brought to the mountain everyone along the way, even if the distance is forty miles or more, is killed by the sword of one of the escorts, who cries: 'Go and serve your lord in the next world.'

They really believe that people killed like this will serve the Khan in the afterlife, and they also kill the Khan's best horses, so that he can have them in the next world. Whe Mongu Khan died more than 20,000 men who had encountered the funeral procession were killed.

There is much more to be said about the Tartars and their way of life.

In winter, they live in warm places on the plains where there is good pastureland for their livestock. In summer they move to the cool mountains and valleys where there are woods as well as plenty of grazing and water. Another reason for this is that there are no gadflies or horseflies to annoy them in the uplands. They climb continuously higher over a period of two or three months, for if they remained in the same place all the time there would not be enough grass for their animals.

They have round wooden tents made of stakes covered in felt which they load onto carts and take everywhere with them. The tents are easily transportable and are always pitched with the entrance facing south. There are also fine two-wheeled carts, well covered with black felt so that not a drop of water could get inside even if it rained forever. These carts are pulled by oxen and camels and carry the women and children and household goods. The women do all the buying and selling and attend to the needs of their husbands and families because the men only hunt, fight and train falcons and goshawks. These people live on meat, milk and game; they eat gerbils, of which there are plenty in the plains during summer, as well as horsemeat, dogmeat and other animals, and they drink mare's milk.

A man would never touch another man's wife, for this would be considered very wicked. The women are good-natured, faithful and hard-working. A man may have as many wives as he pleases – 100 if he can afford them. The husband pays a dowry to his wife's mother, but the wife gives nothing to the husband. The first wife is always regarded as the most important. Since the men have so many wives, they also have more children than other people. If the father dies, the eldest son may marry his father's wives except, of course, his own mother; he may

Medieval Tartar transportable wooden tents

also marry his brothers' widows. Marriages are always celebrated with great festivity.

LXX THE TARTAR LORD AND HIS LAWS

With regard to their religion, the Tartars believe in one almighty God to whom they burn incense and from whom they ask only for good health and wisdom. They have another god called Natigai who is concerned with earthly matters and watches over their children, their flocks and their harvests. They must be very devoted to this god because every household has a felt and cloth model of him standing beside likenesses of the wife and children. The wife is on the left of the god and the children are in front, worshipping him. At mealtimes the men grease the mouths of the images with a small piece of fatty meat; then they sprinkle some broth out of doors as an offering to the other spirits. They begin to eat and drink only after performing these rites. They drink mare's milk, prepared so that it seems like white wine, and they call it *koumiss*.

The rich are dressed in sumptuous clothes of gold and silk with precious furs of ermine, sable, squirrel and fox; all their belongings are beautifully made and very valuable.

Their arms consist of bows and arrows, swords and cudgels; but mostly they

56

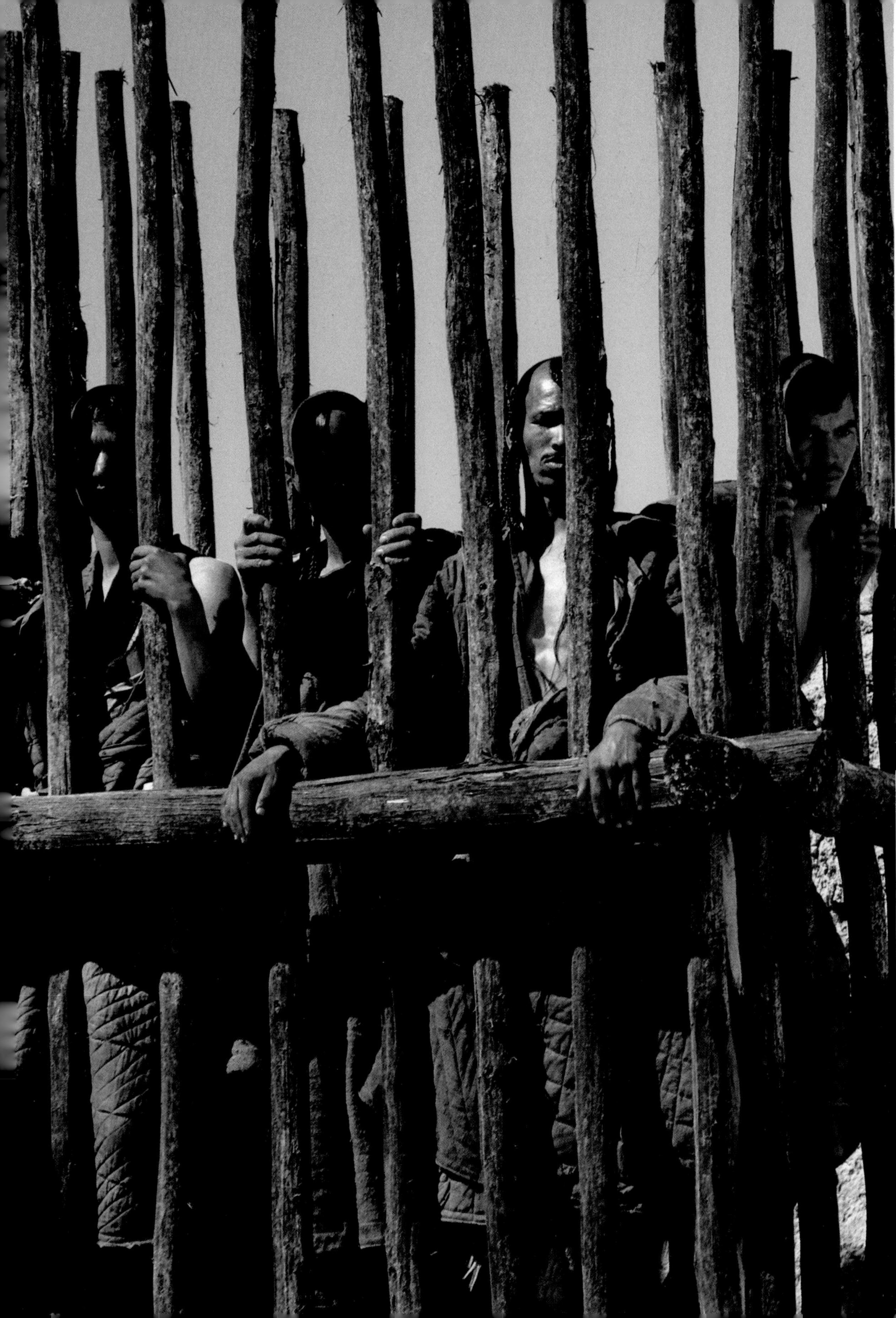

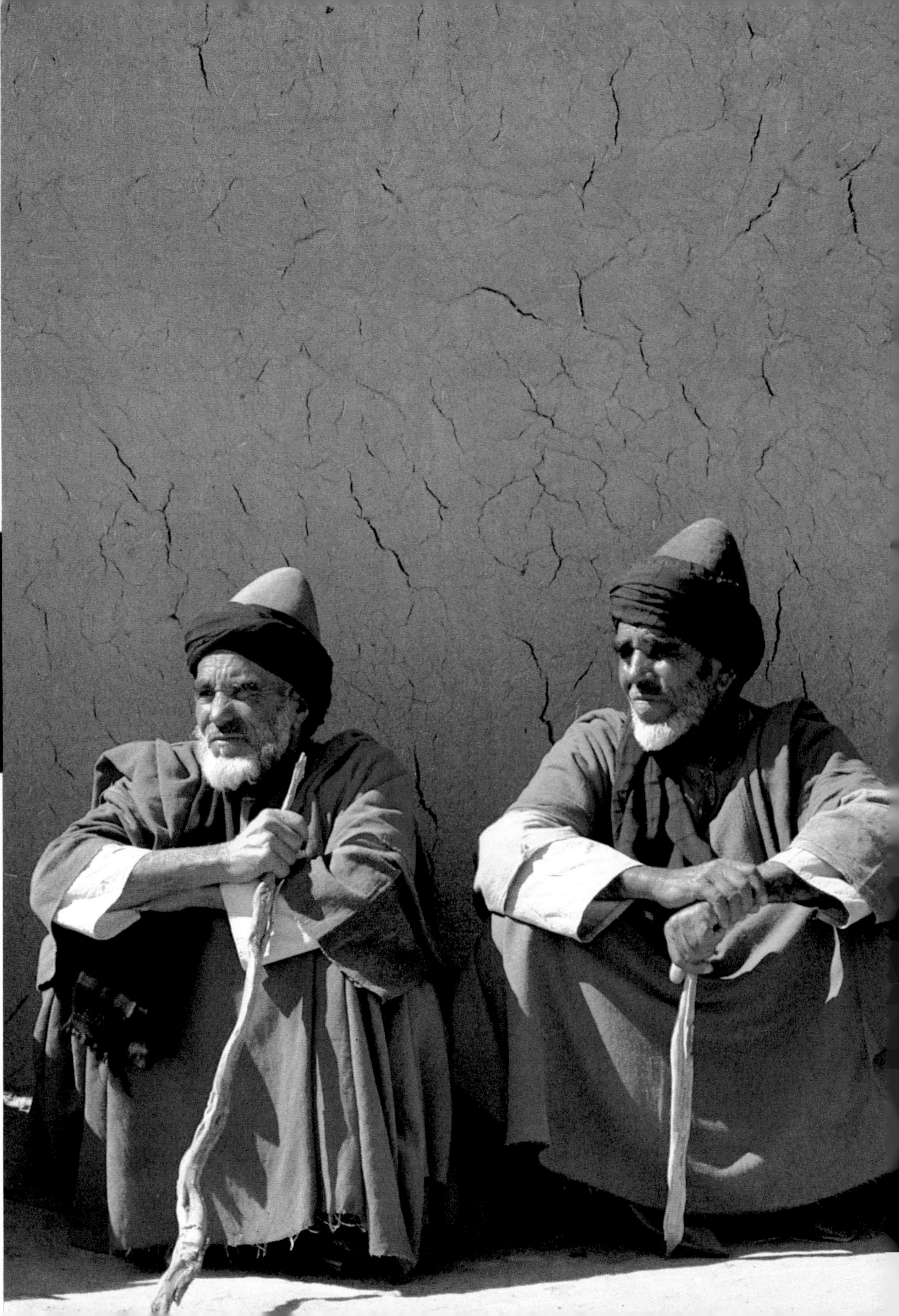

use bows and arrows, for they are fine archers. They wear armour made of buffalo skin and other tough hides which are boiled. The men are excellent fighters and bold in battle. They value their lives so little that they expose themselves to any danger. They are certainly the hardiest soldiers in the world. They often, when necessary, spend a whole month with nothing to sustain them but mare's milk and whatever game they are lucky enough to catch, while their horses are able to manage without barley or straw and can live on just grass. The men are very disciplined in war and can, if needs be, ride all night with their armour on. The horses eat whatever grass they find as they travel. No army is more resistant, cheaper to maintain or better adapted to conquer foreign lands.

The armies are marshalled in the following way. If a Tartar leader goes to war – with, say, 100,000 men and horses – he nominates a commander for every 10,000 men, another for every 1,000, yet another for every 100, and a last one for every ten. In this way each commander need deal with only his ten immediate subordinates. The supreme head consults with the ten men commanding units of 10,000 each, who in turn deal with the commanders in charge of units of 1,000, and so on down to those with only ten men under their command. The men themselves are answerable to their own leader. And if the supreme commander wishes to mobilize a force and orders one of the commanders of 10,000 to let him have 1,000 men, the commander orders each leader of 1,000 to send him 100; and so the order is passed down, each commander supplying his quota without delay since they are all well disciplined and obedient. A unit of 100,000 is known as a *tuk*, one of 10,000 is called a *tomaun*, and the other units also have names.

When the troops are marching to war, a reconnoitring party of some 200 men is sent ahead, and an equal number is deployed to the rear and on each flank of the army in case of sudden attack from unexpected quarters. If the march is a long one the army carries neither tents nor bedding and the men live on mare's milk; there are eighteen horses, both mares and stallions, per man. The men have two flasks for their milk, a little saucepan in which to cook meat, and a small tent to protect them from rain. They can ride for ten days without eating or lighting a fire, merely living on blood drawn from their horses. They also dry their milk into a paste, of which each man carries ten pounds. Every morning they put half a pound of dried milk into a leather flask, with as much water as they want. The galloping of the horses shakes the flasks and the milk dissolves in the water. They then drink this for breakfast.

In battle they never join totally with the enemy army; their tactic is to surround it. Unashamed of being thought to be in flight, they move with great speed, darting from one place to another. Their horses are so well trained that they can turn as quickly as a dog. The Tartar army can fight with the same agility and spirit when it is being chased as it can when attacking. Just as the enemy thinks itself near victory the fleeing Tartars turn and shoot arrows at their foe, littering the battlefield with dead men and horses. After this massacre they suddenly wheel round and violently attack and overcome the enemy. This is how the Tartars have won so many battles and defeated so many large armies.

It must be said, however, that the Tartars of today have degenerated. Those who live in Cathay have adopted the customs and even the religion of idolaters, and the Levantine Tartars have made the Saracen way of life their own.

Justice is administered as follows. A man who has committed a minor crime, not punishable by death, is condemned to seven, seventeen, twenty-seven or thirty-seven strokes of the cane, and so on up to 107, depending on the gravity of the crime. If, however, a man has stolen a horse or something else deserving the death penalty, he is cut into pieces by the sword – unless he can make reparation by paying nine times the value of the stolen property, in which case he can escape death.

Many people brand their livestock – horses, camels, oxen, cows and other large animals – and allow them to graze alone on the plains and in the mountains, knowing they can be identified. But sheep and rams are watched over by a shepherd. All the animals are fat and choice.

The Tartars have one very strange custom. If a man has lost a young son of about four or five years old, and another has lost a daughter of the same age, the two fathers arrange a marriage for the dead children. They draw up a marriage contract which they then burn, believing that the smoke will convey to their children in the other world that they have become man and wife. Then a great feast takes place and food is put out for the married couple in heaven. Paper drawings of slaves, horses, rich cloth, gold coins and household goods are burnt in the belief that the children will then possess these goods in the afterlife. From that time the relationship between families of the children is as though the boy and girl were really married.

Much has now been said about the Tartar way of life, but the wonder of the Great Khan, absolute Lord of all the Tartars, and the supreme imperial court itself have not been touched on. This will all be dealt with in time, for there is much of interest to describe. But for the moment we must return to the great plain.

LXXI THE PLAIN OF BARGU AND THE CUSTOMS OF ITS INHABITANTS

On leaving Karakorum and Altai where the Great Khans are buried, the traveller crosses the plain of Bargu to the north – a journey of forty days. The inhabitants of the plain are a wild people called the Mekrit. They live on game, particularly deer, which they also ride. They are subjects of the Great Khan and their way of life is similar to the Tartars'. Neither corn nor wine is grown on the plain, which in summer is full of wild animals and birds. But in winter it is so cold that no living thing is to be found there.

After forty days the traveller comes to the Ocean, and here, high up in the mountains by the sea, peregrine falcons nest. There is no other living thing here, no men or women or animals, except birds called *bargherlacs** on which the falcons feed. They are the size of partridges and swift of flight with claws like parrots and tails like swallows. When the Great Khan wants peregrine falcons taken from their nests he sends here for them, which is so far north that the Pole Star seems to be slightly to the south. Gerfalcons breed on the islands in this sea. There are as many as the Great Khan could possibly want, so those who export them from Christendom do not send them to him but to Arghun and other Levantine lords.

Having dealt with the northern province as far as the sea, let us turn to other provinces which lie on the way to the Great Khan's court.

LXXII   THE GREAT KINGDOM OF ERGUIUL

Before reaching Erguiul the traveller leaving Kan-chau passes for five days through places where the voices of spirits can be heard, especially at night. Erguiul is one of the many kingdoms in the great province of Tangut and is subject to the Great Khan. The population consists of Nestorians, idolaters and Mohammedans. The main city is called Erguiul. The south-eastern road from here leads to Cathay. In the direction of Cathay is the city of Sinju in the province of the same name. This province is also part of Tangut and is subject to the Great Khan. There is a large number of fine, black and white wild oxen here, which are nearly as big as elephants and are covered with very long, soft, silky hair, except on their backs. They are wonderful animals and can be tamed. They are used as beasts of burden and can do the work of two ordinary oxen.

The finest musk in the world is found here. It comes from a small animal, no bigger than a gazelle, with the tail and hoofs of a gazelle but with the thick pelt of a deer. It has no horns but four slender, curved teeth about three spans long. The two bottom ones bend downwards and the two top ones bend upwards. It is a beautiful animal. The musk is found near its navel at full moon when a small clot of blood forms there. The huntsmen remove the sac of blood with the skin intact round it and leave it to dry in the sun. This blood forms the musk which has such an exquisite scent.

*Sand grouse.

The people in these parts live by trading and craftsmanship; they also have plenty of corn. It takes twenty-five days to cross the province. The pheasants here are nearly the size of peacocks with tails up to ten spans in length. There are also smaller pheasants, like ours, and many different kinds of highly-coloured birds.

The men, who are idolaters, are fat with small noses and black hair. They have only a few hairs on their chins and the women have none at all on their bodies except on their heads. They have beautiful complexions and fine limbs. Both men and women delight in sensual pleasures. The men are allowed as many wives as they can afford, and a beautiful woman, even if she is very poor, can be married to a great lord if the sum paid to her mother can be agreed upon.

Let us now move on towards the east.

LXXIII   THE PROVINCE OF EGRIGAIA

An eight-day ride eastwards from Erguiul brings the traveller to the province of Egrigaia with its many towns and cities. It is part of Tangut and the main town is Kalachan. Although the people are mainly idolaters, there are three Nestorian Christian churches. They are all subjects of the Great Khan.

The best and most expensive camel-hair cloth is made in this city. A fine white woollen material of excellent quality is also made here. Large amounts of this are exported all over the world, in particular to Cathay.

Now we move further east, into territory formerly belonging to Prester John – the province of Tenduc.

LXXIV   THE GREAT LAND OF TENDUC

Tenduc is an eastern province with many cities and castles, subject to the Great Khan. The capital city is also called Tenduc. The King of Tenduc, a descendant of Prester John, is a Christian priest called George. Most of the inhabitants are also Christians. He rules in the Great Khan's name over part of the land which used to belong to Prester John. The Great Khan is in the habit of marrying one of his daughters or relations, to the kings of Tenduc of Prester John's lineage.

Beautiful lapis lazuli is found in these parts and various colours of camel-hair cloth are made; the people live by stockraising and agriculture. There are also merchants and artisans.

Although the ruler is a Christian, there are many Mohammedans and idolaters. There is a race of men known as *Argons* or half-breeds. They are a cross between Tenduc idolaters and Mohammedans. These people are far better looking than anyone else in the country and are highly intelligent and excellent merchants.

Prester John lived in this province when he ruled the Tartars and the surrounding lands and provinces. Besides the ruler, George, other descendants of his still live here. It consists of two kingdoms, known to us as Gog and Magog but which the inhabitants call Ung and Mungul. A different race lived in each kingdom. The Gog lived at Ung and the Tartars at Mungul.

Eight days further east, towards Cathay, are a number of cities and castles inhabited by Mohammedans, idolaters and Nestorians who live by trading and craftsmanship. They make very fine cloth of gold and many different silks in which they dress as we dress in various types of wool.

All military equipment is made in a town called Sindachu. In the mountains, at a place known as Yaifu, large amounts of silver are mined. Animals and birds of all kinds are plentiful.

From here a three-day journey leads to the town of Chagon-nor which means 'white pond'. The Great Khan has a large palace here where he likes to stay because of the many lakes and rivers, which are full of swans, and the beautiful plains with their cranes, pheasants and many other birds. The Great Khan enjoys hunting the rich variety of birds with his falcons and gerfalcons.

There are five different types of crane in these parts. Some are black like crows and very large. Others are white, their wide, richly-coloured wings covered with huge, bright-gold eyes like peacock feathers. Their heads are red and black, their necks black and white and they are bigger than all the others. The third kind is like ours, and the fourth is small with tufts of long, attractive, vermilion and black feathers on each side of its head. The fifth variety is grey and very large with a beautifully-shaped red and black head.

There is a valley near this town where the Great Khan has huge numbers of great partridges, called *cators*, reared under the supervision of guards. In the summer he has millet, panic grass and other grain for the birds sown on the slopes. No one may harvest these crops because they are for the birds to feed on at will. In winter millet is scattered on the ground for them. The birds are so used to being fed in this way that they flock to the keeper as soon as he whistles. The Great Khan has plenty of birds here, but he does not stay on the plain during the winter when they are good and plump because of the cold. Wherever he goes, however, he has large quantities of these fat birds sent to him on the backs of camels.

Now we must travel for three days to the north-east.

LXXV   THE CITY OF XANADU AND THE GREAT KHAN'S FABULOUS PALACE

A further three days' ride takes the traveller to a city named Xanadu built for the present Great Khan, Kublai Khan. Here there is a stone and marble palace with gilded rooms wonderfully decorated with magnificent and delicate paintings of birds, trees and flowers of every kind. Leading away from the palace is a wall which encloses sixteen miles of fertile ground with rivers and streams running through it. Here the Great Khan rears every sort of animal, including fallow deer and roebuck which are fed to the many gerfalcons and falcons, and at least once a week he goes to look at them. He often rides through these gardens with a leopard squatting on his horse's hindquarters. Sometimes he unleashes the leopard and sends it to catch a deer or a roebuck for his falcons. This is a pastime much enjoyed by the Great Khan.

In the middle of the enclosed garden there is a beautiful wood where Kublai Khan has had a royal palace built of gilded and painted reed columns. On top of each column is a gilt dragon, its tail wrapped round the column and its head and outstretched paws supporting the roof. The palace is gilded inside and decorated with the most beautifully painted birds and animals. The ceiling is also made of reeds, which are sealed with paint to prevent water from getting in.

The reeds used to build such a palace are three spans in girth and from ten to fifteen paces long. They are split down the middle from one knot to the next to form a shingle; these long, sturdy shingles can be used not only for roofing but for building a whole house. The reeds are fastened with nails so that they can withstand the wind. The Great Khan has had his splendid reed palace made so that he can erect it when he pleases: it is held together by more than 200 silk cords. Kublai Khan spends three months in Xanadu – June, July and August. It is not too hot then and he enjoys himself a great deal. At the end of these three months the reed palace is dismantled.

On 28 August the Great Khan leaves the beautiful palace. He always departs on the same day, for a strange reason. He breeds snow-white horses of which he has an enormous number. He has more than 10,000 mares alone and their milk may be drunk only by people of Genghis Khan's lineage, except for the Horiat. These are people who were granted the honour by the Great Khan in gratitude for victories they had won for him. So great is the respect inspired by these fine horses that no one, not even a nobleman, would dare to get in their way. Astrologers and idolaters have told the Great Khan that every year, on 28 August, he must, with his own hand, throw the milk of some of these mares in the air and on the ground for the spirits to drink. He has been told that if he does not do this the spirits will not look after his women, animals, birds, harvests and all his other possessions.

If it rains when the Great Khan is in his palace at Xanadu he summons his astrologers and magicians to dispel the smallest cloud from above the palace. So the sky is always blue there even when it rains elsewhere. The magicians are called Tibetans and Kashmiris, for these are the names of the idolatrous races to which they belong. They are better versed in black magic and necromancy than anyone else, and although they worship the devil they claim that their miracles are wrought through the sanctity of their divine power. The magicians are foul and filthy. They have no self-respect and do not care about anyone. Their faces are always dirty and they neither wash nor comb their hair. If a man is justly condemned to death by the authorities, these men cook and eat the body. They do not, however, eat anyone who has died a natural death.

These Bakhshis work other miracles. In the main hall of the palace the Great Khan's table is raised eight cubits above the level of the floor; on the floor, at least eight paces away from his seat, are cups filled with milk, wine and other delicious drinks. These Bakhshi magicians can make the cups rise without being touched and move them to where the Great Khan is sitting. When he has drunk from them, the empty cups return to their places. This has been witnessed by 10,000 people; it is absolutely true and anyone with any knowledge of magic could confirm it.

When the time comes for the Bakhshi to honour one of their idols they go to the Great Khan and say: 'Sire, the feast day of such and such an idol is about to take place and, as you know, Great Khan, this idol can cause bad weather and damage to our animals and crops. So we beg you to give us blackheaded rams, incense, timber, aloes and many other things to offer to our god so that he will protect our livestock and crops.'

They repeat all this to the barons at court and so manage to get everything they want for their idol. Then, with much chanting, they burn incense made from all the good spices they have been given and cook the meat, which they offer to the idol. They then sprinkle broth around for the spirits who, according to the Bakhshi, are glad of it. This, then, is how they honour their gods.

Every idol, like our Christian saints, has his own feast day. There are monasteries and abbeys the size of small towns where more than 2,000 monks may live. They are better dressed than other people, are clean-shaven and have short hair. They celebrate their idols with lights and singing such as it would be hard to find elsewhere.

Some of the Bakhshi are allowed wives by the rules of their religion and have children.

There are other holy men called Sien-seng who abide by a strict rule of abstinence and who lead a very hard life. Throughout their lives they eat nothing but bran, that is the husks of corn left over after the flour is made. They put the bran in hot water for a little while before eating it. And although that is all they eat, they also fast several times a year. They have many large books, and some of the holy men are fire-worshippers. Strange though it may seem, the other monks regard the ones who live so strictly as heretics. Not all idolaters follow the same rules. The Sien-seng, for instance, never marry, and they shave their heads as well as their chins. Their robes are always coloured black and blue, and are usually made of hemp. They sleep on rush or wicker mats and their lives are unbelievably hard. All their monasteries and idols have women's names.

But enough of this. It is time to speak of the marvels of the great King of all the Tartars, the most noble Kublai Khan.

Cho-khang, the Grand Temple of Buddha, at Lhasa

III

Kublai Khan

LXXVI THE GREAT KUBLAI KHAN AND HIS POWER

The time has come to relate the extraordinary facts concerning the present Khan, a title which means Lord of Lords. He has every right to be called the Great Khan as no man since Adam has ever ruled over so many subjects or over such a vast territory, nor has any ruler ever been possessed of such treasure or of so much power. This book will prove that he is without doubt the greatest Lord ever to rule.

LXXVII THE GREAT WAR BETWEEN KUBLAI KHAN AND HIS COUSIN, KING NAYAN

Kublai is, like every supreme lord of the Tartars, a direct descendant of Genghis Khan. He is the sixth Great Khan and he came to power in about 1256. He owes his throne to his spirit, his courage and his superior intelligence. His brothers and other relations have attempted to usurp his throne, but he overcame them all. The kingdom was in any case his by right.

It is now, in 1298, forty-two years since he began his reign. He must be at least eighty-five years old. Before he was king he participated in many wars. He was an excellent soldier and a fine captain, but since his succession he has only been to war once, in 1286, for reasons which will be explained.

Nayan was a very young cousin of Kublai Khan's. He ruled over a fairly large territory and could muster an army of 400,000 men and horses. His ancestors had long been vassals of the Great Khan, as he himself was. But on becoming king at the age of thirty, he decided to do everything possible to be independent of the Great Khan. He sent ambassadors to Kaidu, a powerful lord and Kublai's nephew, who hated his uncle and had rebelled against him. Nayan suggested Kaidu should attack the Great Khan from one side while he, Nayan, attacked from the other. Kaidu could raise 100,000 men and horses. He agreed to the plan and promised to be ready with his army on a specified date. The two of them began to mobilize their cavalry and their infantry.

LXXVIII THE GREAT KHAN AGAINST NAYAN

When the Great Khan heard what was happening he was not at all alarmed. Wise and brave man that he was, he immediately began to prepare his army and swore that unless he could put an end to the two traitors he would renounce his throne and his kingdom. He sent scouts to the borders of Nayan's and Kaidu's land to watch for spies and prevent them from discovering his preparations. He ordered the men of Khan-balik, a ten-day journey away, to be ready as soon as possible.

He raised an army of at least 360,000 men and horses and 100,000 infantrymen. He raised only his armies which were at hand. His other twelve armies were far away, conquering new lands, and would not have been able to arrive in time. Had he mustered his entire forces, the multitude of cavalry would have been beyond counting. The 360,000 came from neighbouring regions and many of them were falconers. It would have taken the army guarding Cathay twenty to thirty days to return and the news would have got out. Then Nayan and Kaidu would have had time to join forces and position themselves to advantage. But the Great Khan chose speed – victory's ally – with which to anticipate Nayan and catch him off his guard.

When Kublai Khan's men, who were fewer in number than the enemy, were ready he summoned the astrologers to tell him the outcome of the battle. When the astrologers told him that the enemy would be beaten, the Great Khan set out with his army. They marched for twenty days until they reached the wide plain where Nayan was entrenched with no fewer than 400,000 cavalry.

Kublai arrived early in the morning with his army and caught the enemy completely by surprise. The Great Khan had already had the routes leading to the plain carefully surveyed and had taken any strangers prisoner. Nayan himself was still in bed with his much loved wife.

LXXIX THE BEGINNING OF KUBLAI KHAN'S BATTLE AGAINST NAYAN

When dawn broke on the day of the battle the Great Khan appeared on the crest of a small hill overlooking the plain where Nayan's army was encamped. Nayan and his men were quite unaware of the danger.

They felt so secure that they had neither posted sentries nor sent patrols ahead or to their rear. The Great Khan was on the hill in a small wooden tower full of crossbowmen and archers, supported by four elephants. His standard with the emblem of the sun and the moon flew from the top of the turret, visible from every direction. The four elephants were protected by armour made of impenetrable boiled leather over which were draped cloths of silk and gold.

The Great Khan ordered his army, which was marshalled into three divisions composed of thirty ranks of 10,000 mounted archers each, to advance on the left and the right so as to surround the enemy. The order was quickly carried out. In front of every rank of cavalry was a corps of 500 infantrymen armed with short spears and swords. Their tactics were as follows: when the cavalry broke into a gallop the infantrymen jumped onto the backs of the nearest horses, behind the riders, and stayed there until the horses stopped. Then they dismounted and killed the enemy horses with their spears.

That, then, is how Kublai Khan's troops were deployed, ready to fight, outside Nayan's camp. Nayan and his men were amazed when they saw this. They hurriedly armed themselves and ordered their ranks.

Both sides were ready for the attack. Anyone present would have heard pipes and other instruments, including a beautiful two-stringed one, all playing while men sang at the tops of their voices. The Tartars never attack until they hear their commander's drums, but while waiting for the battle to begin, they always play and sing. So music echoed from both sides.

Kettledrums, one of the instruments used by the Tartars to herald a
battle

When everything was ready the Great Khan's drums were heard. At this sound, without delay, the soldiers hurled themselves against each other with bows, swords, clubs and some spears; the infantrymen had crossbows and many other weapons. The cruel and bloody battle began. The sky seemed to be raining arrows. Horses and men fell to the ground. The din and screaming were loud enough to drown the noise of thunder. It is worth noting that Nayan was a baptized Christian whose banner bore the cross of Christ.

Suffice it to say that this was the most savage battle ever fought. So many men, especially cavalrymen, had never been on one battlefield before. The number of dead was staggering. Fighting continued right into the afternoon, victory always in the balance. Nayan's men loved their king for his great liberality and were ready to die for him rather than give in. But eventually Kublai Khan won the day. Nayan and his men, realizing they were defeated, tried to flee, but in vain. The King was taken prisoner and the barons and soldiers surrendered to the Great Khan.

LXXX   THE DEATH OF NAYAN

When the Great Khan learned that Nayan had been taken prisoner, he sentenced him to death. Nayan was wrapped very tightly in a carpet and flung about violently until he died. This method was used because imperial blood cannot be shed on the ground, neither must it be exposed to the sun or the air.

Nayan's barons and soldiers then made an act of obeisance before the Great Khan and swore an oath of loyalty. They came from the provinces of Charcha, Kanli, Barskol and Sikintinju.

After Nayan's death, the Saracens, idolaters, Jews and men of no religion who had all fought for him, mocked the cross on his flag and said to the Christians: 'Look how your God helped Nayan, and he was a Christian!'

When the Great Khan heard about these taunts he summoned the men involved, as well as many Christians, and told them: 'If your God did not help Nayan it was because He is good and acts justly. Nayan was a traitor, he rebelled against his ruler. What happened to him was just and the cross of your God was right not to help him in his wicked ways.'

The Christians replied: 'Great Khan, what you say is true, the cross of the Lord cannot support evil. The treacherous Nayan deserved punishment.'

LXXXI   WHY THE GREAT KHAN DID NOT CONVERT TO CHRISTIANITY

The Great Khan usually sent his sons and barons into battle but he took part personally in the rout of Nayan because his young cousin's arrogance was a very serious matter and seemed particularly wicked.

After his victory Kublai Khan returned to his capital, Khan-balik, to rejoice. There was no need to worry about Kaidu because when he heard of Nayan's defeat he was so discouraged that he withdrew from the war for fear of meeting the same fate as his ally.

Kublai Khan stayed in Khan-balik from November until February or March – that is to say until the Christian Easter. Knowing Easter to be a very important festival he summoned all the Christians and asked them for the book containing the four Gospels. Then, with a great deal of ceremony, he burnt incense before it several times. He kissed the book devoutly and asked his barons who were present to do the same. This is something which he does on all important

Christian holidays like Christmas and Easter. He does the same thing on Saracen and Jewish feast days and at the feasts of the idolaters, and if anyone asks him why, he replies: 'There are four prophets who are worshipped and venerated throughout the world. The Christians worship Jesus Christ; the Saracens worship Mohammed; the Jews, Moses; and the idolaters, Sakyamuni Burkhan. I honour and respect all four and through them I honour Almighty God who is in heaven and to whom I pray for help.'

But judging by appearances, Kublai Khan thought that the truest of all faiths was the Christian because he said that it asked for nothing was was not good and holy. He would never allow Christians to carry a cross, however. This was because so good a man as Christ had suffered and died on it.

People might ask why, if the Great Khan thought the Christian religion was the best, he did not convert to it. When he was sending Niccolò and Matteo Polo as ambassadors to the Pope and they were telling him about Christianity, he said to them: 'How can I become a Christian? As you can see, the Christians in these parts are totally ignorant and can achieve nothing. But the idolaters do whatever they like. When I am at table they can make cups full of wine move across the room to me without being touched, and then I drink. They can control bad weather and do many miraculous things, and, as you know, the idols speak to them and make predictions when asked to do so. If I convert to Christianity my barons and other people will ask why I have been baptized and what miracles I have seen performed in the name of Christ. You know that the idolaters claim that their power lies in their saintliness and the holiness of their idols. I would have no answer and that would be a great mistake. These idolaters can do so many things; they could easily make me die. Go to the Pope and beg him to send me 100 wise men of your religion who will know how to condemn what the idolaters do and will tell them that they too can work miracles but do not do so because it is the work of the devil and of evil spirits. Let your priests prove themselves by making the idolaters powerless to work their charms in front of them. Then I shall be able to condemn the idolaters and their laws and I will be baptized. When I am baptized, all my lords and barons will be baptized too and then my subjects. There will be more Christians here than in your own country.'

If the Pope had sent men capable of preaching our religion Kublai Khan would indeed have become a Christian because it is well known that he very much wished to do so.

Let us turn now to how Kublai Khan rewards his barons who have fought well and how he treats cowards. He has twelve wise and courageous men whose duty it is to observe and report how the commanders and soldiers behave in battle. The Great Khan promotes good captains as follows: if they have led 100 men he increases their command to 1,000, and those who have led 1,000 he promotes to command 10,000, and according to their rank he gives them silverware, tablets of command, fine armour, gold and silver jewels, pearls, precious stones and horses. Captains commanding 100 men receive silver tablets, whilst those commanding 1,000 receive gilt ones. The leaders of units of 10,000 are given gold tablets with a lion's head. The tablets belonging to captains of units of 100 or 1,000 weigh 120 *saggi*,* and the ones with the lion's head weigh 220. Each tablet bears the following inscription: 'In the name of God and of the grace He has bestowed on our Emperor, may the Great Khan be blessed; death and destruction to those who disobey him.' Special privileges are granted with these tablets.

Mongol tablets with Uighúr inscriptions found near the River Dnieper in 1845

The commander of 100,000 men or the general of a large army has a gold tablet weighing three hundred *saggi* bearing the same inscription. Beneath the inscription a lion, the sun and the moon are represented. These leaders are given many privileges and considerable authority. Anyone possessing the tablets is obliged, when out riding, to carry a small umbrella over his head as a sign of his rank under the Great Khan, and when he sits, to do so on a silver seat. The most important barons are given tablets with gerfalcons on them and are allowed to exercise power equivalent to the Great Khan's own. Anyone bearing a tablet with a gerfalcon can commandeer a great prince's army to escort him and can also requisition horses from kings and other men.

LXXXII THE GREAT KHAN'S WAY OF LIFE

Kublai Khan, the Lord of Lords, is a man of medium height, well built but not fat, with well-formed limbs. He has a pink and white complexion like a rose, fine

*One *saggio* weighed about ¹/₆ oz.

Portrait of Kublai Khan, from a Chinese engraving

black eyes and a handsome nose. He has four legitimate wives. His eldest son is heir apparent to the empire. The wives are all called empresses, and each one has her own court with no less than 300 beautiful girls in attendance, as well as many eunuchs and other men and women. Each court consists of about 10,000 people. When the Great Khan wishes to sleep with one of his wives, he either goes to her room or summons her to his.

Besides his wives he has many young concubines who come from a Tartar city called Kuagurat where the people are very beautiful and fair-skinned. About once every two years the Great Khan sends ambassadors to Kungurat to select the most beautiful girls and bring them to the court. Here they are looked after by ladies of the court who observe them at night in their rooms and check that their breath is sweet, that they are virgins and perfect in every way. If they are beautiful, good and healthy they are sent to attend on the Great Khan. For three days and three nights, six of these girls wait on the Khan in his room and his bed, doing whatever he requires. At the end of this time the six girls are replaced by another six, and so on in rotation.

LXXXIII THE GREAT KHAN'S CHILDREN

The Great Khan's four wives have borne him twenty-two sons. The eldest was called Genghis after the illustrious Genghis Khan and he was to inherit his father's empire. But he died, leaving a son called Temur who, being the son of the Khan's eldest son, will succeed his grandfather. Temur is wise and courageous and has already proved himself in battle.

The Great Khan's concubines have given him a further twenty-five sons, all good and brave soldiers. Every one of these is a powerful lord.

Of his twenty-two legitimate sons, seven are kings of vast provinces which they rule wisely and well. This is not surprising, for their father is wise and gifted, the best ruler the Tartars have ever had.

Let us now turn to the court and how the Great Khan lives.

LXXXIV   THE GREAT KHAN'S PALACE

For three months every year Kublai Khan lives in the capital of Cathay, at Khan-balik, where he has a great palace. It is surrounded by a square wall, each side of which is a mile long. The wall is very thick and ten paces high, painted white and crenellated. At each of the four corners of the square there is a splendid and beautiful palace where the Great Khan's arms are stored. Half-way along each side of the square there is another similar palace, making eight in all. Every palace houses different equipment. For example, in one there is harness for the horses; in another there are bows, ropes, arrows, quivers and all the implements for archery; in a third there are breastplates and armour made of boiled leather; and so it goes on.

There are five gates in the south side of the wall. The central one is only opened for the Great Khan himself. Two small gates on either side of the main gate and two large ones near the corners of the wall are for citizens and other people.

Inside this wall is another one, slightly longer than it is wide. It has eight palaces like those in the outer wall, and, like the outer wall, it has five gates in the south side. There is one door in each of the other three sides of both walls.

Within the second wall is the Great Khan's palace – the biggest palace ever to be seen. It abuts onto the northern wall, but to the south is a wide open space where barons and soldiers parade. It is built on only one floor, with a very high roof, and is raised at least ten spans from the ground, surrounded by a marble wall two paces wide within which are the foundations of the palace. The protruding edge of the wall provides a terrace on which people can walk round the palace. The outside edge of the wall supports a very fine loggia on columns. On each side of the palace a large marble staircase leads up to the top of the wall, forming entrances to the palace.

The walls inside are covered with silver and gold and there are paintings of horsemen, dragons and every kind of bird and animal. The vaulted ceiling is also entirely covered with paintings and gold ornamentation. The main reception room can seat more than 6,000 people. There is an overwhelming number of rooms; no architect in the world could have designed the palace better. The roof is beautifully painted in many colours – vermilion, green, blue, yellow and so forth – so that it shines like a jewel and can be seen from afar. This roof is solidly built to withstand the passage of time.

The Great Khan's palace at Khan-balik (Peking)

In the rear of the palace are large halls and rooms containing the Great Khan's private possessions – his personal treasure, gold and silver, precious stones and pearls, silver and gold vases. His concubines live in this part of the palace and his private apartments are also here.

Between the inner and outer walls are parks planted with beautiful trees, where white harts, musk deer, squirrels and many other animals live. The paths which cross the fields are paved and raised at least two cubits so that they are never muddy and puddles cannot form, the water draining off into the fields where the grass grows thick and green.

Between the two walls on the north-west side there is a deep, wide and very well-built artificial lake which is fed by a small river. Kublai Khan has stocked the lake with many kinds of fish. Iron grills at the river's entrance to the lake and at its outlet prevent the fish from swimming away. Between the walls to the north the Great Khan has had a hillock made from the soil excavated from the lake. It is a good 100 paces high, a mile in circumference, and covered in evergreen trees. If the Great Khan learns of a beautiful tree, he has it dug up, its roots still in earth, and carried to the hill by an elephant. He will have trees of any size transplanted and has a plantation of the finest trees in the world. The whole hillock is covered with a precious bright-green powder, so that not only the trees,

A. D. 1290.

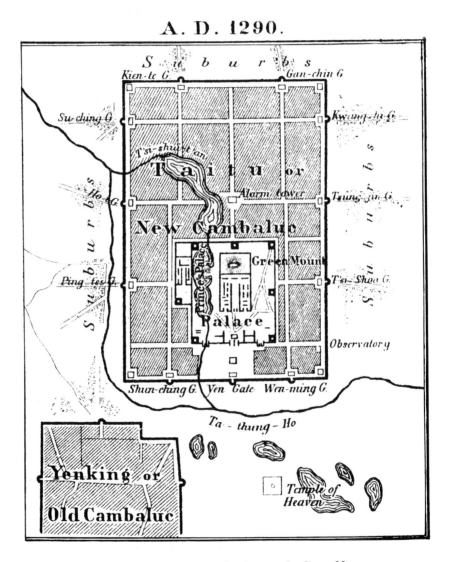

Detailed plan of Khan-balik, showing the Green Mount

but everything which meets the eye is green; hence its name, the 'Green Mount'. And at the top of the Green Mount is a green palace. The hillock, the trees and the palace are so beautiful that they delight all who see them. Indeed, Kublai Khan had them put there for this reason.

LXXXV THE PALACE OF THE GREAT KHAN'S SON

Near to his own palace the Great Khan has had another one built exactly like it for his heir. It is the same shape, the same size and has similar walls. The water connecting the two palaces can be crossed by a bridge. At the time when the Polo brothers left the court, the Khan's grandson, Temur, was living there. He emulates the Great Khan in every way and the imperial seal is his, but he cannot exercise absolute power until his grandfather's death.

Now let us turn to the city of Taidu where the palaces stand and see why and how they were built. The Great Khan's astrologers had told him that the large and important city of Khan-balik, which means the Lord's City, would rebel and overthrow the empire. So he built a new city across the river from the old one. The inhabitants of the old city were sent to live in the new city, only those who were suspected of rebellious intentions being left behind.

The new city is not as big as the old one was. It is built in an exact square with a perimeter of twenty-four miles. The city wall is crenellated and painted white; it is twenty paces high and ten paces thick at the bottom, narrowing to only three paces wide at the top. There are twelve gates to the city and over each is built a large and fine palace. Another palace is built at each corner of the city walls. So there are three gates and five palaces on each side. The arms for the defence of the city are stored in large rooms in the palaces.

The city's streets are wide and straight and designed so that one gate can be seen from another. There are many fine houses and palaces with shops on either side of the larger streets. Every building site is an exact square.

In the middle of the city there is a palace, larger than any others, over which hangs a great bell which rings a curfew every night. After the third stroke the citizens are not allowed on the streets except in cases of emergency – if someone is ill or a woman is in labour – and then a lantern must be carried.

Each of the twelve gates is guarded by 1,000 men. This is not because surprise attacks are feared, but in honour of the Great Khan who lives there, and also to deter thieves. There is, however, a lingering wariness of rebellion due to the astrologers' predictions.

More people live outside the city walls than inside, in houses which spread for three or four miles in each direction. There are many fine lodgings, all about a mile from the city, for the merchants who come there from all over the world.

Every nationality has its own lodging house; there is one for the Lombards, one for the Germans, one for the French, and so on.

There are over 20,000 prostitutes living in the suburbs. A captain is in charge of these women, and under him other captains each control groups of 1,000 or 100 women. These courtesans are carefully supervised because ambassadors coming to the Great Khan's court are his guests and they and all their retinue must be welcomed hospitably and supplied with a new woman every night. The women are not paid for their service as this is how they pay tax to the Great Khan.

All night groups of about thirty guards ride through the city looking for people who have defied the curfew. If they find anyone, he is immediately thrown into prison. In the morning he is interrogated and if he is found guilty of any offence he is given so many strokes of the cane, depending on the gravity of his crime. Men have been known to die from these beatings. Since the priests and astrologers decree that blood cannot be shed inside the city, this is how criminals are punished.

A Cathay rebellion did eventually take place in the following way. Twelve men in the city are responsible, at their own discretion, for the administration of land and other matters of public concern. One of the twelve was a Saracen called Ahmed, a shrewd, brave man who had more influence with Kublai Khan than any of the others. So much so, that the Great Khan allowed him every liberty. After Ahmed's death it was discovered that he had been giving the Great Khan magic potions so that the Khan not only believed everything his minister said, but obeyed him in everything. Ahmed had power over everything, even over punishing criminals. Whenever he wanted to get rid of someone he hated for whatever reason, he went to the Great Khan and said: 'So and so deserves to die because he has offended Your Majesty . . .' and Kublai Khan would reply, 'Do as you see fit.'

No one dared to interfere with Ahmed. Everyone was afraid of him. Furthermore, there was not a beautiful woman in the land whom Ahmed could not have if he wanted her. He would send his henchmen to the girl's father and they would say to him: 'Give your beautiful daughter to the Bailo (by which title, meaning viceroy, Ahmed was known) and such and such an office will be yours for three years.' The father would then relinquish his daughter and Ahmed would recommend him for the post to Kublai Khan. Once again the Khan would tell Ahmed to do as he saw fit. By exploiting men's ambitions and because he was so feared, Ahmed had all the women he wanted, as wives or concubines. He also had twenty-five sons who held all the highest positions in the country and many of whom, like their father, committed adultery or other dishonest deeds.

Anyone wanting an official position had to bribe Ahmed, so he managed to amass a large amount of treasure. Finally, when his reign of terror had lasted twenty-two years, the Cathayans, disgusted by his injustice and the crimes committed against themselves and their women, decided to rebel and kill him. One of the Cathayans, a man named Ch'ien-hu, whose wife and daughter had both been raped by Ahmed, commanded 1,000 men. With the aid of a certain Wan-hu, who commanded 10,000 men, he planned to kill the tyrant when Kublai Khan left Khan-balik after his three-month stay and returned to Xanadu with his son Genghis. In the Khan's absence Ahmed would be left in charge of the city. If anything untoward happened, Ahmed would send envoys to the Great Khan for his advice.

Ch'ien-hu and Wan-hu confided their plot to various leading Cathayans, and it was agreed to spread word of the plan to other cities as well. On the appointed day a great fire would be the signal for the Cathayans to kill all bearded men, for Cathayans are clean-shaven but Tartars, Saracens and Christians all have beards. The signal would be passed from city to city, and all bearded men would die:

The Cathayans hated the reign of the Great Khan because he mistrusted them and installed Tartars and Saracens to rule over them; they felt they were being treated like serfs. Furthermore, the Great Khan had no legal right to Cathay for he had conquered it by force.

On an agreed day, Ch'ien-hu and Wan-hu broke into the palace at night. Wan-hu sat on the throne and had the lamps lit. He then sent a messenger to Ahmed, who lived in the old city, with the news that Prince Genghis had arrived unexpectedly and wanted to see him. Ahmed was surprised, but he was afraid of Genghis so he set out immediately. When he reached the city gate he met the Tartar Kogatai, commander of the city's 12,000 guards, who asked him where he was going so late. Ahmed said he was going to see Genghis who had just arrived.

'How can he have arrived without my knowing?' Kogatai asked, and with some of his men he followed Ahmed. Meanwhile, the Cathayans were thinking that if they could manage to kill Ahmed they would have nothing else to fear.

When Ahmed entered the palace he was dazzled by the bright lights and knelt in front of Wan-hu, thinking he was Genghis. Wan-hu, who was ready and waiting, simply cut off his head with a sword. Kogatai arrived at the palace just in time to see what happened. Without hesitation he shot an arrow straight into Wan-hu's heart, killing him instantly. Ch'ien-hu was taken prisoner and a group of guards was sent into the streets to warn the citizens that anyone found out of doors would be killed immediately.

The Cathayans, realizing their plot had been discovered and finding themselves without a leader, shut themselves up in their houses and failed to give the signal of rebellion to the other cities. Kogatai immediately sent envoys to Kublai Khan to inform him of what had happened. The Great Khan replied with instructions that the conspirators be suitably punished. In the morning, Kogatai interrogated all the Cathayans. Many of them were subsequently put to death as accomplices, and the same thing happened in the other cities when it was discovered that they had also planned to revolt.

When Kublai Khan returned to Khan-balik he wanted to know what had caused the rebellion. He then discovered the crimes committed by Ahmed and some of his sons. Not all the sons were bad, but seven of them had, with their father, violated innumerable women. So the Great Khan requisitioned Ahmed's treasure and had it brought to the town from the old city. He then ordered Ahmed's body to be dug up and thrown to the dogs. The sons who had participated in their father's crimes were flayed alive. All these events took place while Marco Polo was there.

LXXXVI THE GUARD OF 12,000

For reasons of prestige rather than because he is afraid, the Great Khan has a personal bodyguard of 12,000 cavalrymen. They are called the Keshikten, which means the Lord's loyal guard. These 12,000 men have four captains, one for every 3,000. Each group of 3,000 guards the palace for a period of three days and three nights, eating and drinking there. At the end of that time 3,000 fresh guards take their place for the same length of time, and so on in turn throughout the year. The 9,000 men not on duty stay in the palace in the daytime, unless they are sent elsewhere in the service of the Great Khan or have special authority to leave, but they are permitted to go home at night.

When the Great Khan holds court and has a banquet he sits facing the south at a table raised above the others. His first wife sits beside him on his left; on his right, lower down, so that their heads are level with his feet, sit the Khan's sons in order of age, beginning with the eldest, followed by his grandsons and other members of the imperial family. The barons sit on a lower level still. The same arrangement applies to the women. The Great Khan's daughters-in-law, grand-daughters-in-law and other royal women sit below him on the left; below them sit the wives of barons and court officials. Every place is designated by Kublai Khan himself and the tables are set out so that he can see everyone. Most of the barons and soldiers in fact sit on carpets without a table. There are huge numbers of them, but they, too, are seated so that the Great Khan can see them. During a banquet there will be, in addition, more than 40,000 people eating outside the dining hall; they arrive in their hundreds from many different countries bringing strange gifts, and some who hold important positions come seeking further advancement. All these people arrive when the Great Khan is holding court.

In the middle of the hall where the Great Khan sits is an enormous square casket of very fine gold, each side about three paces long, decorated with a beautiful bas-relief of animals. Inside the casket is a large and precious gold urn which holds as much as a butt of wine, and in each corner are vessels filled with mare's milk, camel's milk and other drinks. The casket also holds the cups from which the Great Khan drinks. A gold vessel with enough wine for eight or ten people is put between every two guests. Everyone has a gold cup with a handle and helps himself from the vessel. The women have exactly the same as the men. All the vessels, cups and other objects are very valuable.

Foreigners who are unused to the ways of the court are appointed barons to show them to their seats and ensure that the servants bring them everything they need in the way of wine, milk or meat.

On either side of each of the hall's doorways stand two gigantic men, each holding a staff. They are there to see that no one touches the threshold, for everyone must step over it. The barons warn foreigners that it is considered unlucky to touch the threshold. If anyone touches it by mistake, his robes are taken away and he has to pay a fine before he may have them back; if he keeps his clothes he must receive a beating instead. This rule does not, however, apply to people leaving the hall since they may be somewhat affected by the amount of wine they have drunk and incapable of walking steadily.

Those who wait on the Great Khan have to wear fine gold or silk cloths over their noses and mouths to prevent their breath from contaminating his food. When the Great Khan indicates that he wishes to drink, all the instruments in the hall begin to play, and as he takes his cup from the cup-bearer all the barons and guests kneel to him. Only then does he drink. These marks of respect are repeated every time he drinks. There is, of course, an abundance of every kind of food.

No baron or lord may come to the banquet without his first wife, who eats with the other ladies. When the meal is over, jugglers, acrobats and similar entertainers come to amuse the Great Khan. Everyone enjoys these displays, which are occasions for much laughter. Finally the guests all return to their own houses.

LXXXVII KUBLAI KHAN'S BIRTHDAY CELEBRATIONS

The Tartars always celebrate their birthdays. The Great Khan was born on 28 September, which is therefore the most important feast day apart from the first day of the year.

On his birthday Kublai Khan dresses in beaten gold. At least 12,000 barons and knights dress in the same fashion and colour, although their clothes are less valuable, being made of gold and silk cloth. They all wear wide gold belts. These clothes are given by the Khan to his barons. The jewels and pearls which decorate them are alone worth more than 10,000 gold bezants. Thirteen times a year the Great Khan gives sumptuous clothes resembling his own to these 12,000 barons, gifts on a scale that no other ruler on earth could afford.

LXXXVIII   FURTHER CELEBRATIONS OF THE GREAT KHAN'S BIRTHDAY

Every single one of Kublai Khan's Tartar subjects gives him a magnificent birthday present according to his means and position. Gifts also come from other people, particularly those seeking advancement. Twelve barons are put in charge of these applications. On this day, all idolaters, Saracens and people of other religions pray repeatedly to their idols or gods that the Great Khan may be given a long life, health and happiness.

This, then, is how Kublai Khan's birthday is celebrated. Let us now turn to the other great feast at the beginning of the year which is known as the 'white feast'.

LXXXIX   THE FEAST OF THE NEW YEAR

The new year begins in those parts in February and it is celebrated by the Great Khan and all his subjects. The custom is for everybody to dress entirely in white, as far as they can afford it. White is thought to bring good luck and by wearing white on the first day of the year the people believe they ensure their happiness throughout it. On this day gifts of gold, silver, precious stones, pearls and rich white cloth are sent to the Khan from every province and kingdom in the empire so that he may be rich and happy all the year. The barons, lords and other people also give each other white presents, greeting each other joyfully and wishing each other good luck.

It is traditional for the provinces to send presents numbering nine times nine, that is eighty-one white horses, pieces of gold or lengths of material. The Great Khan has occasionally received as many as 100,000 white horses of great value. On this day there is always a procession of elephants draped in white cloth embroidered with birds and animals. Each elephant bears a beautiful casket filled with plate and white clothing for the court. Next come camels, also draped in white and carrying things for the festival. They all file past the Great Khan. It is one of the most magnificent spectacles imaginable.

In the morning, before the tables are ready, all the kings, dukes, marquesses, counts, barons, knights, astrologers, doctors, falconers, army officers and other officials gather in the great hall in Kublai Khan's presence. Those for whom there is no room must stay outside, but still within sight of the Khan. The hierarchy is as follows: first come the Khan's sons, grandsons and other members of the imperial family; next come kings, dukes and so forth. When everyone is finally seated a priest stands up and says in a loud voice: 'Kneel and adore.'

The people immediately obey, touching the ground with their heads and worshipping Kublai Khan as if he were a god.

Then the priest says: 'God save and protect our lord for many years, and grant him happiness.'

'So be it,' the people reply.

'God grant that the empire may increase in prosperity and protect obedient subjects, granting them peace. May peace and goodwill dwell in the land.'

'So be it,' the people again reply.

This is repeated four times. Then everyone moves towards a richly-decorated altar on which is a vermilion tablet, engraved with the Great Khan's name, and a beautiful censer. The priest, as the people's representative, censes the tablet and the alter most reverently, then everybody bows respectfully and returns to their places.

Chinese conjurers and acrobats, who performed before the Great Khan
at the 'white feast' to celebrate the new year

After this the gifts are presented to the Great Khan. When he has seen them all the tables are prepared and everyone sits down according to their rank. Kublai Khan sits at the high table alone with his first wife. All the ladies sit on the empress's side of the hall. The banquet is arranged in the same way as for the Khan's birthday, with jugglers and acrobats, until at last everyone returns home.

We will now turn to the clothing of some of the barons who attend the festivities.

XC   THE 12,000 BARONS

There are thirteen festivals during the year, one for each lunar month. The 12,000 barons, who are called the Keshikten (the Khan's personal guard), have to attend them all. The Great Khan gives each of these men thirteen different coloured outfits embroidered with pearls and precious stones. He also gives each of them a priceless gold belt and fine leather boots embroidered with silver thread. Their robes are adorned with so many jewels that when the barons are dressed in them they look like kings. There is a special outfit for each of the thirteen feast days. They are always well kept and usually last for about ten years. The Great Khan also has thirteen feast-day robes. They are the same colour as those he gives his barons, but made of richer materials with even finer jewels.

The thirteen robes belonging to each of the 12,000 barons, a total of 156,000 garments, are of such magnificence that it is impossible to estimate their worth. The Great Khan insists on all this in order that his feasts should be as lavish and splendid as possible.

It is worth noting, too, that on these festive occasions a large lion is led into Kublai Khan's presence, and it is an amazing sight to see the lion, without a chain, go and lie down in front of the Great Khan as though acknowledging its ruler.

Let us now turn to the Great Khan's hunting.

XCI   THE GREAT KHAN'S SUBJECTS AND THEIR TRIBUTE OF GAME

From December until February, when Kublai Khan is in Taidu, everyone in the region is ordered to hunt both animals and birds and present their larger game to the Great Khan. The ruler of every province within a thirty-day journey rallies his huntsmen and they go wherever beasts are to be found, which they surround and kill with dogs and arrows. Vast quantities of animals reserved for the Great Khan are disembowelled and sent to him on carts. Provinces further away, however, send only the skins, cured and prepared for use in making army equipment.

XCII THE GREAT KHAN'S WILD ANIMALS

Kublai Khan owns a large number of leopards trained to hunt, and lynxes which are taught to catch animals. He also has lions, far bigger than the lions of Babylon, with beautiful striped pelts of orange, black and white. They are used to attack wild boar, wild oxen, bears, wild asses, deer and roebuck. It is an extraordinary sight to watch the lions catch their prey. The lions are carried out in cages on wagons, with a little dog for company. They are kept in cages because they are very ferocious and it would be impossible to hold them otherwise. They have to be transported against the wind as any animal getting a scent of a lion would immediately flee.

The Great Khan also has a large number of eagles for catching wolves, roebuck and deer. The ones which catch wolves are very large and powerful – no wolf is too big for these eagles.

Now for the Great Khan's dogs.

XCIII THE TWO BROTHERS IN CHARGE OF DOGS

The Great Khan has among his barons two brothers called Bayan and Mingan. They are known as *kuyukchi*, which means 'keeper of hounds'. Each of the brothers has 10,000 men under his command. Whenever they go hunting one of these units of 10,000 dresses entirely in red, the other in blue. Two thousand men from each unit lead the dogs – no less than one, two or even three large mastiffs per man. When Kublai Khan goes hunting, one brother rides on one side with 10,000 men and as many as 5,000 dogs. The second brother rides on his other side with the same number of men and dogs. They march in two lines spread out over a distance of a day's journey. Then, little by little, they close in so that no animal can escape. Such a hunt is an amazing event. The Great Khan rides across the countryside hawking with his barons and all of a sudden packs of hounds burst out from one side or the other in pursuit of bears, deer and other wild beasts. It is truly a magnificent sight.

The brothers are bound to deliver 1,000 head of game per day to the court from October to March. This does not include quails and fish, which they deliver when they can. A head of fish is the amount three people would eat in a meal.

Now for how Kublai Khan spends the next three months.

XCIV THE GREAT KHAN OUT HUNTING

At the beginning of March the Great Khan leaves Khan-balik and travels south towards the sea, which is two days' journey away. He is accompanied by 10,000 falconers with their 500 gerfalcons and a multitude of peregrine and saker

83

falcons. He also takes many goshawks to hunt along the river banks. All these falconers are dispersed in groups of 100 or 200. When they return from hawking they present most of their game to the Great Khan.

When he goes hawking himself with gerfalcons and other birds of prey he takes no fewer than 10,000 men, whom he calls 'watchmen', who spread themselves out in pairs over a vast stretch of countryside. They each have a call and a hood. When the Great Khan orders his birds to be freed, the falconers do not have to follow them because with so many watchmen the birds are never lost sight of and can be helped if they are in trouble.

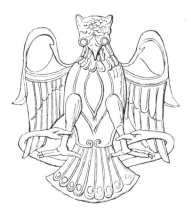

Carving of a gerfalcon

All the birds have small silver medallions, inscribed with their owners' names, attached to their feet. Thus they can easily be returned where they belong. Unidentified birds are given to a baron known as the *bularguchi*, which means 'controller of lost property', who concerns himself with all unclaimed objects – horses, swords, birds or whatever. Anyone keeping lost property is considered a thief. The baron is easily found since he always positions his tent, with his flag flying, on the highest ground in the camp.

Many fine hunting expeditions take place on this journey south towards the Ocean. Because he suffers from gout, the Great Khan always travels, when hawking, in a beautiful wooden shelter carried by four elephants. It is lined with beaten gold and the outside is covered with lion-skins. Kublai Khan always has twelve of his best gerfalcons with him and a number of barons and ladies to keep him company. As he travels along on top of the elephants his barons ride beside him drawing his attention to passing birds, such as cranes. The cover of the shelter is then thrown back and Kublai Khan sends out his best gerfalcons. They fight with the cranes for a long time and nearly always manage to capture them.

Meanwhile the Great Khan lies back, delighting in the spectacle, with his barons and knights riding around him.

No ruler on earth has so many pleasures so easily available to him.

After a long journey, the Great Khan comes to a place called Cachar Modun where his pavilions, and those of his sons, his barons and his women have been pitched in advance. In all, there are about 10,000 ornate pavilions.

The imperial pavilion contains several tents. The one where Kublai Khan has his court is large enough to hold 1,000 knights. This tent opens to the south and serves as a hall for the barons and other courtiers. It is connected to another tent which faces west, where the Great Khan holds private audiences. At the back of the hall is a large and beautiful room where Kublai Khan sleeps. There are other tents as well, but they are not connected to the main one. The two large tents and the Khan's bedroom are supported by carved and gilded wooden posts and are covered on the outside with fine lion-skins striped black and white and orange.

The tents are made very cleverly so as to be weatherproof, and are lined with sable and ermine – two of the most sumptuous furs in the world. A man's sable coat can, if the quality is good, be worth as much as 2,000 gold bezants. The Tartars call sable the queen of furs. One skin is about the size of a marten. The Great Khan's apartment is lined with these two furs most beautifully and carefully sewn together. The tent ropes are all made of silk. These tents are so costly that no minor king could even begin to afford them.

All the other tents are pitched round the Great Khan in an orderly fashion. His women also have magnificent pavilions and there are even tents for the gerfalcons, falcons and other birds. The camp is enormous and resembles a well laid-out town. It is occupied by a multitude of people; Kublai Khan has his whole retinue with him – doctors, astrologers, falconers and a great number of court officials. Everything goes on exactly as it does in the capital city.

The Great Khan remains here until the spring, around the time of our Easter. All the time he is there he goes hawking by the rivers and lakes, hunting swans and other birds. Everyone in the area sends him game and he has a very happy time. The splendour and enjoyment of these hunting parties is beyond description.

No merchant, artisan or peasant dares to keep goshawks or hounds in any of the Great Khan's territory. And no nobleman who is not a head falconer would dare to hunt within a five- or ten-mile radius of the Great Khan without special permission. Furthermore, no king or nobleman throughout the empire hunts hare, does, roebuck, stags or suchlike animals between the months of May and October because this is the breeding season. Anyone doing so would be severely punished. The law is so well established that during these months animals often come very near to men without fear of being harmed.

When the hunting season comes to an end, the whole party returns to Khan-balik, hawking and hunting on the way.

XCV   THE GREAT KHAN HOLDS COURT AND CELEBRATES

The Great Khan stays for three months in his magnificent principal palace in Khan-balik where he amuses himself and celebrates with his ladies.

XCVI   THE GREAT CITY OF KHAN-BALIK

There are more houses than can be counted in Khan-balik. The population is very dense, especially in the outskirts where traders and anyone coming to the city on business lodge. The houses there are as fine as those inside the city walls.

The city is the mercantile centre of the world. All the most precious stones and pearls from India are brought there. The strangest and most valuable things come from Cathay and other provinces. All these rarities reach Khan-balik because the court is there with all its fine ladies, noblemen, soldiers and others who attend the Great Khan. At least 1,000 cartloads of silk are sent to Khan-balik every day. Vast quantities of silk and cloth of gold are woven there because there is a scarcity of flax, cotton and hemp. There are more than 200 cities in the surrounding area from which the people come to Khan-balik to buy and sell produce, which is why the city is such an important trading centre.

The dead may not be buried within the city or anywhere near it. Idolaters are taken outside and their bodies are burned. Others are buried a long way away. Prostitutes, of whom there are at least 20,000, may not live in the city, only in the suburbs. These women make a good living from the foreign traders who are continually coming and going. The number of prostitutes gives some idea of the size of the population of Khan-balik.

It is now time to consider the money which is manufactured in the city.

XCVII   THE GREAT KHAN'S PEOPLE SPEND PAPER, NOT COINS

The Great Khan's mint is situated in Khan-balik and the way it functions might lead one to suppose that the Khan had mastered the art of alchemy.

Money is made from bark collected from mulberry trees on whose leaves the silk worms feed. The bast — a black, fibrous, inner layer of bark — is removed, shredded, and pounded and flattened with glue into a kind of paper which is as fine as papyrus. It is then cut into squares and rectangles of different sizes. The small pieces are worth the equivalent of half a Venetian silver groat, bigger ones are worth a groat, and others equal five groats and ten groats. There are larger

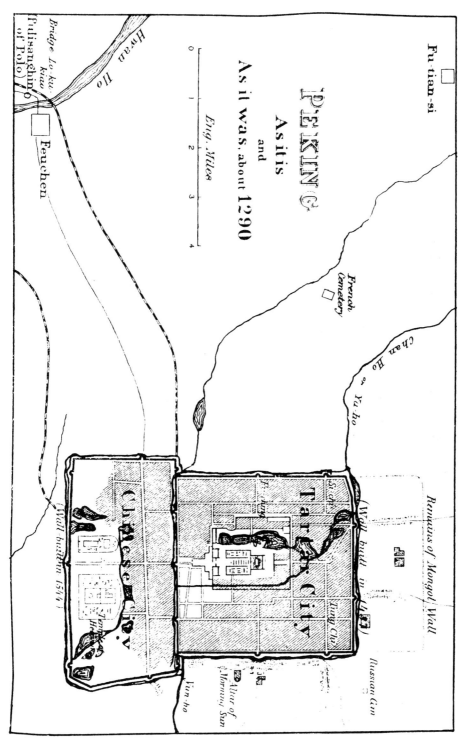

Peking (Khan-balik) as it was in about 1290, with later additions superimposed

ones still which correspond to one, two or three bezants, and so on up to ten. Each note is stamped with the Great Khan's seal. This money carries as much authority and validity as gold or silver. Special officials write their names on the notes and then the chief official nominated by the Great Khan authenticates the money by sprinkling some red pigment on a seal entrusted to him for the purpose and stamping the notes. Anyone found forging them is put to death. So much of this money is made that Kublai Khan could buy all the coins in the world.

Throughout the empire this paper money is used in every transaction. To refuse it would be to incur the death penalty. In fact the Great Khan's subjects are perfectly willing to be paid in paper money since with it they can buy anything, including pearls, precious stones, gold or silver. Yet paper money worth ten bezants does not weigh as much as even one bezant.

XCVIII THE GREAT KHAN'S TWELVE ADVISERS

Kublai Khan has twelve barons in charge of his army, who supervise military manoeuvres and dispatch men wherever necessary. They are also responsible for rewarding good and courageous soldiers and punishing cowards. If the commander of 1,000 men proves inadequate in battle, he will be degraded to the command of only 100 men. If, on the other hand, he acts bravely, he will be promoted. Nothing, however, is done without the Great Khan's consent, and when a man is promoted Kublai Khan gives him magnificent gifts to encourage bravery in others. These barons have jurisdiction over what is called the *Thai*, which is the supreme court, with only the Khan above them.

The Great Khan also has twelve dignitaries to administer the thirty-four provinces. They live in Khan-balik in a beautiful and spacious palace. Every province has its judge and clerks, each of whom has his own house, and between them they deal with all the affairs of the province. They are, however, responsible to the twelve barons. It is the barons who select the administrators of the thirty-four provinces. When they have done so, they inform the Great Khan who gives a gold tablet of authority to each governor according to his rank. The barons are also responsible for the collection of taxes and for expenditure in the provinces — indeed for everything in the provinces directly concerned with the Great Khan, except military matters.

The twelve barons live in a palace called *Shieng* and preside at the supreme court of the same name. Again, there is no higher authority except Kublai Khan himself. Of the two supreme courts, the *Thai*, or military court, is considered to be more prestigious.

There is no point in enumerating the provinces here. We will turn instead to Kublai Khan's envoys and how they find fresh horses on their journeys.

25

29

30

XCIX   THE POST HOUSES ON THE WAY TO KHAN-BALIK

Many roads lead out of Khan-balik towards different provinces; each road bears the name of the province to which it goes. Kublai Khan has seen to it that his envoys are supplied with everything they need when they ride along these roads. This particular service is organized in the most amazing fashion. Every twenty-five miles there is a beautiful, palatial post house where the messengers can stay in magnificent beds with silk sheets and every other luxury suitable for a king. There are always 400 well-kept horses ready, which are supplied and fed by nearby towns. There are more than 10,000 such palaces, all beautifully furnished, and more than 200,000 horses in all. It is hard to imagine so grandiose an organization – the only one of its kind.

Travellers can even find post houses in the wilder parts of the empire, for Kublai Khan has had them built there and has himself supplied them with horses and harness. However, there may be as many as forty miles between them. The Great Khan sends people to cultivate the land around these post houses and as a result villages develop. In this way Kublai Khan's messengers can travel in any direction, always finding lodgings and a change of horse.

Anyone asking where the Khan finds enough people to run this organization and what they live on should remember that idolaters and Saracens all have between six and ten wives each and an unlimited number of children, so one man may have as many as thirty sons. We, on the other hand, have only one wife each, and, in cases of sterility, no children.

There is no shortage of rice, panic grass and millet on which the Khan's people can live. The Tartars, the Cathayans and the people of Manzi harvest particularly rich crops. They do not make bread, but cook their cereals with milk or meat. Wheat, which produces a smaller harvest, is only eaten in the form of noodles. Every possible piece of land is cultivated. The animals breed well and every man can take at least eight horses with him when he goes to war.

This then is why these parts are so densely populated and why the people are so well off.

Between the post houses there are also small villages of about forty houses where the Great Khan's unmounted couriers live. They wear wide belts hung with bells so that they can be heard from afar. They carry messages in relays, each courier running three miles at great speed. Three miles from the first courier a second one, alerted by the sound of the bells, is waiting to take over. As soon as the first arrives, the second one takes whatever he is carrying, and also a note from the clerk, and immediately begins to run. This process is repeated every three miles and by this method the Great Khan can receive news from places which are ten days' journey away in a day and a night. Neither the couriers nor the men servicing the post stations have to pay tax; they are very well supported by the Khan.

In cases of emergency, like bringing Kublai Khan news of a rebellion, the horsemen can cover 200 to 250 miles a day. In these cases they carry a tablet stamped with the gerfalcon to show that speed is essential. These messengers wrap up well, covering their heads, and ride at full gallop on strong horses. As they near the next post house they blow a special horn which can be heard from a long way off, so that fresh horses will be ready for them. They immediately leap onto the fresh horses and gallop off, continuing in this way until night falls — and if they gallop on through the night they can even cover 300 miles by the morning. If there is no moon at night, men from the post houses run ahead of them carrying torches, but this, of course, slows them down considerably.

These strong, enduring messengers are highly prized men.

C   THE GREAT KHAN HELPS HIS PEOPLE

The Great Khan is in the habit of sending his messengers all over the empire to enquire after his subjects and to find out if their crops have suffered from drought or been ravaged by locusts. If he discovers a famine, he not only exempts the sufferers from tax, but gives them grain to eat and to sow. This is an act of great bounty. If, during the winter, the Great Khan learns that a man has lost his livestock through some misfortune, this man is also exempted from tax. In this way Kublai Khan looks after his subjects.

CI   THE GREAT KHAN HAS TREES PLANTED ALONG THE ROADS

The Great Khan has ordered trees to be planted on either side of the roads frequented by messengers and traders. They are large trees which are visible from a distance and help the traveller to follow the right path.

These trees are planted everywhere, even in desert regions, where they are a great comfort to the traveller. The Great Khan is only too happy to plant trees because diviners and astrologers have told him that anyone planting trees lives a long time.

CII   THE CATHAY WINE

In the province of Cathay, most people drink wine made from rice and flavoured with delicious spices. It is so well made that it tastes better than any other wine. It is clear and a great stimulant which quickly intoxicates people.

CIII THE BURNING STONES

There is a black stone to be found throughout Cathay which, like other stones, is cut out of the mountains, but it burns like wood and, in fact, gives out far more heat than wood while making a low flame like charcoal. It burns slowly and will keep burning all night. These stones are used throughout Cathay even where there is plenty of wood. This is necessary because there are so many bath-houses, where everyone has a bath at least three times a week, and in winter one a day, that there is probably not enough wood to heat all the water. In addition, the rich have stoves for hot water in their own houses. So the black stones are used a lot, to save wood and because they are cheap.

CIV HOW THE GREAT KHAN CARES FOR HIS PEOPLE

When the harvest is good and corn is cheap, the Great Khan buys huge quantities which he stores in large buildings designed for the purpose, where it can be preserved for a good three or four years. In every province vast granaries are filled with wheat, barley, millet, rice, panic grass and so forth. In cases of famine the grain from these warehouses is sold at a quarter of the current price, so that no one need go without.

CV THE GREAT KHAN'S CHARITY TO THE POOR

Not only does the Great Khan supply his people with grain, he also cares for the poor. In every city he has had a list drawn up of people who are poverty stricken because of illness or other misfortunes which prevent them from working. Throughout the year, poor families, even with ten members, are given free grain. Large numbers of families are helped in this way; furthermore, bread and alms are never refused by the palace. It is the duty of certain officials to hand out bowls of rice, panic and millet every day of the year.

Before the Tartars learnt the ways of the idolaters, no one was given alms and beggars were chased away. 'Be off!' they would be told, 'and take your God-given illness with you. If God loved you as much as he loves us, he would have looked after you.' But the idolaters' priests convinced the Great Khan that charity was good and the idols would bless him for it. Since then, Kublai Khan has taken pity on the poor and been very generous to them, for which the people are grateful and they worship the Khan like a god.

In Khan-balik the Great Khan provides food and clothing for a further 5,000 or so astrologers and soothsayers who practise their arts in the city. These people have an almanac in which the movements of the planets are written. Every year the astrologers of all denominations – Christians, Cathayans and Saracens – trace the course of the year with reference to each moon and work out how conditions will be affected by them. One moon will bring gales, another earthquakes and another thunder, lightning, torrential rain, sickness, the plague, or war. They say that all these things will happen in the natural course of events, but they can be either exacerbated or mitigated by God.

The astrologers write down everything that will happen in small notebooks which are sold for a groat each to people who want them. The best and most proven soothsayers are honoured accordingly. Anyone wanting to know in advance the outcome of a long journey or an important venture will consult the astrologers, telling them the year, month, day, hour and place of his birth.

The years are divided into twelve cycles, in which every year has its own sign, such as the lion, the ox, the dragon and so forth. When someone is asked his date of birth, he will reply: 'In the year of the lion, on such a day or night, in the hour of such a moon.' When the twelve-year cycle has ended, it begins again at the first sign. An astrologer, then, can study the constellation and the planet under which someone was born and compare them to the constellation and planet at the time of the undertaking, by which means he can foretell the outcome of any venture. If a planet then in the ascendant indicates ill luck, a merchant may have to wait for a more auspicious planet to be in the ascendant before setting out on his journey. If the constellation over a city gate is in opposition to the merchant's own, he must leave by a different gate, or wait for the constellation to change. The astrologers can tell the traveller where and when he will be attacked by thieves, whether there will be storms, whether his horse will break its leg and whether or not the outcome of the venture will be successful. All the events of the return journey can likewise be foretold.

The Cathayans are superior to any other people in good manners and wisdom. They devote themselves to learning and to all the scientific disciplines. They speak politely and greet people cheerfully. They behave with dignity and eat cleanly. They treat their mothers and fathers with great respect; there is even an officially appointed council which deals with and punishes ungrateful children.

These people are idolaters and every one of them has a tablet hung in his house on which is written the name of their most high, heavenly and divine god. This they worship every day with incense, holding their hands above their heads and gnashing their teeth. They pray to him for health of body and mind only, asking for nothing else. But on the floor they have a statue called Natigai, god of earthly matters, to whom they pray for fine weather, a good harvest, their children and so forth, and whom they worship in the same way as their most high god.

They do not care for their souls, but only for the pleasures of the flesh. They believe, however, that the soul of a dead man passes into another body. If a poor man has led an honest life he will be reborn as a gentleman, then as a nobleman, and so on until he finally becomes part of the absolute deity. On the other hand, if a gentleman has led a bad life, he will be reborn as a peasant, and after that as a dog, and so on down to the lower forms of animal life.

We must now leave Khan-balik for the riches of Cathay.

IV

From Peking to Bengal

CVI   THE GREAT PROVINCE OF CATHAY

Marco Polo was sent by Kublai Khan on a four-month journey to the west, during which he saw many things.

Ten miles from Khan-balik there is a large river called Pulisanghin which flows into the Ocean. Traders sail up and down it with their merchandise. An extremely fine stone bridge spans the river. It is at least 300 paces long and eight paces wide so that ten horsemen can ride across it abreast. It is beautifully built

The bridge over the Pulisanghin, from a Chinese original

94

of grey marble slabs dovetailed together and has twenty-four arches and twenty-three columns supporting it. Along each side is a parapet made of marble slabs and columns. The columns are set one and a half paces apart, each with a lion at the top and another at the foot. Between the columns is a wall of grey marble slabs to prevent people from falling into the water. At the top of the ramp leading on to the bridge there is a huge marble column resting on the back of a marble tortoise. The bridge is indeed a very fine sight.

CVII   THE CITY OF CHO-CHAU

Beyond the bridge a thirty-mile journey takes the traveller through gardens, lush vineyards and flowering meadows with clear streams to the beautiful city of Cho-chau. There are many idolaters' temples here and the population lives by trade and by weaving cloth of gold and fine sendal. The city is full of lodging houses for travellers.

A mile beyond this city the road divides. One fork leads west to Cathay, the other south-east to the province of Manzi. After a journey of ten days along the road to Cathay the traveller reaches the city of T'ai-yuan-fu.

CVIII   THE KINGDOM OF T'AI-YUAN-FU

T'ai-yuan-fu is a ten days' ride from Cho-chau. It is the capital of the kingdom, a beautiful city, rich in merchandise and artisans' workshops. Much harness for the Great Khan's army is made here and fine vineyards produce an abundance of wine. This is the only part of the province in which wine is made from the grape. A vast amount of silk is also produced as there are numerous mulberry trees and silk worms.

To the west of T'ai-yuan-fu the lovely countryside is dotted with towns and castles. There are many traders in these parts who go from town to town making large profits.

After a seven-day journey the traveller reaches the remarkable city of P'ing-yang-fu which is also crowded with merchants. A lot of silk is produced here and the people live by trading.

CIX   THE CASTLE OF CAICHU

The beautiful castle of Caichu, built by the so-called Golden King, is a two-day journey to the west of P'ing-yang-fu. Inside the castle walls is a magnificent palace with a hall full of priceless portraits of the old rulers of the province. The hall itself is exceptionally fine, decorated in gold, with wonderfully depicted scenes of the lives of the kings. The people here tell a story concerning the Golden King and Prester John.

The Golden King, from a manuscript in the Royal Asiatic Society's
collection

The Golden King was a very great and powerful man and only beautiful young women – of whom there were many at court – were allowed to wait on him. He travelled about the countryside in a small and very light cart pulled by young girls. Nothing delighted the King more. Nevertheless, he was a capable and just ruler. He was at war with Prester John whom he managed to hold off by the strength of his army. This made Prester John so angry that seven of his men offered to capture the Golden King and hand him over alive to Prester John, who gratefully accepted the offer. So the seven men set off with a good company of men and went to the Golden King to whom they offered their services. The King welcomed them gladly. At the end of two years these seven men had become, by virtue of their good service, favourites of the King. He trusted them as though they were his own sons. But no one is safe from traitors, and one day the Golden King went out with only a small retinue, which included these seven wicked men. When they had crossed a river about a mile from the palace, the seven, knowing that the King's escort was not strong enough to defend him, decided that the time had come to act. They drew their swords and said: 'Either come with us, or be killed.'

The King, quite bewildered, replied: 'What do you want? And where do you want me to go?'

'You must come with us to our lord, Prester John,' they answered.

CX   PRESTER JOHN AND THE GOLDEN KING

When the King heard this, he was shocked and sorely pained by the treachery. He begged the men to take pity on him. 'Haven't I honoured you under my roof? Why do you want to hand me over to my enemy? Such action would be wicked and treacherous.'

But the seven were adamant, and they led him to Prester John, who was delighted by their arrival and greeted the King with a sneer. The Golden King did not respond to the greeting and Prester John sent him to look after the animals. So, because Prester John wanted to show his contempt and prove his own superiority, the King became a herdsman. After two years, he was summoned to Prester John and told to put on rich clothes. Then Prester John paid homage to him and said: 'Your Majesty, now do you realize that you cannot set yourself against me?'

The King admitted that he knew and had always known that he could not oppose Prester John. Having nothing more to ask, Prester John gave him horses, harness and a guard of honour and let him go. From that time the Golden King became the friend and loyal vassal of Prester John.

We shall now move on to other matters.

CXI   THE GREAT KARA-MORAN RIVER

Twenty miles to the west of the Golden King's castle is the Kara-moran river which is so wide and deep that no bridge crosses it. It flows into the Ocean and many busy trading towns and villages are built along its banks. Ginger is grown in abundance in these parts and large amounts of silk are produced. There are so many birds that one Venetian groat will buy at least three pheasants. Canes, which the inhabitants put to good use, grow along the river banks. Some of them are a foot and a half thick.

A two-day journey to the west beyond the river, takes the traveller to the imposing city of Ho-chung-fu. Like all Cathayans, the people are idolaters. The city is a rich commercial centre with many artisans' shops. There are a lot of exotic spices including ginger, galingale and lavender, and various qualities of cloth of gold are woven here. This is all that is worth recording about Ho-chung-fu.

CXII   THE CITY OF SI-NGAN-FU

A further eight days' journey to the west takes the traveller through more busy trading towns, flowering fields and gardens, and countryside full of mulberry trees. Apart from a few Turks, Nestorian Christians and Saracens, the people are idolaters. There is a rich variety of wildlife. At the end of the eight days the large and fine city of Si-ngan-fu, capital of the province of the same name, is reached. The province was given by the Great Khan to one of his sons, called Mangalai, who has been crowned King. It is a city of merchants and artisans, and silk and arms are made there. Almost everything can be found there at a reasonable price.

Mangalai's palace is beyond the city. It rises out of a great plain with rivers, lakes, marshes and springs where there are many wild animals and birds, and is surrounded by a well-built, crenellated and very high wall with a five-mile perimeter. The palace itself is very large and decorated in the finest possible way. It has many beautiful rooms with legends depicted on the walls in beaten gold, exquisite azure, and marble inlay. Mangalai is a good and just king, much loved by his subjects. The soldiers stationed around the palace amuse themselves by hunting.

Let us now turn to the mountainous province of Han-chung.

CXIII THE PROVINCE OF HAN-CHUNG ON THE BORDER OF CATHAY AND MANZI

Leaving Mangalai's palace the traveller will take three days to cross a fine plain with innumerable busy cities and villages and plenty of silk before reaching the great mountains and valleys of Han-chung. There are castles and cities in these mountains where the people are mostly idolaters, although there are some Nestorians and Saracens. They live on game and the fruits of the land and woods. There are huge forests inhabited by many wild animals, including lions, bears, wolves, does, roebuck, deer and so forth, which are a joy to the huntsmen. Riding for twenty days, through mountains, valleys and woods, the traveller will always find towns, villages and good lodgings.

CXIV THE PROVINCE OF AK-BALIK MANZI

Twenty days further west lies the province of Ak-balik Manzi, which is a plain. There are many cities and villages inhabited by idolatrous tradesmen and artisans. Enough ginger grows here to supply the whole province of Cathay and the people earn considerable income from it. The land is very fertile, and wheat, rice and other cereals are also grown. The capital city is called Ak-balik Manzi, which means 'the white city near Manzi'.

The plain extends for a distance of two days' journey. It is a pleasure to cross as every city and village is a delight. At the end of the two days there are more mountains, valleys and extensive forests.

Riding west for yet another twenty days the traveller will find more towns and villages and an idolatrous population living on the land, hunting and keeping sheep. Vast numbers of lions, bears, wolves, does, roebuck, stags and musk deer live here.

CXV   THE PROVINCE OF CH'ENG-TU-FU

A further twenty days' ride westward through the same mountains leads to a plain in another province bordering on Manzi, called Ch'eng-tu-fu. The capital city bears the same name and was once an important place ruled over by rich and powerful kings. The city has a twenty-mile circumference, but it has been divided up.

When the King of the province died, he left three sons and the city was divided between them. Each part has its own city wall within the outer wall. In this way each of the sons inherited a kingdom with extensive lands and vast wealth from their rich father. But the Great Khan conquered the whole area, dispossessed the Kings and took control of the kingdom.

Many fresh-water rivers full of fish rise in the distant mountains, and flow through and around the city. Some are half a mile wide and others only 150 paces, but they are all deep. Beyond the city they flow into each other making one mighty river called the Yangtze which runs into the Ocean, eighty to a hundred days' journey away. The river is navigable and crowded with ships carrying an enormous quantity of merchandise up and down it. The river is so wide that it looks almost like the sea.

Inside the city a huge stone bridge spans the river. It is eight paces wide and 2,000 paces long – the breadth of the river. All along both sides are marble columns which support the wooden roof of the bridge. The roof is richly decorated with legendary scenes. Every morning collapsible wooden shops selling a variety of goods are put up along each side of the bridge. The Great Khan's officials collect about 1,000 gold bezants' worth of taxes from the traders on the bridge every day.

A five-day journey from this city, where the people are idolaters, leads through plains and valleys with many villages and dwellings where the people live on the land, although there are also artisans who weave the loveliest sendal and other materials. The plain belongs to the province of Ch'eng-tu-fu and is full of wild beasts such as lions and bears. But at the end of the five days the traveller reaches the totally devastated province of Tibet.

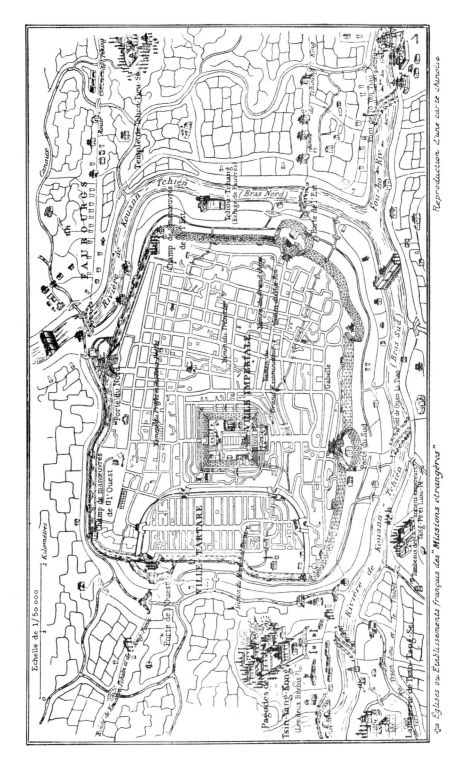

Nineteenth-century French map of Ch'eng-tu-fu

CXVI THE PROVINCE OF TIBET

Tibet was laid waste by Mongu Khan's wars. Everywhere cities and villages are in ruins and houses have been demolished.

For twenty days the traveller must pass through uninhabited villages where roaming lions, bears and lynxes make the journey very dangerous. Merchants travelling through these regions use the very large canes growing here to defend themselves. The canes have a circumference of three paces and are a good fifteen paces high. The knots in them are about three spans apart. At night, travellers make a huge pile of these green canes which they then throw on to a wood fire. As they burn they begin to twist and split in half making a loud crackling noise and occasionally exploding. This terrifies the wild animals and they run off into the countryside. These explosions can be heard ten miles away, so the animals do not often even approach. When the horses hear the noise for the first time they are so frightened that they sometimes break loose and gallop off. In fact horses which have never heard the noise before must have their eyes and ears bandaged and their legs tied to prevent them running away. This is the only way in which travellers can spend the night safely. Furthermore, they must take with them plenty of provisions for they will find habitations where they can stock up only every third or fourth day if they are lucky.

Finally, after twenty days' journey through country roaming with dangerous animals, the traveller reaches houses and castles built on mountain slopes. The people here have strange customs concerning marriage. No man will marry a virgin on the grounds that if a woman has not had several lovers she must be undesirable to men and unloved by the gods. So when foreigners or strangers pitch their tents in the area, as many as forty young girls may be brought by their mothers from the village and offered to them. The more attractive girls are welcomed and the others go sadly home. A traveller may keep a girl with him as long as he stays in the village, and when he leaves he must give the girl a jewel to prove she has had a lover. If a girl has twenty jewels, she has had as many lovers. The girls with most jewels are then chosen as wives because, by common accord, they must be the loveliest. Once they are married their husbands cherish them and regard it as a great sin to touch another man's wife. This peculiar practice is certainly worth commenting on and it goes without saying that any young man between the ages of sixteen and twenty-four would be delighted to go to this place.

These people are idolaters and savagely wicked. They do not regard thieving or murder as wrong; they are the worst brigands in the world. They live by hunting and on the fruits of the land, and they also keep sheep. There are so many musk deer in these parts that their scent can be smelt throughout the province. These

101

evil men keep excellent hounds to catch huge quantities of musk deer from which they take the musk. They have neither coins nor paper money. Salt is their currency. The people are miserably dressed in animal skins, canvas or coarse cloth, and have their own language called Tibetan.

CXVII   MORE ABOUT TIBET

This huge province of idolaters borders on Manzi. The people are consummate thieves. The province is so large that it contains eight kingdoms and innumerable towns and castles. In several parts there are lakes, rivers and mountains with vast quantities of gold dust. Cinnamon grows freely and the people pay large sums for amber and coral to decorate the necks of their women and idols. Camel hair is woven here as are silk and cloth of gold. Spices which are quite unknown to us grow in Tibet.

The magicians and astrologers are cleverer here than in any other province; by their diabolical spells they work the most astounding miracles which cannot be related for fear of frightening the reader. Tibetans have the most unpleasant habits. They own mastiffs as large as donkeys which are trained to hunt every type of animal, but particularly the huge and fierce wild oxen. There are many different kinds of hounds, and excellent lanner and saker falcons.

Let us now move on to the province of Kaindu, for enough has been said of Tibet which, it should be remembered, belongs like all the other provinces in this book to the Great Khan. Only the ones mentioned at the beginning belong to Arghun's son.

CXVIII   THE PROVINCE OF KAINDU

Kaindu is situated to the west of the provinces just described. It used to have its own king but the land is now subject to the Great Khan. The population is idolatrous. There are many towns and villages and there is a lake where large numbers of the whitest pearls are to be found. But the Great Khan will not allow them to be collected because there are so many that they would swamp the market. When Kublai Khan wants some, he orders them to be fished up for him. Anyone else fishing for them would be killed. There is also a mountain in the province where a great many exceptionally fine turquoises can be found.

The attitude to women in Kaindu is unusual. Men do not mind if foreigners, or anyone else for that matter, make love to their wives, daughters, sisters or other female relatives. In fact they are very pleased because they think their gods and idols will be glad and shower them with wealth. So when a stranger lodges in these parts, or even when he merely crosses a man's threshold, the householder immediately leaves, ordering his wife to do absolutely everything the stranger asks. He goes to his fields and vineyards where he remains as long as the lodger is in his house. Sometimes the lodger stays for two or three days, sleeping with the wretched fellow's wife. The stranger signifies his continued presence in the house by hanging a hat or some such object outside. This practice is common throughout the province although the Great Khan has forbidden it. Furthermore, in the castles and post houses on the mountain roads, there are men with very beautiful wives who offer them freely to passing merchants. When a merchant has satisfied himself with the wife he gives her a piece of material or other object of little value and rides off. As he leaves the husband and wife usually stand and jeer at him: 'Show us what you've gained from us, you fool! You've left us this,' and they hold up the piece of cloth, 'but you've taken nothing with you.'

For currency the people of Kaindu use gold bars which are valued by weight. But they have no small change. Instead they use salt. They boil salt water to a paste which they then put in moulds to make slabs weighing about half a pound which are flat on one side and rounded on the other. The slabs are then put on hot bricks by the fire to dry and solidify. Special officials stamp the Great Khan's seal on this money. Eighty of these slabs are worth one gold bar. But merchants make enormous profits by exchanging forty, fifty or perhaps sixty slabs of salt for one gold bar in isolated parts of the province where gold is found in rivers and lakes and where there are few people to buy it.

There are huge numbers of musk deer in Kaindu, and much fishing in the salt lake where the pearls come from. There are lions, wolves, bears, does, roebuck and many different types of birds. There is no grape wine but an exquisite liquor is made from corn and rice mixed with spices. A great many cloves are grown here on small bushes not unlike laurels, with little white flowers. Ginger, cinnamon and other spices alien to us are plentiful here.

A ten-day journey from Kaindu takes the traveller through many towns and villages with similar customs, until he reaches the river Yangtze which forms the boundary of the province. The river, which flows on down to the Ocean, is full of gold dust, and cinnamon grows along its banks.

CXIX   THE PROVINCE OF KARA-JANG

The province of Kara-jang lies on the other side of the river. The people are idolaters and subjects of the Great Khan. But he has made his son, Essen-temur, King. Essen-temur is a rich and powerful king and a wise and prudent man who rules justly.

Five days' journeying west of the river takes the traveller through many towns and villages where a fine breed of horse is raised. The people live on the land and

103

by their livestock. They have their own language which is very difficult to understand.

After five days the traveller reaches the capital city of Yachi with its many merchants and artisans. Here there are Mohammedans, idolaters and some Nestorian Christians. There is wheat and rice, but wheat bread is not eaten here as it is not very healthy. A lot of rice is eaten and a fine, clear, alcoholic drink is made from rice mixed with spices. Their currency is cowrie shells. Eighty of these shells are worth a silver bar, the equivalent of two Venetian groats. Eight silver bars are worth one gold bar. There are salt-water wells from which salt is extracted – in fact the whole province lives from the sale of salt, and the King makes an enormous profit from it. It does not matter if a man sleeps with another man's wife provided it is with the consent of the woman.

There is a lake full of the finest and largest fish in the world here; it has a circumference of 100 miles. The people eat raw chicken, mutton, ox and buffalo meat. The poor buy raw liver which has just been taken from the dead animals and which they dip in a garlic sauce and eat immediately. This, in fact, is how they treat all meat. Even the rich eat raw meat which they slice up very finely and marinate in a sauce made of garlic and spices. They eat it with as much pleasure as we eat cooked meat.

CXX   MORE ABOUT KARA-JANG

The kingdom of Kara-jang is a ten-day journey to the west of Yachi. The capital city is also called Kara-jang. The people are idolaters and subjects of the Great Khan who has sent them his son, Hukaji, as King. Gold dust is found in large quantities in the rivers and in the mountain lakes. They have so much gold here that they will exchange one gold bar for only six silver ones. Cowrie shells are also used as currency here. The cowries are not local, but come from India.

Kara-jang is full of snakes, some of them very large and frightening. They are a horrible sight, the largest being as much as ten paces long with a girth of ten spans. Near their heads they have two short legs without feet, but with three claws – two small and one large – like falcons or lions. Their heads are enormous with eyes bigger than loaves of bread and mouths large enough to swallow a man whole; their teeth are huge. These animals are so vast and dreadful that they terrify both men and beasts. There are other smaller ones, about five to eight paces long.

The snakes stay in hiding underground during the day and only come out at night to catch and eat any animal they can find and to drink from the rivers, lakes and springs. They are so heavy that they leave a deep furrow wherever they go as though a full barrel has been rolled through the sand. Traps are set at night to catch these serpents. Along their tracks strong wooden stakes are put into the ground with razor sharp steel blades like iron lances sticking out of them. These are then covered with sand. Several of these traps are laid in a row. When the snakes come out and begin to move faster and faster down the slope towards the water, the blades cut into the whole length of their bodies and kill them. The crows seeing them die begin to screech, which alerts the trappers who come and fetch the bodies. The trappers cut open the serpents' bellies and remove the bile, which they sell for a high price as it is used in medicine.

If a man is bitten by a rabid dog, he has only to drink a small quantity of this bile to be cured. If a woman is a long time in labour and is screaming, she will immediately give birth if she drinks some of it. The bile is also used to reduce swellings, which subside quickly when bathed in it. Not only is the bile of these creatures very valuable, the flesh is also sold for a good price as it tastes excellent and is much sought after. These serpents are fearless; they will go into the dens of lions and other wild beasts and devour their young and even the lions themselves.

Fine horses are bred in this province and exported to India. But first two or three bones are removed from the horses' tails so that they cannot shake them while being ridden because it is thought that the tail of a galloping horse should not move. In these parts the men ride in the French fashion with long stirrups, unlike the Tartars who ride with short stirrups, standing up in them to draw their bows. Here they have armour made of buffalo hide, lances, shields, crossbows and poisoned arrows.

Warriors of Kara-jang

Before they were conquered by the Great Khan, they used to murder gentlemen of quality who happened to lodge in their houses, not in order to rob them, but because they thought the traveller's shade would stay with them and his goodness and wisdom would become part of their home. A great many people were murdered in this way until thirty-five years ago, when the Great Khan threatened the assassins with severe punishment.

CXXI THE GREAT PROVINCE OF ZAR-DANDAN

Five days' journey to the west of Kara-jang takes the traveller to the province of Zar-dandan, where the population is subject to the Great Khan and idolatrous. The capital city is called Vochan. The teeth of all the men here are covered in gold. They make a kind of mould out of gold, which they fit over their top and bottom teeth. The women's teeth, however, are natural. The men also decorate their arms and legs with patterns of indelible black dots made with needles. They consider these marks to be very distinguished and beautiful. The men here are fine horsemen and spend all their time hunting and hawking. The women and slaves do all the household tasks.

When a woman has given birth, and the baby is washed and swaddled, the husband takes the wife's place in the bed and stays there for forty days with the baby beside him, only getting up if it is absolutely necessary. All his friends and relations come to see him and to congratulate him. The husbands do this because they say that the woman has had all the trouble of carrying the child and there is no reason why she should continue to labour for it for another forty days. So the mother gets up immediately, after giving birth, does the housework and waits on her husband in bed.

These people eat all kinds of meat, raw and cooked in their own way, and special dishes of rice mixed with meat; they drink excellent spiced rice wine. Gold coins are the common currency although they also use cowrie shells. One gold bar is worth five silver ones because the silver mines are five months' journey away. So merchants who come here with a lot of silver make a good profit.

These people are idolaters without temples; they have no idols but worship the eldest member of the family because they are the fruit of his loins. They have no alphabet or any form of writing, which is not surprising as they live in quite isolated places amongst huge forests and high mountains where the air is so foul in summer that no stranger could survive it.

When they trade with one another, they take a round or square piece of wood which they split in two and each one keeps a half, having first made as many notches in the halves as necessary. When one of them pays what he owes he takes back the other half of the piece of wood.

In none of these places – Kara-jang, Vochan or Yachi – are there any physicians. When an important person is sick magicians who work black magic and who guard the idols are called, and when the sick man has explained how he feels, the magicians begin to play instruments and to twirl and dance until one of them falls flat on the ground, foaming at the mouth as if dead. This signifies that the devil has entered his body. He stays there like a corpse and all the other magicians, seeing him in this state, start to ask him what is wrong with the patient. He replies: 'Such and such a spirit has struck him because of some wrong he has done.'

The other magicians answer: 'Please forgive him, and tell us what you want in order to preserve his life.'

After a lot of discussion and prayer, the spirit in the fallen magician eventually speaks. And if the sick man is destined to die, he says: 'This patient has so offended the spirit and is so wicked that the spirits do not wish to forgive him.'

This is a death sentence, but if the patient is going to recover, the spirit inside the magician stretched on the ground replies: 'The offence was a serious one, but it is forgiven. If the patient wishes to recover he must sacrifice two or three rams and prepare ten or more rich and exquisite drinks to offer to such and such a spirit or idol. Magicians and women who serve the idols must also participate at the sacrifice and a great feast must be prepared.'

The friends of the sick man do everything they are told to do. They prepare the drinks and kill the rams whose blood they sprinkle in different places in honour of the spirits. Then they cook the rams in the sick man's house and invite the correct number of magicians and women. When everything is ready they begin to play instruments, and dance and sing praises to the spirits. The broth from the meat and the drinks are sprinkled everywhere, incense and aloes are burnt, and large numbers of lights are lit. Then they ask if the patient is forgiven and if he will recover. The spirit does not immediately answer, but asks for further sacrifices. When they have been made the patient will be forgiven and will soon recover. When more broth has been sprinkled, lights lit and incense burnt, the spirit is finally satisfied and the magicians and women sit down to eat and drink with great rejoicing. Then everyone returns home and the sick man recovers.

Let us now move on to other places.

CXXII   THE GREAT KHAN CONQUERS THE KINGDOMS OF
MIEN AND BENGAL

In about 1272 the Great Khan sent a large army to Kara-jang and Vochan to defend the people there against invaders. This was before he had sent Essen-temur to be King. The very rich and powerful King of Mien and Bengal who ruled over a vast kingdom and who was not subject to the Great Khan – although he was soon to have his kingdom confiscated – decided to send a huge army to attack Kublai Khan's soldiers in Vochan. He planned to slaughter the enemy and to teach Kublai Khan not to send in any more men. So he mustered 2,000 gigantic elephants and on top of each he put a small but well-built wooden turret so his soldiers could fight from a height. There were between twelve and sixteen armed men in each of these turrets. He also mobilized 40,000 cavalrymen and infantrymen – the infantry being in the minority. The army was certainly prepared for a memorable battle.

As soon as everything was ready the army set out to take the Great Khan's men by surprise. They came without difficulty to within a three days' march of the Tartar army and then pitched their tents so that the men could rest before the battle.

CXXIII   THE BATTLE BETWEEN THE GREAT KHAN AND THE KING OF MIEN

The commander of the Tartar army, called Nasr-uddin, was amazed when he heard that the King was advancing with so great a force since he himself had only 12,000 cavalrymen. But he was a brave man and a good leader. He began to deploy his men as best he could and to encourage them to defend the country to their utmost. The 12,000 Tartar cavalrymen wisely gathered in the plain with a dense wood behind them, and awaited the enemy.

When the King of Mien's army was rested the men started marching again, and they marched until they reached the Volchan plain where the Tartars were waiting for them. About a mile in front of the enemy the King lined up his elephants ready for the battle. An experienced general, he deployed his cavalry and infantry with ingenuity. Then he began to advance on the enemy.

When the Tartars saw him coming they showed no sign of fear whatsoever, but rather demonstrated their courage by marching calmly forward in perfect order. The two armies were very close and the battle was about to begin when the horses saw the elephants and took fright, refusing to advance any further. But the King marched on with his men and his elephants.

CXXIV   THE BATTLE

The Tartars were furious when they realized what was happening and they had no idea what to do. But they reacted very intelligently. Accepting that nothing would make the horses advance, they dismounted and hurriedly tied the animals to the trees in the wood behind them. Then they drew their bows and began to shoot at the elephants. They succeeded in wounding an unbelievable number. The King's men were, meanwhile, aiming at the Tartars, attacking as ferociously as possible, but the Tartar soldiers were more skilled and managed to defend themselves valiantly. Many of the elephants were so riddled with wounds that they began to crash back into the King's ranks, causing chaos. Then the elephants charged into the wood, breaking the turrets on their backs and destroying everything as they ran wildly hither and thither. When the Tartars saw the elephants in flight they jumped without hesitation onto their horses and charged the King and his men. The King's soldiers defended themselves gallantly and a furious battle raged. When there were no more arrows, the men resorted to clubs and swords. The struggle was long and bitter. Harsh blows were struck. Horses and men fell to the ground, hands, arms, bodies and heads flew through the air. The god of thunder himself could not have been heard over the din. The battle was growing more intense, but there was no doubt that the Tartars had the upper hand. It was a bad hour for the King and his people when the battle began; so many of them were killed that day.

The fighting lasted until after mid-day when the King and his men, realizing the extent of their casualties, decided that they could hold out no longer. They saw that soon they would all be killed, so they turned and fled as quickly as they could with the Tartars chasing them, cruelly massacring as many as possible. It was a truly pitiful sight. When the Tartars had chased them some way, they returned to the wood for the elephants, but although they cut down huge trees to block the elephants' way, they were quite unable to catch them. They had to ask some captured prisoners to round them up because elephants are the most intelligent of animals and would never give themselves up to strangers. In this way the Tartars managed to capture 200 elephants and after that battle the Great Khan was able to use plenty of elephants himself.

CXXV THE GREAT DESCENT

The road winds downhill for two and a half days out of this province. The only thing worth mentioning about the journey is the huge plateau where a rich and varied market attracts people from round about for three days every week. Merchants come from all over the place to exchange five silver bars for one gold bar with great advantage to themselves. As for the people with gold, they live in such inaccessible places that no one can rob them.

At the bottom of the great descent, bordering on India to the south, lies the province of Mien. The traveller then comes to impassable mountains and dense woodland inhabited by elephants, unicorns and other wild beasts but with no sign of human life.

CXXVI   THE CITY OF MIEN

After fifteen days in these remote parts the traveller reaches the town of Mien, the large and imposing capital of the kingdom. The people are idolaters, subjects of the Great Khan, and have their own language.

A rich and powerful king used to rule here and when he was about to die he ordered two towers, one of gold and one of silver, to be built over his mausoleum. The first tower was made of fine stone covered in a thick layer of gold which made it look like a massive construction of solid gold. It was very broad and at least ten paces high. The top was dome-shaped and all around it hung gold bells which tinkled in the wind. The silver tower was built exactly like the gold one, and the tomb itself was covered in gold and silver plate. These two towers were as fine as any in the world and extremely valuable. They shimmered in the sunlight so that they could be seen from far away.

There were a great number of acrobats and jugglers in the Great Khan' court and when he told them that he wanted to send them to conquer the kingdom of Mien with the aid of his captains, they replied that they would willingly go, and set out with the captains and troops provided. In fact, it was these jugglers and acrobats who conquered Mien. When they had taken the city, they were so amazed by its riches that they sent messages to the Great Khan describing the precious towers and asking if he wanted the gold and silver from them. But the Great Khan knew that the King had had them built for the repose of his soul and to be remembered after death, so he said that he did not want them destroyed. In fact, he particularly wished them to remain as the King had designed them. This is not surprising as the Tartars never touch things belonging to the dead.

There are many fine wild oxen in this province, as well as deer, roebuck and many other animals. But we must now move on to the province of Bengal.

CXXVII   THE GREAT PROVINCE OF BENGAL

The province of Bengal lies to the south, and around 1290, when Marco Polo was at Kublai Khan's court, it had not yet been conquered. There are several kingdoms and a number of different languages spoken within the province, which borders on India. The people are keen idolaters. There are many eunuchs; in fact the province supplies them to neighbouring courts. The oxen are as large as elephants, although not so fat. Milk, meat and rice are eaten and a large amount of cotton is produced. Spikenard, galingale, sugar and many rare spices make for active trading. Indian merchants come to buy eunuchs; they also buy slaves whom they sell again elsewhere. There are many slaves and eunuchs in these parts because anyone taken prisoner is immediately castrated and sold.

There being no more to say about Bengal, let us turn to Kaugigu.

CXXVIII   THE PROVINCE OF KAUGIGU

Kaugigu is situated to the east. It is ruled over by a king. Its people are idolatrous, they have their own language and are subject to the Great Khan to whom they pay a tax every year. The King is so lascivious he has more than 300 wives; he only has to see a beautiful woman to marry her.

The country is rich with gold, and there are many rare spices, but because it is so far from the sea, prices are low. There are a lot of elephants and other animals and there is a great deal of game. The people live on meat, milk and rice; they have no grapes but make an excellent wine from rice and spices. Both men and women have their skins painted, that is to say they have pictures of lions and dragons indelibly drawn by needles on their bodies, faces, necks, hands, stomachs, legs and arms. They regard tattooing so highly that the more a person has, the more distinguished he is considered to be.

CXXIX   THE PROVINCE OF ANIN

Anin is another province to the east, also subject to the Great Khan, where the people are idolaters with a language of their own. The women wear very valuable gold and silver bracelets and anklets, and the men wear even more valuable ones. They sell a lot of excellent horses to the Indians who re-sell them at a vast profit. The land is fertile with excellent grazing, so there are a great many buffaloes, oxen and cows. The province is fully self-sufficient.

Bengal, Kangigu and Anin are situated in a row. It takes thirty days to cross the first and fifteen to travel across the second to the third.

Let us now travel thirty days east towards Toloman.

CXXX   TOLOMAN

Toloman is an eastern province. The people are idolatrous, they speak their own language and are subjects of the Great Khan. They are extremely beautiful, although hardly fair-skinned; in fact they are quite dark. The men are excellent warriors. There are a great many towns and a particularly large number of castles built high up in great mountains. The dead are burnt and the bones that remain are collected in small caskets and hung in mountain caves where neither man nor beast can get at them. There is gold, but cowrie shells are common currency. In all these places, Bengal, Kangigu and Anin, gold and cowrie shells are used for money. Not many traders come here, but those who do are rich and manage to do a lot of business. The people live on milk, meat, rice and excellent rice wine. They have no vines.

111

Natives of Toloman

CXXXI THE PROVINCE OF KUIJU

If the traveller sails down the river from Toloman for twelve days he will reach the great city of Kuiju in the province of the same name. The people are idolaters and are subject to Kublai Khan; they make their living by trade and craft. Beautiful materials for summer clothing are made from the bark of trees. The men are warlike and the only currency is the Great Khan's paper money. it is dangerous to sleep out at night because of the lions. Even travellers in boats must take care to moor a long way from the river banks as the lions are quite capable of jumping into the boats from the shore, snatching their prey and running off eating it. But

112

the men can defend themselves from these dangerous beasts with their own particular breed of dogs which are brave enough to attack the lions – but it takes two dogs to one lion.

If a man meets a lion while he is riding along carrying his bow and arrows, followed by his two large dogs, the swift and strong dogs throw themselves at the lion as soon as they see it. One attacks it from behind, the other from the front. The lion hurls itself backwards and forwards between the two, but the dogs can look after themselves, and the lion, knowing that it cannot win, tries to run off. The dogs chase it, biting its tail and hind legs. The lion turns angrily, but the dogs react so quickly that it can never catch them. What more is there to say? The terrified lion tries to face the dogs with a tree behind it for protection, but they still manage to go on biting. While the lion twists and turns, the man draws his bow and shoots as many arrows as are needed to kill the beast. Many lions are killed like this as it is almost impossible for them to defend themselves against an armed man on horseback with two dogs.

There is a lot of silk in Kuiju which, with all sorts of other merchandise, is carried down the river to other countries. The river winds on for twelve days through towns and villages where the people are idolatrous and subject to the Great Khan. They use the Khan's paper money, live by trade and craft, and are good fighters.

At the end of twelve days the traveller finds himself back in Ch'eng-tu-fu. A further seventy days' journey through countries and provinces which have already been described takes the traveller to Cho-chau.

113

V

From Peking to Amoy

CXXXII Ho-kien-fu

Ho-kien-fu, which is in Cathay, lies four days' journey to the south of Cho-chau beyond trading towns and villages, all subject to the Great Khan, where the people are idolaters and use paper money.

Ho-kien-fu is a fine Cathayan city inhabited by idolators who burn their dead, but there are some Christians who have built a church. The people are subject to the Great Khan and spend his paper money. They live by trade and produce much silk, cloth of gold and sendal. Many towns and castles depend on Ho-kien-fu.

Three days' journey further south is Changlu.

CXXXIII Changlu

Changlu is a very large southern city, subject to Kublai Khan; his paper money is used here. The people are idolaters who burn their dead. Enormous quantities of salt are produced here. Great piles are collected of a particular salty soil, over which a lot of water is then poured. The water drains through the earth washing the salt away with it, and is collected in trenches. Then it is boiled in large, shallow, iron containers until a beautiful, fine, white salt is formed. This salt is carried inland and sold at a great profit, some of which is paid to the Great Khan. Large fish weighing two pounds each are caught in these parts.

Let us now move on to Changli.

CXXXIV Changli

Changli is a Cathayan city to the south. It is subject to the Great Khan and paper money is used. The people are idolaters. It is a five-day journey from Changlu through a region of many towns and castles. Through the city a wide, deep river flows, up and down which valuable silks, spices and other goods are carried.

There is no more to be said about Changli; let us move on to Tandinfu.

CXXXV TANDINFU

From Changli to Tandinfu the traveller goes south for six days through many rich towns and cities subject to the Khan where the people are idolatrous, spend paper money and live by trading and craft. They are quite self-sufficient.

Tandinfu itself is a very large city which was conquered by the Great Khan's army. It is the finest city in the whole region. A lot of extremely rich merchants trade here, and there is an unbelievable amount of silk. There are many well-kept gardens with an abundance of fruit. At least eleven rich, historical cities known as imperial cities, are dependent on Tandinfu. All these cities are exceptionally busy commercial centres with unlimited supplies of silk.

In 1272 the Great Khan sent one of his barons, Litan Sangon, to defend the city and the province with an army of 80,000 cavalrymen. While Litan lived in the province he considered rebelling against Kublai Khan. When he eventually felt that the whole population was behind him, he revolted. Whe Kublai Khan heard what had happened he sent two more barons, Ajul and Mongotai, with 100,000 horsemen. These two barons with their cavalry and a large contingent of infantry attacked Litan. Litan was unlucky; he lost the battle and was killed, along with many of his men. After Litan's defeat the Great Khan wanted to discover who was involved in the revolt and everyone found guilty was put to death most cruelly. But Kublai Khan did not punish the innocent native population, which has been loyal to him ever since.

Some of the Cathayan customs are worthy of further comment; the way of life is interesting and the young girls are especially well brought up.

No girls are better mannered or more modest in their behaviour than the Cathayans. They never indulge in immoderate mirth, they do not dance or aggravate others. Neither do they spend their time at windows watching passers-by and hoping to be admired; they never listen to immodest talk, nor do they go to festivals. When they do go out, they go to respectable places like the temples of their idols or to visit relatives. They are always accompanied by their mothers and they never look brazenly in people's faces, but wear elegant hats which oblige them to look at the ground, so they only look where they are putting their feet. They are quiet in the presence of their elders and never speak unnecessarily; in fact they only speak when they are spoken to. They spend much of their time working in their rooms and rarely see their fathers and brothers or the older people in the house. They do not entertain suitors.

The young boys do not speak in front of their elders either unless they are spoken to. They are so modest, even among members of their own family, that two of them would never take a bath together.

When a marriage is arranged, either a girl's father offers her to another family, or the other family asks for her. The father has to guarantee that his daughter is a virgin; he signs an agreement with the bridegroom and if the bride is not a virgin, the marriage is not valid. When the agreement has been signed the girl's chastity is put to the test. She is taken to the baths where her mother, the bridegroom's mother, the relations of both families and certain matrons versed in these matters are waiting for her. These women test her virginity with a pigeon's egg. If this experiment does not satisfy the women of the bridegroom's family – who know that lost virginity can be disguised – then one of the matrons wraps a cloth around her finger and inserts it into the girl until it is stained with blood. This blood can never be washed clean, so if the stain disappears when the cloth is rinsed, the girl is not a virgin. If her virginity is proved, the marriage is valid. If not, the father has to pay compensation.

In order to keep their virginity intact, the girls in these parts avoid all violent movement and walk with the tiniest possible steps. The Tartars in Cathay, however, are not concerned with such details and allow their wives and even their daughters to go riding with them, which could easily damage them. But the people in Manzi abide by the same customs as the Cathayans.

CXXXVI THE GREAT CITY OF SINJU MATU

If the traveller rides south of Tandinfu through numerous busy towns and villages, and countryside rich with game and fish, he will, after three days, reach the imposing city of Sinju Matu, a great trading centre with many artisans' workshops. Paper money is used here, the people are idolaters and subjects of the Great Khan.

A river of great importance flows from the south through the town. The people of Sinju Matu have diverted the river into two streams, one of which flows eastwards to Manzi and the other westwards to Cathay. The traffic on this river is very heavy. The boats are not particularly large since their size is suited to the river, but they carry vast quantities of merchandise to Manzi and Cathay and return loaded with more goods. The sight of so much traffic on the river is really amazing.

CXXXVII THE GREAT CITY OF LINJU

A further eight days' travel southwards through more large trading towns and villages leads to the city of Linju. The towns and villages are subject to the Great Khan, their inhabitants are idolaters who burn their dead and who use paper money. The people of Linju are expert soldiers, but they are also great traders

116

and craftsmen. There is an enormous amount of game in the region and it is fully self-sufficient. The area is full of jujubes which are twice the size of dates, and the people bake a lot of bread. Linju is built on the same river as Sinju Matu and large ships full of rare goods sail by.

Let us now move to the huge and extremely rich city called Piju.

CXXXVIII   PIJU

Beyond Linju the traveller passes southwards through more rich towns and castles for three days. This is all part of Cathay; the people are idolaters and burn their dead. Like the inhabitants of the other regions, they are subjects of the Great Khan and use his paper money. They have the best possible land for hunting and hawking, and they are fully self-sufficient.

After three days the traveller comes to the huge and imposing trading city of Piju where many different crafts flourish and there is a great deal of silk. The province borders on Manzi and the people load their carts with goods and travel from town to town and from village to village. Kublai Khan collects considerable taxes from here. There is not much else to say about it, so we will move on, south, to Siju.

CXXXIX   THE CITY OF SIJU

Siju is a two-day journey from Piju. The countryside is rich and beautiful, and alive with every sort of animal and bird. Siju is large, wealthy and busy. The inhabitants are idolatrous, they burn their dead and use the paper money of their overlord, the Great Khan. Wide, fertile plains producing every kind of grain lie in all directions.

To the south of Siju is a further stretch of beautiful countryside with villages and hamlets, fine gardens, an abundance of game and bird life, and fields of wheat. The people are idolaters and use the Great Khan's paper money.

After three days the traveller reaches the Kara-moran river which flows down from Prester John's territory. It is nearly a mile wide and is deep enough for large vessels to navigate. As many as 15,000 ships carry the Great Khan's armies down this river to the islands in the Ocean, which is only one day's journey away. These ships are each manned by twenty sailors and can take fifteen horses and men with all their arms and provisions.

The two cities of Hwai-ngan-chau and Kaiju face each other across the river. One is large, the other small. On the far side of the river lies the province of Manzi which was conquered, as we shall see, by the Great Khan.

117

CXL THE GREAT KHAN'S CONQUEST OF MANZI

The vast province of Manzi was formerly ruled by a very rich and powerful king called Facfur. His kingdom was so extensive and his subjects so numerous that he was undoubtedly one of the most important kings in the world. Only the Great Khan was richer and more powerful. But Facfur was not a very warlike man and delighted only in the company of women and in caring for the poor.

During his reign there was not a warhorse in the land and no one knew anything about battles or military strategy; this was because Manzi is a place of great natural strength. The cities are all surrounded by stretches of water at least a bow-shot wide and renowned for their depth. Every city is reached by a bridge, so that, had the people been trained in battle, they could never have lost. Having no warlike skills at all, however, they were defeated.

In 1268, Kublai Khan sent a baron called Bayan Ching-siang, whose name means a hundred eyes, to the province of Manzi. The King of Manzi had been warned that only a man with a hundred eyes would be able to usurp his kingdom. Bayan took with him a large cavalry and infantry escort, and he also had a big fleet at his disposal to transport the soldiers. When Bayan and his men reached the city of Hwai-ngan-chau, the gateway to the province (of which we will speak later), he asked the people to surrender. The people refused, so Bayan continued his march until he came to another city where he repeated his demand and was met with the same refusal. So he advanced, taking his time while waiting for the reinforcements which he knew the Great Khan was preparing. One after the other, five cities refused to surrender. But the sixth city Bayan took by storm, and the seventh and the eighth, and so on until he had taken twelve cities in a row and reached the capital, Kinsai, where the King and Queen lived.

When the King saw Bayan and his army he was so frightened that he abandoned the city with a large number of men and, with a fleet of 1,000 ships, set sail for the Ocean where he planned to take refuge on the islands. But the Queen with many of her followers remained in the city and prepared to defend it. When the Queen asked Bayan's name and learnt that it meant a hundred eyes, she remembered the astrologers' prophecy and immediately surrendered. After this all the cities in the kingdom capitulated without a murmur. This was, indeed, a fine victory for Kublai Khan, as there was no richer kingdom in the world.

But the King of Manzi was a very magnanimous man. Every year he paid for 20,000 babies to be looked after and fed; this was necessary because the poor women used to abandon their newborn babies. The King ordered all the foundlings to be collected and horoscopes made for them. Then he sent them to various parts of the kingdom where they were fed and cared for. If a rich man was childless, he went to the King and was allowed to choose as many children as he wanted. When these children grew up the King arranged marriages between them and provided them with a livelihood.

Furthermore, if, when he was riding through the street, he saw a little house standing between two fine large ones, he would ask why it was smaller than the others. If he was told that it belonged to a poor man, he ordered it to be rebuilt so that it was as large and handsome as the two on either side.

The King was waited on by more than 1,000 young boys and girls. He ruled so justly that everyone lived together peacefully, houses were left open at night, goods were left unguarded and nothing was ever stolen. It was just as safe to go out at night as it was during the day. To describe the vast riches of the kingdom would be impossible.

Having spoken of the King, let us turn to the Queen. She was taken to the Great Khan who, when he saw her, ordered that she be treated with all the respect and honour due to a great lady. But her husband never returned from the islands, and it was there that he died.

The time has come to talk of the way of life of the people of Manzi. Let us start with the city of Hwai-ngan-chau.

CXLI , THE CITY OF HWAI-NGAN-CHAU

Hwai-ngan-chau is a large and rich city on the north-western border of Manzi. The people there are idolaters who burn their dead. As the city is built on the Kara-moran river, there are a great number of ships, and goods are continually being brought here. Merchandise is deposited from a number of places, to be sent on to other cities by boat. Enough salt is made at Kwai-ngan-chau to supply at least forty other cities, so the Great Khan manages to collect considerable tax here from salt and other goods.

Now we will move on to the city of Pao-ying.

CXLII   THE CITY OF PAO-YING

On leaving Hwai-ngan-chau, the traveller goes south along a causeway leading into the province of Manzi. The causeway is built of stone and washed on either side by deep, navigable waters. This is the only way of entering the province by land. Bayan and his men arrived by boat. After a day's journey, the traveller reaches the large and beautiful city of Pao-ying. There are a few Nestorian Christians who have built a church here, but, on the whole, the people are idolaters. They are subjects of Kublai Khan and use his paper money, living by trade and craft; they have a great deal of silk and are fully self-sufficient.

Now let us go on to Kao-yu.

119

CXLIII   THE CITY OF KAO-YU

Kao-yu is a day's journey to the south-east of Pao-ying. It is a fine and large city where the people are idolaters who spend paper money and are subjects of the Great Khan. They live by trade and craft and they, too, are self-sufficient. They have a great deal of fish, game and birds and animals of all kinds. One Venetian groat will buy three pheasants.

We will now move on to Tai-chau.

CXLIV   THE CITY OF TAI-CHAU

A day's journey south-eastwards from Kao-yu takes the traveller through fields and smallholdings until he reaches Tai-chau, a city which, although not large, is overflowing with riches. The people are idolaters who use paper money and are subject to the Great Khan. The town thrives by trade and craft. There are many boats and the fishing is excellent. The Ocean is a three-day journey to the east of Tai-chau, and salt is produced in great quantities everywhere between the town and the coast. There is a large, beautiful and rich city called Chinju here where enough salt is made to supply the whole province. Without seeing this region it is impossible to imagine the revenue the Great Khan gets from it.

Let us now return to Tai-chau and go from there to Yang-chau.

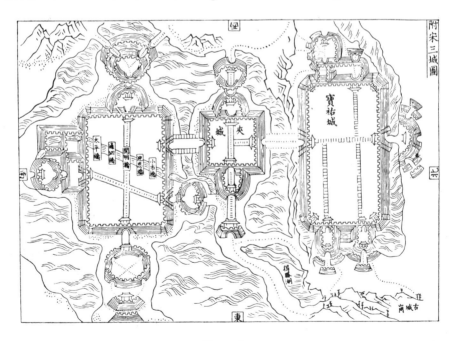

Yang-chau

120

CXLV   THE CITY OF YANG-CHAU

From Tai-chau the traveller goes south-east for one day through very beautiful countryside with a large number of villages and hamlets until he reaches the city of Yang-chau. This town is so large and powerful that twenty-seven rich trading cities depend on it. It is one of the twelve cities chosen as seats for the Khan's twelve barons. The people are subjects of the Great Khan, they use paper money, and are idolaters. Marco Polo himself was sent here by the Great Khan to govern the city, instead of one of the barons.

There is much trade and craft, and military equipment is made here in vast quantities. A great many soldiers live in and around the city.

There is nothing more to be said about Yang-chau so we will move on to two other provinces which are part of Manzi.

CXLVI   THE PROVINCE OF NGAN-KING

Ngan-king is a rich province to the west of Manzi. The people are idolaters, they use paper money, are subjects of the Great Khan and live by trade and craft. They have a great variety of silks and they weave cloth of gold. They also grow much corn and are self-sufficient since the province is very fertile and full of game, including lions. There are many very rich merchants and the tax paid by the city to the Great Khan is enormous.

Now for Siang-yang-fu which is a grand city worthy of consideration.

CXLVII   THE CITY OF SIANG-YANG-FU

At least twelve other large and rich cities are dependent on Siang-yang-fu. Trade flourishes in the city, which is full of artisans' workshops. The people are idolatrous and subject to the Great Khan. They burn their dead. There is a lot of silk of every kind as well as cloth of gold and there is no shortage of fish and game. In fact nothing is lacking in this great city.

After the rest of Manzi had surrendered, Siang-yang-fu resisted the Tartars for a good three years. The Great Khan sent a large army to besiege the city, but it could only occupy the north side because Siang-yang-fu has deep water on every other side. Supplies reached the city across the water from all directions and it managed to resist the besieging Tartar soldiers. After three years the army was frustrated beyond endurance. The city would never have fallen but for Niccolò, Matteo and Marco Polo, who declared: 'We will find a way of taking the city.'

The besieging army replied that they would like nothing better. Discussions took place in the presence of the Great Khan, who had received messengers from the Tartar army, complaining that the city was impossible to take because there was no way of preventing the delivery of provisions across the water.

The Great Khan had replied: 'It is essential that the city be taken.'

At this point the Polo brothers and Marco made their suggestions: 'Great Khan, we have with us men from our country who can make mangonels which can hurl stones. If they are used against the city the people will be terrified into surrendering immediately.'

Kublai Khan ordered some mangonels to be made immediately. The three Venetians had with them a German and a Nestorian who were masters in the art of building these machines. They were told to make three very large mangonels capable of throwing weights of up to 300 pounds, which were then tried out in the presence of the Great Khan and his court.

The mangonels were sent to the men who were besieging Siang-yang-fu. The Tartars had never seen such an amazing invention. As soon as the machines were set up a huge stone was hurled into the city where it crashed down with a terrible noise causing great damage. The people inside were so astounded they did not know what to do. A council was formed to decide what measures to take, but its members could think of no way of escaping the terrible new weapon, so, thinking they would all be killed, they agreed to surrender under the same conditions as the other provinces and agreed to submit to the Great Khan's rule. The enemy commander accepted their conditions and so, thanks to Niccolò, Matteo and Marco Polo, the citizens of Siang-yang-fu capitulated. And this was no small thing since the city and its province are among the finest in Kublai Khan's empire, and he receives a large revenue from it.

Let us now pass on to Sinju.

CXLVIII   THE CITY OF SINJU

Fifteen miles to the south-east of Yang-chau stands the city of Sinju. It is not a large city, but many ships dock there and it is a busy trading centre. The idolatrous people are subjects of the Great Khan and use paper money. The city stands on the largest river in the world, the river Yangtze. Its breadth varies from six to eight miles and its length extends for more than 100 days' journey. Many navigable tributaries flow into it from different areas. Enormous numbers of ships are used to carry a great variety of goods up and down it. This is why it produces so much revenue for the Great Khan.

The river is so long and flows through so many towns and cities that it is true to say that more ships laden with precious goods sail on it than on all the rivers of Christendom and the sea put together. Marco Polo himself saw 5,000 ships sailing near the city at one time and was told by the Great Khan's customs collector that more than 200,000 ships travel upstream every year, not counting those which return. Sinju is not a very big town and it is hard to imagine how many ships the larger cities must have. This river flows through at least sixteen provinces and more than 200 important towns, all with more shipping than Sinju. The ships have a deck and only one mast but they have a large capacity and can carry up to 12,000 *cantari**, according to our measurements.

Before turning to another city, called Kwa-chau, it is worth mentioning that all the ships have hemp rigging on the mast and sails, but the towropes are made of the canes described earlier, which are fifteen paces long. These canes are split and joined at the ends to make lengths of up to 300 paces, and they are stronger than hemp ropes. Every ship has between eight and twelve horses to tow it upstream.

CXLIX KWA-CHAU

Kwa-chau is a small town to the south-east, built on the banks of the river. It is inhabited by idolaters who are subject to the Great Khan and who use his paper money. Large quantities of grain and rice are collected in this town and sent by water to Khan-balik where the Great Khan lives. It is not transported by sea but by rivers and lakes. Most of the food for the Great Khan's court comes from this city and it was Kublai Khan who had the waterway to Khan-balik built. He had wide and deep canals dug to connect one river to another. The water flows along them as if they were broad rivers, and large ships sail down them. Thus Khan-balik can be reached from Manzi. A road runs parallel to the waterway so the same journey can, in fact, be made overland. In the middle of the river, right opposite the city, there is a rocky island on which the idolaters have a monastery for some 200 monks. The monastery is full of idols and is the most important of many, like an archbishopric.

Now we must cross the river and move on to the city of Chin-kiang-fu.

CL CHIN-KIANG-FU

Chin-kiang-fu is a city in Manzi. The people are idolaters and subjects of the Great Khan. They have paper money and live by trade and craft. They produce a considerable amount of silk and they weave cloth of gold and every kind of silk. Many very rich merchants live in Chin-kiang-fu. The citizens thrive on all sorts of game and fish. The countryside is fertile, producing everything necessary for the people's welfare. Since 1278, there have been two Nestorian churches.

*One *cantar* equals about 150 lbs.

Until 1278, not only was there no Christian monastery in Chin-kiang-fu, there was not even one Christian. But in that year Kublai Khan sent a Nestorian, Mar Sergius, to govern the town for three years and he had the two churches built.

CLI CHANG-CHAU

On leaving Chin-kiang-fu the traveller goes south-east for three days through rich trading towns and villages, where the people are idolaters and use paper money, until he comes to the huge city of Chang-chau. Here the people are also idolatrous subjects of the Great Khan and use paper money. There are many artisans and the city is a rich trading centre where silk of every kind and cloth of gold are produced. There are birds and animals and the land is very fertile.

The inhabitants of Chang-chau had to pay dearly for one treacherous action. At the time of the conquest by the Great Khan, Bayan sent some Alan and Christian soldiers to capture the city. The Alans took it and when they entered Chang-chau they found so much good wine that they all got drunk and fell into a very heavy sleep. When the men defending the city saw their enemy reduced to such a state, lying on the ground as though dead, they quickly killed them all. As soon as Bayan, the commander-in-chief, heard about this treachery, he sent a large force to storm the city and put the inhabitants to the sword. This is why so many people died in the siege.

Now for the city of Su-chau.

CLII SU-CHAU

Su-chau is a large and fine city. The people are idolatrous and are subject to the Great Khan. They have vast quantities of silk which they use for clothing. Rich and important merchants live in the city, which is very large, having a circumference of sixty miles. It is so densely populated that it would be impossible to count the inhabitants. If the people of Manzi were warlike they would have no difficulty in conquering the world. But instead they are clever traders, men of intelligence and understanding, with many great philosophers and learned doctors of medicine. They have an enormous number of astrologers and soothsayers.

There are at least 6,000 stone bridges in the city under which one or two galleys can sail. Quantities of rhubarb and ginger grow in the mountains round about – one Venetian groat will buy sixty pounds of excellent fresh ginger. Sixteen other large and busy trading cities depend on Su-chau.

A day's journey away is a city called Vuju. It is a very large, rich trading city, but as there is no more to say about it, we will move on to Vughin, another huge

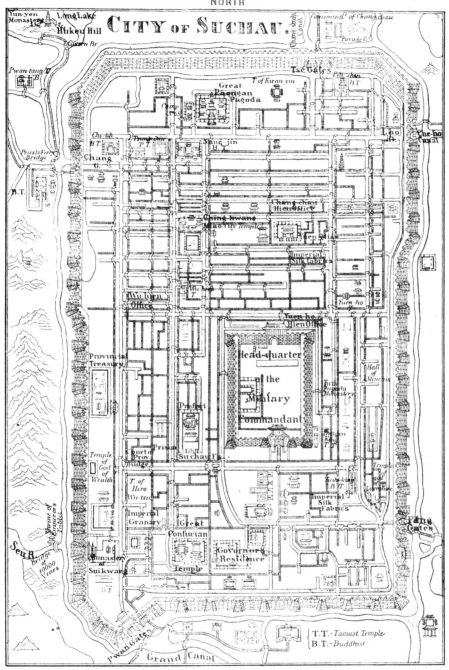

Su-chau

and rich city. The inhabitants are subject to the Great Khan, they are idolaters and use the Khan's paper money. They have a lot of silk and other merchandise. They are clever merchants and excellent craftsmen. From Vughin we will go to another large and wealthy city, Changan, where once again the people are idolatrous subjects of the Great Khan whose paper money they use. They live by trade and craft, making many different qualities of sendal. Game and fish are plentiful in the area. But there is nothing more to add, so we will move on towards Kinsai, the capital of the kingdom of Manzi.

CLIII   KINSAI, THE CAPITAL OF MANZI

On leaving Changan, the traveller goes for three days across a very beautiful region with many fine and rich towns and villages where the people live by trading and craft. They are idolaters, subjects of Kublai Khan and use paper money. They are fully self-sufficient. At the end of these three days the traveller reaches the magnificent city of Kinsai, which means 'the city of Heaven'.

Kinsai must be described in detail since it is, without a doubt, the most majestic and wealthy city in the world. When Bayan conquered Manzi, the Queen of Kinsai sent him a written description of the city to pass on to the Great Khan, so that Kublai Khan would know of its splendour and save it from sacking and destruction. Marco Polo saw this letter with his own eyes so that everything here is absolutely true.

First, the Queen wrote that the city had a circumference of 100 miles, which is not altogether surprising because the roads and canals are wide and the markets are vast because of the large numbers who gather there. On one side of the town there is a lake of clear fresh water; on the other, a huge river from which branch numerous canals of all sizes which wash the waste out of the city. The river flows into the lake and eventually on down to the Ocean. The air is fresh and healthy. It is possible to travel in the city by land or water, the roads and canals being wide enough for carts and boats carrying goods.

There are 12,000 stone bridges as well as other wooden ones. Large boats can sail under almost all the bridges, and under the others there is room for small boats. It is not surprising that there are so many bridges because the town is situated in water and entirely surrounded by it.

On one side the city is bounded by a water course about forty miles long which is fed by the river. It was built by former kings of the province to collect the water from the river when it threatened to burst its banks; it also acts as a defence. The earth dug out of it was piled up on the city side of the watercourse like a high dyke or barrier.

There are ten main marketplaces and an infinite number of smaller ones. They are square and the sides of the larger ones are half a mile long. They open on to a main street which is forty paces wide and which runs straight from one end of the town to the other, crossed by many smoothly sloping bridges. Every four miles along this street there is one of these marketplaces with a perimeter of two miles. There is also a wide canal behind the squares, which runs parallel to the main street and on the banks of which merchants from India and other countries store their goods in warehouses.

Three times a week 40-50,000 people come to the markets and buy many excellent provisions – roebuck, deer, does, hares, rabbits, partridges, pheasants, francolin and Greek partridges, chickens, capons, and innumerable geese which are raised in huge numbers near the lake. One Venetian groat will buy two geese or four ducks. Then there are the butchers who sell veal, beef, goat and lamb, mostly bought by the rich.

Every kind of fruit and vegetable is available in the markets, including huge sweet pears with white flesh weighing ten pounds each, and delicate yellow and white peaches. They import raisins from elsewhere, and wine, which is not particularly appreciated by the locals who are used to rice and spice wine. Huge quantities of fish are brought in every day up the river from the Ocean. There are also fish from the lake where many fishermen are employed. The fish are fat and tasty, of varying kinds depending on the season. It seems impossible that all these fish will be sold, but in fact they go very quickly because there are so many people used to eating fish and meat at the same meal.

The ten squares are surrounded by tall houses under which are shops providing every sort of luxury – spices, jewels, pearls, and some selling only inexpensive wine freshly made from rice and spices.

Many streets open on to the marketplaces and there are numerous public cold-water baths where servants wash both men and women who come there from an early age because they are accustomed as children to washing in cold water at all times of the year. This is regarded as being very healthy. Some rooms have hot water for foreigners who cannot bear the cold water. The people here wash every day and would never go to a meal without washing.

Courtesans live in other houses. There are too many of them to count, and they live not only around the squares, in the areas especially reserved for them, but all over the city. They are richly dressed and scented and have plenty of servants and elegant houses, and are highly accomplished in the arts of seduction, flattery and caresses suited to every sort of person. Foreigners are so delighted by the agreeable sweetness of these ladies that once they have visited them they never forget them and when they go home they say they have been to Kinsai, the city of Heaven, and dearly wish to return there.

In other streets there are doctors, many artisans, and astrologers who teach

127

people how to read and write. They all have their proper places around the squares. In each of the large marketplaces there are two big palaces facing each other, where the King's officials and magistrates live. If there is a quarrel between merchants or other citizens, it is the duty of these men to administer immediate justice. It is also their job to ensure that the men who guard the bridges are in the right place every day. If they are not, suitable punishment is meted out.

On either side of the main street are large houses and palaces with gardens and artisans' workshops. So many people pass up and down the street all day that it seems impossible that there is enough food for them all, and every day the marketplaces are full of people who have arrived by boat or cart bringing food of every kind. As an example of the quantities of food which are consumed, forty-three cartloads of pepper, each weighing 223 pounds, are sold every day in Kinsai. This was told to Marco Polo by one of the Great Khan's customs officers and gives some idea of the amount of spices and other foods which must be sold.

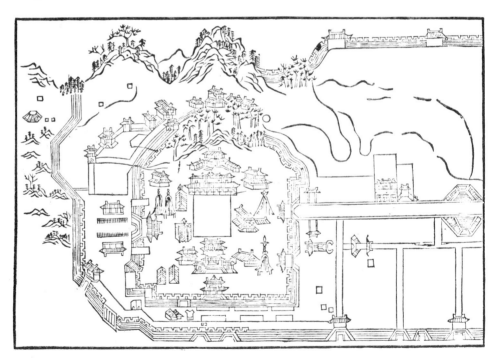

Plan of Kinsai, 'the city of Heaven'

The Queen of Manzi's letter said that there were twelve guilds in Kinsai, one for each of the main crafts. Twelve thousand workshops, each employing between ten and forty men, belong to each guild. Of course not all these men are master-craftsmen; some are apprentices. All this work is necessary as Kinsai supplies many of the cities in the province. There are an untold number of merchants carrying out innumerable deals all the time. Rich men, like their wives, do no manual work whatsoever, but live the refined life of kings. The women are refined and delicate. The King of Manzi had decreed that every man should practise the same craft as his father. Even if he had 100,000 bezants, he had to continue in that craft. The rich did not, of course, have to do the actual manual labour, but they had to manage the workshops and supervise the work.

To the south lies the lake with its thirty-mile circumference. Many fine palaces and noblemen's houses are built on its banks. They are magnificently designed and beautifully constructed; indeed, they could not be more luxurious. There are also a large number of idolaters' monasteries and abbeys. In the middle of the lake are two islands on each of which stands a magnificent, ornate palace suitable for an emperor. These palaces are used for banquets where people may celebrate weddings and other feasts. China, household goods, bowls, tables and fine things made by the Kinsai craftsmen are kept there. One hundred banquets can be held in these palaces at a time, but they take place in separate rooms and loggias and do not interfere with each other.

In addition to this, the lake is filled with pleasure boats of all kinds so that between ten and twenty people can go boating together. The boats are from fifteen to twenty paces long with wide flat bottoms, and they float without rocking. Anyone wanting to enjoy the company of women or friends hires one of these boats, which are always beautifully decorated and have little tables and chairs and everything necessary for guests. The boats have deck roofs from which men navigate the craft by means of long poles which they push into the bed of the lake, for it is not very deep. Inside the boats the walls and ceilings are brightly painted with figures, and there are windows which can be opened, allowing the diners to appreciate the beautiful views. This boating is an extremely agreeable way of passing the time; the city seen from the lake is magnificent with its palaces, temples and monasteries, and its gardens along the banks with their tall trees. When the people of Kinsai have finished their work, they can think of nothing better than boating on the lake with their ladies or courtesans, or taking carriage rides about the city.

There are many fine, ornate houses in Kinsai and the people there spend monumental sums of money on decorating them. There are also tall stone towers in which valuable goods are stored in case of fire, and there are many fires because the houses are built of wood. The inhabitants of Kinsai are, of course, idolaters and subjects of the Great Khan whose paper money they use. They eat all kinds of meat, even dogs and other foul animals which no Christian would dream of touching.

129

The men and the women are white-skinned and beautiful. They dress in silk for the most part because they have so much of it – some being produced in the region and even more being imported.

The natives, like their king, are peaceful people. They do not know how to handle arms, nor do they keep them in their houses. They carry on their businesses honestly and live in such mutual respect that the people in any one neighbourhood seem like a large family. Their friendly sociability is remarkable and there is no jealousy or suspicion concerning women, as it would be considered disgraceful to make improper conversation to a married woman. They are equally fond of visiting foreign traders whom they welcome warmly to their homes, helping and advising them in their business affairs. But they dislike soldiers, even the Great Khan's guard, whom they hold responsible for the loss of their rightful king.

The Great Khan has ordered each of the 12,000 bridges to be guarded day and night by ten men. The men watch over the city to guard against crime and revolt. In the centre of the city there is a tower built on high ground, and on top of this tower is a wooden drum which a man strikes with a small hammer so that it can be heard at a distance. This drum is sounded whenever a fire breaks out or there is some form of civil disorder.

The Great Khan keeps a large guard here with many of his faithful barons because Kinsai is the capital of Manzi, a province of immeasurable riches. He keeps it under particular surveillance for fear of rebellion.

All the streets of Kinsai are paved in stone or brick, as are the roads throughout the province, so it is possible to travel anywhere without getting covered in mud.

There are more than 3,000 hot baths in the town where people gladly go several times a month because they treat their bodies with the greatest care. And these baths are the largest, the finest and the best equipped in the world. One hundred men and women can bathe there at one time.

Twenty-five miles to the north-east of Kinsai lies the Ocean and on its shores stands the city of Kan-p'u, a fine port where huge ships arrive laden with precious goods from, amongst other places, India. Ships can sail up the river from Kan-p'u to Kinsai.

The Great Khan has divided Manzi into nine large kingdoms, each with its own king. Each of these nine kings is independent of the others, although they are all vassals of Kublai Khan to whose agents they must give a yearly account of taxes and other matters. The agents, like other officials, are changed every three years. The King at Kinsai rules over more than 150 large, rich cities.

It is amazing to think that there are no less than 1,200 cities in Manzi, all governed by the Great Khan's officials and all heavily guarded. No city has a garrison of fewer than 1,000; some have 10,000, others 20,000, and some even

130

30,000 – it is impossible to count them all. These soldiers are not all Tartars, some are Cathayans, cavalrymen and infantrymen, but they are all part of the Great Khan's army. The Tartar cavalrymen are not posted in the cities surrounded by water, but in drier places where they can exercise their horses. Kublai Khan sends Cathayans and any natives of Manzi who may be trained soldiers to the watery places. Every year there is a levy of those subjects practised in carrying arms, and they are made to join the Khan's army. Men from Manzi are never sent to guard their native cities, but are always posted to towns at least twenty days' journey away, where they stay for four or five years before returning home and being replaced by others. The same arrangement is made in Cathay.

A large part of the Great Khan's revenue from these cities goes to supporting his troops. Kinsai itself has a permanent garrison of 30,000 soldiers.

The fabulous riches of Manzi cannot be spoken of too highly and the profit the Great Khan gains from them is enormous. No one can truly believe all these things until he sees them, for it is almost impossible to describe the magnificence of this province.

When a baby is born in Manzi, the parents make a note of the day and the hour of its birth, and of the constellation and planet under which it was born, so everyone knows the details concerning its birth. So when a person wants to travel, he goes to an astrologer with his horoscope and the astrologer advises him whether or not to set out. The same thing happens for a marriage. The astrologers decide by the planets if two people are suited to each other, and if they are not, the marriage is called off. The astrologers are very learned in their art. They work such clever spells, and so many of their prophecies come true, that people pay great attention to them. Numerous astrologers are to be found in every square of the city.

When the dead are taken to be burnt, all the relations take part in the funeral procession dressed in rough cloth to denote mourning and accompanied by musicians with instruments, who chant prayers to their idols. Paper cut-outs are made of male and female slaves, horses, camels, cloth of gold, coins and so forth. All these things are thrown into the flames with the dead body and it is thought that the deceased will benefit from them in the next world, and that the idols will honour them accordingly.

The palace of Facfur, the former King of Manzi, who fled the city, is in Kinsai. It is quite the grandest palace in the world and therefore worthy of mention.

The kings who came before Facfur enclosed a vast tract of land, ten miles in circumference, with a high crenellated wall. The wall was divided into three and in the middle was an enormous gateway. Inside, at ground level, were twenty large loggias all the same size, their ceilings painted in gold and supported by columns decorated most delicately in gold and blue. In front stood the main

131

pavilion painted with scenes from the lives of former kings and with figures of knights and ladies, birds and beasts and many beautiful things. It was indeed a wonderful sight. Every wall and ceiling was covered with brilliant colour and gold. Every year on the idols' feast days King Facfur used to hold court here, inviting lords and the city's richer craftsmen to dine. Ten thousand people could sit down with ease in the pavilions. They were a fine sight in their silk clothes and precious jewels.

Behind the main pavilion, opposite the great gateway, was a wall with a door leading into a kind of cloister with a portico supported by columns. Here were several finely decorated apartments belonging to the King and Queen. There was also a covered way leading to twenty more courtyards – ten on each side, all built like long, narrow cloisters. On to each of these cloisters opened fifty rooms occupied by the King's 1,000 serving maids. Some of these young girls occasionally accompanied the King when he went sailing with the Queen in boats covered with silken awnings, or when he visited the temples of the idols.

The other parts of the enclosure were cultivated with woods and beautiful fruit trees, and there were fountains and lakes full of wonderful fish. There were roebuck, does, deer, hares and rabbits, and here the King went riding with his young girls – sometimes in carriages and sometimes on horseback. No men ever accompanied them. The King made the girls run with the hounds, as he liked to watch them chasing the wild animals. When they were tired they went into the copses by the lake and took off all their clothes. Then, quite naked, they plunged into the water and swam about while the King watched them with great delight. Facfur spent his time enjoying himself with women in this way, uninterested in and quite ignorant of military matters, so that finally, due to his ineptitude and greatly to his disgrace, his kingdom was conquered by Kublai Khan.

All this was told to Marco Polo by a rich old merchant from Kinsai who had been a favourite of Facfur's. He had known the King and his palace in all its splendour. Now the palace, of which only part is still standing, is lived in by the new King nominated by Kublai Khan. The young girls' pavilions have been knocked down and so has the crenellated wall around the garden. The copses and trees are all gone.

Nowadays in Kinsai there are 1,600,000 houses, and among them many grand palaces. There is only one Christian church. There is a practice in Kinsai, indeed throughout Manzi and Cathay, whereby everyone writes his name on the door of his house, as well as the names of his wife, his sons, his daughters-in-law, his slaves and any other member of the household, and the number of horses he owns. If a person dies, his name is removed from the door. In this way, the governor of the city knows how many people are under his command. Anyone with a hostel or lodging house must record the names of his guests, and the date of their stay. The Great Khan can then know who is coming and going. This law shows great prudence.

Let us now turn to the revenue which the Great Khan collects from Kinsai and its dependent cities which make up one of the nine kingdoms of Manzi.

CLIV   THE GREAT KHAN'S REVENUE FROM KINSAI

The Great Khan's income from Kinsai and its surroundings is vast. Salt is the most profitable of all goods. Every year the sale of salt produces 5,600,000 *saggi* of gold, one *saggio* being worth more than a florin or a gold ducat.

So much for salt. Twice as much sugar is produced in these parts as in the rest of the world. So sugar too brings in an enormous revenue. There is a levy of 3 ⅓ per cent on all spices and other goods which are exported. Charcoal and rice wine are also highly taxed, as are the 12,000 workshops for each of the crafts. Every item is separately taxed, and there is a 10 per cent tax on silk and many other products. Hence the total is enormous. Marco Polo was told several times that the sum total of all taxes was 14,700,000 pieces of gold. This must be the largest revenue ever heard of.

Let us now leave Kinsai for Tanpiju.

CLV   THE GREAT CITY OF TANPIJU

On leaving Kinsai, a day's journey to the south-east takes the traveller through country full of fine houses, villages and fertile gardens producing all the necessities of life until he reaches the great city of Tanpiju which is dependent on Kinsai. The people are subjects of the Great Khan, they spend paper money and are idolaters who burn their dead. There is nothing else worth mentioning about this place.

From Tanpiju, the traveller goes south-east for three days, through large and busy trading towns. The people are idolatrous and subjects of the Great Khan, although they come under the immediate authority of the King of Kinsai. They live by trade and craft. After three days the traveller reaches Vuju, a large city where the people are idolaters, subjects of the Great Khan and have paper money. They are craftsmen and live by trading. They also come under the authority of the King of Kinsai. There is little else to say about them, so we will move on to Ghinju.

On leaving Vuju the traveller passes south-east through so many towns and villages, one after another, they seem like one large city. Every good thing can be found in this region. The tallest and thickest canes grow here. Some have a circumference of as much as four spans and are fifteen paces long. There is

133

nothing else worth recording. At the end of two days the traveller comes to a very large, fine city called Ghinju. Here the people are subjects of the Great Khan, although they are governed by the King of Kinsai. They have a lot of silk and live by trading.

Four days' journey further to the south-east from Ghinju takes the traveller through yet more towns, villages and hamlets where all the necessities of life can be found. The people are idolaters, living by trade and craft. There is game and a great deal of bird life and there are also large numbers of very big, ferocious lions. But throughout the province of Manzi there are no sheep, rams, buffaloes, goats or pigs.

After a further four days' journey the traveller reaches the large and beautiful city of Chanshan. It is situated on a hill surrounded by two branches of a river. The river divides at the foot of the hill, flowing south-east in one direction and north-west in the other. This city is also under the authority of the King of Kinsai and, here too, the people are subjects of the Great Khan and idolaters.

Beyond Chanshan, beautiful countryside stretches out for a further three days. There are hamlets, villages and towns where merchants and artisans live. These people depend on Kinsai and they have a plentiful supply of everything they need. There is much wildlife, with game and birds of all kinds.

Three days further on lies the very large and beautiful city of Kuju. The inhabitants are subjects of the Great Khan and idolaters. This is the last city which comes under the rule of Kinsai. Kinsai has nothing whatsoever to do with any of the places now to be described, for another one of Manzi's nine kingdoms begins here – Fu-chau.

CLVI THE KINGDOM OF FU-CHAU

Kuju is the last city in the kingdom of Kinsai; on leaving it the traveller enters Fu-chau. If he goes south-east for six days he will cross mountains and valleys and pass through towns, villages and hamlets. The people are idolatrous and subjects of the Great Khan but are governed by Fu-chau; they live by trade and craft and are fully self-sufficient. They have game and birds and huge ferocious lions. Amazing quantities of ginger and galingale grow here. One Venetian groat will buy eighty pounds of fresh ginger; there is also a fruit which can be used as a substitute for saffron.

The people here eat revolting things, even human flesh if the man has not died of an illness. If he has been killed by, for instance, a sword, they eat all of him and claim that the meat is excellent. When men go into battle they cut their hair short and paint a blue mark like the blade of a sword in the middle of their faces. Only the leader rides, the rest go on foot. They carry lances and swords and are the cruellest people in the world. They kill as many men as possible, drink their blood and then eat them. They look out for any opportunity to kill, to drink the blood of their enemies and to eat the murdered bodies.

After travelling for three of these six days the traveller reaches the grand and beautiful city of Kien-ning-fu where the inhabitants are subjects of the Great Khan but owe immediate obedience to Fu-chau. It is built on a large river which is spanned by three of the best constructed and most unusual bridges in the world, all supported at one end by the city walls. The bridges are at least a mile long and nine paces wide. They are built of stone with marble columns and are indeed a fine sight. One alone cost an unimaginable sum to build.

The people live by trade and also weave different types of silk and cotton from dyed thread, which they sell throughout the province. Large quantities of ginger and galingale are grown and sold. The women are very beautiful. There is a strange species of featherless chicken here which is covered in fur like a cat and is black all over. These chickens lay excellent eggs just like our chickens.

There is nothing more to say about Kien-ning-fu so we will move on a further three days through more trading towns and villages with many merchants and men-at-arms. There is a great deal of silk, the people are idolaters and subjects of the Great Khan. There is a lot of game and bird life and there are large and ferocious lions which are a danger to travellers. At the end of these three days and after a further fifteen miles the traveller reaches the city of Unken where an enormous amount of sugar is produced. Indeed, all the sugar for the Great Khan's court comes from here. Before Kublai Khan conquered the town, the citizens did not know how to make good sugar. They used to boil it and then skim it, making a black paste. Then some Babylonians from the Great Khan's court were sent to teach the inhabitants of Unken how to refine sugar by using the ashes of certain trees.

Now we will move on a further fifteen miles to the city of Fu-chau.

CLVII THE CITY OF FU-CHAU

Fu-chau is the capital of the kingdom of the same name – one of the nine kingdoms of Manzi. It is a busy commercial city with many traders, artisans and men-at-arms. The inhabitants are subjects of the Great Khan and idolaters. Kublai Khan keeps a large army in the city as there are frequent rebellions in the surrounding towns and villages. At the first sight of a revolt, the army hurries to the town in question and destroys it. The people scorn danger and death partly because they are confident of being honoured in the next world and partly because they live in invincible strongholds in the mountains.

On one side of Fu-chau flows a river which is at least a mile wide. A beautiful bridge spans the river, supported by pontoons held in place by heavy anchors. Huge, strong planks are nailed to the pontoons. Large numbers of river-going ships are built in this city, and an enormous amount of sugar is grown. Ships laden with pearls and precious stones arrive across the sea from India and sail on up the river to Fu-chau, from where the goods are dispersed throughout the region by land or water.

Fox-like animals roam the whole area damaging the sugar cane by gnawing at it; they also creep up on sleeping travellers and steal whatever they can find. The merchants have devised a method of trapping them. In the tops of large gourds they make an opening just large enough for the animal's head. To strengthen the opening they pierce holes round it and thread the holes with a piece of cord. They then put some fat inside the gourds and place them around their camp. The animals smell the bait and greedily force their heads into the gourds, but are then unable to withdraw them. As the gourds are very light the animals can lift them and walk off with them on their heads. But they are unable to see where they are going so the merchants can then catch them easily. Their flesh is delicious to eat and their skins fetch a high price.

Geese weighing as much as twenty-four pounds are to be found in this country. They have large crops under their throats and a protuberance on their beaks between their nostrils, like swans only bigger.

There is an abundance of everything in this city and there are many delightful orchards. It is a quiet and orderly city – a wonderful place in every way.

It is interesting how and why many Christians live here among the idolaters. Matteo and Marco Polo happened to be in the city with a learned Saracen who told them of some people who practised a strange religion. These people, having no idols, were not idolaters, they worshipped neither fire nor Mohammed, and nor did they appear to be Christians. The Saracen suggested that if Marco and Matteo met these people, they might be able to understand their religion.

So they went to question them about their beliefs and customs, but the people were afraid to answer lest their religion be in danger. Matteo and Marco, sensing their fear, spoke encouragingly to them and said: 'Don't be afraid. We have not come to hurt you, but only to help you and to improve your way of life.'

The people suspected that Marco and Matteo had been sent with bad intentions by Kublai Khan. The two Polos stayed patiently among these people, growing used to them and to their ways until they finally discovered that they were Christians who in fact had holy books in their possession. Matteo and Marco began to read these books and translate them word for word, and discovered that they were the words of the Psalter. When they asked how the people had come by the books, they were told: 'From our ancestors.'

In fact there were, in a small temple, paintings of three apostles – three of the seventy who preached the Gospel throughout the world. The people explained that many years before, their ancestors had been instructed in the faith which had been kept alive in those parts for 700 years. But they had been without instruction for so long now that they were ignorant of even the most important teachings of the Church. Only one thing had been handed down from their ancestors, which was that the three apostles should be venerated.

'You are Christians like us,' Matteo and Marco Polo told them, 'and we advise you to send messengers to the Great Khan explaining your religion so that he can recognize it. Then you will be able to practise it freely.'

Two envoys were sent to the Great Khan. Matteo and Marco Polo told them that when they reached the court they should address themselves to the Christian leader there who would be able to deal with the matter. The envoys did as they were asked and the Christian leader went to Kublai Khan and explained that these Christians should be recognized as such in their own land. But when the leader of the idolaters heard about this he said that these people were idolaters and were generally accepted as such. A bitter argument then took place in the presence of the Great Khan who, finally, with considerable irritation, dismissed everyone. Then he summoned the two envoys and asked them if the people in question wanted to be Christians or idolaters. The messengers replied that without wishing to offend or displease the Great Khan, the people would prefer to be Christians like their ancestors. The Great Khan then ordered that they should call themselves Christians and granted them all the rights and privileges due to Christians. And it turned out that, spread throughout Manzi, there were at least 700,000 Christian families.

CLVIII THE CITY OF ZAITON

On leaving Fu-chau the traveller crosses the river and rides south-east for five days through fine towns, villages and hamlets. There are hills and valleys, plains and forests with many camphor-producing trees. There is a great deal of wildlife and there are many birds. The people are subjects of the Great Khan and idolaters, but they owe immediate allegiance to the King of Fu-chau. After five days, the traveller comes to a fine and great city called Zaiton. This is a port where ships arrive from India, laden with rich and rare merchandise, invaluable gems and huge pearls. It is also the main port for the Manzi traders. It is amazing to see so many precious stones and valuable goods passing through one port. The port supplies the whole province of Manzi, and for every ship carrying pepper to Christendom, 100 dock in Zaiton. This is indeed one of the busiest ports in the world.

The Great Khan collects a vast revenue from Zaiton as every ship coming from

India must pay a 10 per cent duty on all its merchandise and precious stones. Payment for the hire of cargo boats is taxed at 30 per cent for small goods, 40 per cent for aloes, sandalwood and other bulky merchandise, and 44 per cent for pepper. So merchants pay, in various taxes, half the value of their goods to the Great Khan. It is clear how much Kublai Khan must profit from this port. The people are idolaters and subjects of the Great Khan. This is a very rich land with plentiful supplies of everything.

In the same province is a town called Tinju where the most beautiful large and small china bowls are made. They are made only here, and are exported throughout the world. They are very cheap – a Venetian groat will buy three of the finest. The inhabitants of this town speak a language of their own.

Fu-chau, then, is one of the nine kingdoms of Manzi and the Great Khan collects a greater income from it than from any other part of his empire except the city of Kinsai. Of the nine kingdoms only Yang-chau, Kinsai and Fu-chau have been mentioned. It would take too long to describe the other six. The three have been spoken of in order as Marco Polo travelled through them, but although he heard and learnt much about the others he did not visit them. Any description of them would, therefore, lack precision.

Much has been said, then, about Manzi, Cathay and other provinces, about the people, the animals, the gold, the silver, the precious stones, the pearls and many other things, but this book cannot be complete without an account of India. The wonders of India are unique and must be described here. And they will be laid down faithfully according to Marco Polo's account.

Marco Polo spent so long among the Indians, learning their customs and everything possible about their way of life, that few people can match his knowledge. He tells of many strange and wonderful things, all of them true, which will be recounted in this book one after another, just as he reported them.

VI

From China to India

CLIX THE BEGINNING OF THE BOOK ON INDIA

We have spoken of many different regions, but the time has now come to move towards India and to tell of its delights. First let us turn to the boats in which the merchants travel. They are built of pine and fir and are partly covered by a deck under which there are usually sixty cabins, each one comfortably large enough for one merchant. They have a tiller and four masts. Occasionally they have two other masts which can be put up or taken down. The boats are built with a double hull, that is to say the inside of the hull is lined with a second layer of planks.

The Khan's fleet sailing through the East Indies

They are caulked inside and out and nailed together with iron nails. Since there is no tar, they cannot be tarred, but they are coated with a substance which is regarded as superior to pitch. The shipbuilders pound lime and finely-chopped hemp with oil from a certain tree until they have a sticky paste with which they cover the boats.

The boats are manned by between 150 and 300 sailors and they are large enough to carry 5-6,000 sacks of pepper. Some have sails and oars; there are four oarsmen to each oar. These large ships sail in convoy with several smaller ones, also laden with goods and with a crew of 80-100. The smaller ships are also often used as tugs, towing the larger ones with ropes of strong hemp. There are usually two of these, one larger than the other. The big ships also carry about ten small boats which they use when anchoring and for fishing, among other things. These little boats are lashed to the sides of the big ships. The larger tugs in the convey also carry smaller boats.

When the ships need repairing, usually after a year at sea, a third layer of planks is nailed to the hull, and this in turn is coated with the lime and hemp mixture. Further layers of planks can be added until there are six in all.

These, then, are the ships which carry merchants to and from India. But there are certain islands in the Ocean which must be mentioned before we reach India.

CLX THE ISLAND OF JAPAN

Japan is an island in the middle of the Ocean, 1,500 miles from the mainland. It is a vast island whose inhabitants have white skins and beautiful manners. They are idolaters and independent, recognizing no ruler but their own.

Gold is mined there in huge quantities. Nobody ever goes to Japan from the mainland so the gold never leaves the island.

The ruler of Japan has a magnificent palace roofed entirely with fine gold, as we might use lead for our houses and churches. It would be almost impossible to estimate the value of this gold. But besides the roof, the floors of the bedrooms are covered with a layer of gold, two fingers thick. The other rooms and the windows are decorated with gold in the same way. The palace is immeasurably valuable; anyone would be amazed by it.

There are vast numbers of very beautiful, large, round, pink pearls which are even more precious than white ones. It is usual when burying a body to put a pearl in its mouth. The Japanese have many other priceless stones. The island is in fact incalculably rich.

When Kublai Khan heard about the riches of this island he decided to conquer it and sent two barons there, one called Abakan and the other Vonsamchin, both capable and brave men. They set sail from Zaiton and Kinsai with their men and reached Japan. They conquered a few places in the plain and some hamlets, but no cities.

Then a most unfortunate thing happened, although it must be stated that there was considerable rivalry between the barons and neither helped the other. A violent gale blew from the north and Kublai Khan's men realized that their fleet was in danger of being smashed to pieces. They immediately boarded their ships and put to sea, but when they were only four miles out the wind became so strong that the ships sailing alongside each other collided and were wrecked. Some of the men were able to save themselves by swimming to a nearby island but the rest were all drowned. The ships which were not sailing too closely together were saved and when the wind dropped and the sea grew calm, they put in at the same island. The two barons in charge of the army allowed only noblemen and captains to board their ships before hoisting the sails. Thirty thousand Tartars were left on the island, all of whom imagined they would die since they had no idea how they could leave the island. They were sick at heart on seeing the ships sail back home. Those on board arrived back safely and returned to the Great Khan. But let us consider those who were abandoned on the island.

CLXI   THE STORY OF THE THIRTY THOUSAND

The 30,000 abandoned Tartars were in despair. But when the ruler of Japan heard that the enemy were in flight and many of them had taken refuge on the

Ancient Japanese Emperor

island, his people were delighted. As soon as the sea was calm enough the Japanese boarded their ships and sailed straight to the island, determined to take all the Tartars prisoner. When the 30,000 saw that the enemy had left their ships unguarded, they, with great cunning, began to run, chased by the Japanese. They ran round the island until they came back to where the ships were moored and swiftly and suddenly boarded them.

They immediately set sail and returned to the large island, where, because they were flying the Japanese flag, they were able to approach the capital city. The natives, seeing their own flag, presumed their soldiers were returning, and allowed the ships to dock. So the Great Khan's men entered the city and finding it full of old men they took it, banishing the younger citizens, apart from some beautiful women whom they kept for their own purposes. In this way the vanquished became the victors.

When the King of Japan and his people learnt that they had lost their capital city, they nearly died of disappointment and sorrow. They returned to the capital with other ships and besieged the port so that no one could enter it or leave it.

The Great Khan's men resisted for seven months during which time they tried to think of a way in which to alert Kublai Khan of their position. But they were unable to send any messengers out. When they realized that there was no way of sending word to the Great Khan they surrendered on condition that their lives were spared, and they resigned themselves to spending the rest of their lives on the island. This all happened in 1281.

The Great Khan, meanwhile, had one of the two barons commanding the army executed; the other he banished to an island where many people were sent to die and where the baron did in fact die. Kublai Khan did this because he heard that the two men had behaved very badly in the cruel war in Japan.

A marvellous event had taken place in a certain castle in Japan when the two barons had captured some men there. These men refused to surrender and were all condemned to be executed. But it turned out to be impossible to cut off the heads of eight of them. This was because they had embedded a special stone in their arms between the skin and the flesh, where it could not be seen. This was a magic stone which prevented any man who had it from dying by the sword. When the barons learnt that the eight men could not be executed, they ordered them to be cudgelled to death. The men soon died, and the magic stone was removed from their arms and kept with great care. But in the end, as we have seen, the Great Khan's men were defeated. So let us now return to the subject in hand and continue with the book.

CLXII   THE CUSTOMS OF THE IDOLATERS

The idolaters in these islands are not unlike those in Cathay and Manzi; they all worship idols with heads like rams, pigs, oxen or other animals. Some have three heads, one in the right place and the others coming out of the shoulders. Some

Fight between Japanese and Chinese soldiers, from a Japanese drawing

have four or ten hands or even as many as 1,000. Those with 1,000 are thought to be the best and are held in the greatest possible veneration. When they are asked by Christians why they make their idols in so many different forms, they reply: 'Our grandparents left them to us like this and so shall we hand them down to our children and grandchildren.'

The lifestyle of these idolaters is such a mixture of extravagance and wickedness that it cannot be recounted in this book – the account would be far too grotesque for Christian ears. Let us say no more about them, except for one thing. When one of these idolaters takes a man prisoner and the ransom cannot be paid, the prisoners' friends and relations are invited to the captor's house. Then the prisoner is killed and cooked and eaten by his friends and relations. Human flesh is regarded as the greatest possible delicacy.

The island of Japan lies in the China Sea, in other words the sea beside Manzi, for China is called Manzi in their language. It is an eastern sea. In it lie, according to the most experienced sailors, some 7,448 islands, most of which are inhabited. On each of these islands there are very sweetly-scented trees whose timber is as useful, if not more so, than aloe wood. There is also a vast quantity of pepper as white as snow, as well as a considerable amount of black pepper. The islands are full of priceless things like gold, but it takes a year to reach them. Nevertheless, when the people of Kinsai and Zaiton go there, they do a lot of business and make great profits. They set out in winter and return in summer because there are only two winds in those parts. One blows the ships towards Japan and the other carries them home. One blows throughout the summer and the other throughout the winter. These places are a very long way from India, and although we say the China Sea, we are really speaking of the Ocean. It is like saying the 'English Sea' or 'La Rochelle Sea'; one can speak of the China Sea or the Indian Sea although both are part of the Ocean.

Japanese archer

But we will leave these islands. Marco Polo did not visit them and they are not our concern. The Great Khan has nothing to do with the people there and receives no taxes from them. So we will go back to Zaiton and continue our journey from there.

CLXIII CHAMBA

On leaving Zaiton the traveller sails with the south-west wind for a good 1,500 miles across the Gulf of Cheynam. It would take two months to sail right across it to the north. The gulf is filled with many small islands, mostly inhabited, where gold and copper are to be found. In many of them, a considerable amount of grain is harvested. The gulf is so large and so many people live there that it seems almost like another world. On the other side of the gulf from Zaiton is a vast and rich province called Chamba. The people have their own king, their own language and are idolaters. Every year they send a tribute of elephants to the Great Khan, but nothing else. There is a good reason why they send elephants.

In 1278 the Great Khan sent one of his barons called Sogatu with an army of cavalrymen and infantrymen to attack Chamba. The King, who was very old and very wise, did not have an army nearly big enough to fight the Great Khan's men in a pitched battle so he defended himself from inside an impregnable fortified town. But when he saw how the enemy were laying waste his country and destroying everything outside the town, he was deeply distressed and sent some envoys to the Great Khan with the following message: 'The King of Chamba pays his respects as he would to his legitimate overlord. He is old and has ruled a long time, and he would like to be your vassal and to send you a rich tribute of elephants and aloe wood. He sends this message in a spirit of peace and begs you to stop your barons and soldiers destroying his land.'

When the messengers had finished speaking, the Great Khan felt sorry for the old King and sent envoys back to his barons, telling them to go and wage war elsewhere. Now, every year, the King of Chamba sends Kublai Khan a great quantity of aloe wood and twenty of the largest and best elephants he can find. And that was how the King of Chamba became a vassal of the Great Khan.

In this kingdom no girl may marry without the King having seen her first. If he likes her, he marries her himself. If not, he gives her a dowry according to her status so that she can marry another baron. When Marco Polo himself was there in 1285, the King had 326 children and at least 150 of his sons were well trained in the arts of war.

The kingdom is full of elephants and aloe wood. There is also a large quantity of very black wood called ebony from which chessmen and inkstands are made.

There being nothing else worth mentioning we will move on to Java.

CLXIV THE GREAT ISLAND OF JAVA

The huge island of Java lies 1,500 miles to the south-west of Chamba. Experienced sailors claim it to be the largest island in the world with a perimeter of more than 3,000 miles. It is ruled by a great and powerful king. The people are idolaters and pay tribute to no one. The island is extremely rich. Pepper, nutmeg, spikenard, galingale, cubeb, cloves and all the rarest spices in the world are found here. A great many ships put in here and the merchants buy goods from which they make a huge profit. It would be impossible to estimate the riches of the island. Kublai Khan was never able to conquer it because it was so far away and the seas were dangerous. But merchants from Zaiton and Manzi were able to bring great riches back from the island, and indeed still do.

Having spoken of Java, we will now travel on.

CLXV   THE ISLANDS OF SONDUR AND CONDUR

A small island and a large island lie seven miles to the south-west of Java. They are called Sondur and Condur and are uninhabited so it is not worth speaking about them. Five hundred miles further south-east of these two islands is a large and rich mainland province called Lokak ruled over by a powerful king. The inhabitants are idolaters and speak a language of their own. They pay tribute to no one since their country is too far from anywhere for them to fear invasions. If it were possible for the Great Khan to send an army there easily, he would already have subjected it. There is an abundance of ebony and brazil wood and also an unbelievable amount of gold. There are elephants, game and every kind of animal and bird. Cowrie shells, which are used as currency in so many parts of the world, come from here.

CLXVI   THE ISLAND OF BINTAN AND OTHERS

Five hundred miles to the south of Lokak lies the island of Bintan, a very wild place with woods of highly-scented and very valuable trees. Sailing on between the two islands for another sixty miles or so, larger ships are obliged to lift the rudder a little because it draws nearly four paces, which is about the depth of the sea. After these sixty miles, there are a further thirty before the island kingdom of Malayur is reached. The capital city has the same name. It is ruled by a king and the people speak a language of their own. The city is large and noble and a great trade in spices and all the necessities of life is carried on there. There is nothing else to be said about this place, so we will move on.

CLXVII   LESSER JAVA

One hundred miles to the south-east of Malayur lies the island of Lesser Java. It is not, however, particularly small since it is more than 2,000 miles in circumference and is made up of at least eight kingdoms. All the inhabitants are idolaters and each kingdom has its own language. The island abounds in riches, and in all the most precious spices including many unknown in our part of the world. There is aloe wood, brazil, ebony, and many other rare things as well. This island lies so far to the south that the Pole Star cannot be seen even fleetingly. We shall speak of all the different peoples on the island in turn. First, the kingdom of Ferlec.

Medieval ship sailing in the Java Sea, from a bas-relief at Boro Bodor

Saracen merchants have converted the people in the cities of Ferlec to the Mohammedan faith, but the mountain people live like animals. They eat human flesh and any other meat, whether good or bad. They worship many things; for instance, when they rise in the morning they worship the first thing they see.

From Ferlec the traveller passes into Basman, an independent kingdom with a language of its own. The people are lawless and live like animals. They profess allegiance to the Great Khan but they pay him no tribute because they live too far away for the Khan's officials ever to be able to go there. Nevertheless, they declare themselves in favour of him and occasionally send him a rich and beautiful gift like some black goshawks of a rare breed. They have wild elephants and unicorns as big as the elephants, with pelts like buffaloes and feet like

147

elephants. The unicorn has one very large black horn in its forehead, but it does not defend itself with it. The unicorn uses its spikey tongue and its knees for this purpose, first crushing its quarry by kneeling on it and then lacerating it with its tongue. Its head, which it always carries low, is like the head of a wild boar. It likes to wallow in mud and slime and is particularly ugly; in fact it bears no resemblance to the idea we have of a unicorn, neither is it anything like the animals which we describe as allowing themselves to be caught by young maidens. It is the very opposite. There are a great many large monkeys of different types, and pitch-black goshawks which are excellent hunters.

It must be noted that merchants who claim to have brought back pygmies as a rarity from India are involved in great deception. There is a breed of tiny monkey on the island, with almost human features. They are caught, killed and skinned. Only their facial hair is left. Then they are dried and embalmed with camphor and other substances. They look like men but it is a great imposture. These 'men' are fabricated in the way I have described. They exist neither in India nor in any other wild country.

Now we will go to Sumatra.

CLXVIII   SUMATRA

The kingdom of Sumatra is on the same island as Basman. Marco Polo was forced to remain here for five months because bad weather prevented him from travelling. The Pole Star cannot be seen from here either, nor can the Plough. The people are savage idolaters whose king is rich and powerful. They claim the Great Khan as their overlord.

The Polos distrusted the native bestial cannibals, so when they disembarked from their ships they built fortifications in the form of deep trenches behind which they and their 2,000 men lived. The natives, however, sold them timber, of which there was plenty in the island, in exchange for foodstuffs and other things.

Sumatra has the best fish in the world, but there is no corn, only rice. There is no wine, but an unusual type of drink made from a certain tree. A branch is cut from the tree and a receptacle hung from the trunk. The receptacle must be quite big as in a day and a night it will be full to overflowing with this most delicious drink. These trees look like small date palms, but they only have four branches and when they have stopped producing wine, the trees are watered thoroughly and after a little while the stumps begin to produce more, but this time it is white rather than red. So there is red and white wine, and it is a wine which can cure dropsy and consumption.

Sumatra is full of coconuts as big as a man's head which are very good to eat.

When they are fresh they have a liquid in the centre which is more delicious and sweet to taste than any wine in the world. The people here eat any meat, good or bad.

We will now move on to the next kingdom.

CLXIX   THE KINGDOM OF DAGROIAN

Dagroian is another independent kingdom with its own language. The people are very wild and claim loyalty to the Great Khan. They are idolaters with bad ways. If one of them, either a man or a woman, is ill, his or her relations call magicians to see if the patient can be cured. These magicians, by their spells and with the help of their idols, can tell if the sick person will recover. If the magicians say the patient is going to die, certain men are called whose job it is to kill the incurable. These men come and suffocate the patient who is then cooked and all his relations gather together to eat him. They even eat the bone marrow, so absolutely nothing is left. When they have finished eating, they collect the bones and put them in a fine casket which they carry off to the mountains and hang in caves where no man or animal can find them. Furthermore, if they capture a foreigner who cannot pay a ransom, they kill and eat him without a second thought – an infamous and evil practice.

CLXX   THE KINGDOM OF LAMBRI

Lambri is a kingdom with its own ruler but which pays allegiance to the Great Khan. The people are idolaters. There is a super-abundance of brazil as well as camphor and precious spices. Brazil is cultivated in the following way: after the seeds are sown the young shoots are transplanted. They are then left for three years after which they are dug up and used. Marco Polo took some of the seed to Venice and planted it there, but nothing grew because the climate is much too cold.

One very extraordinary thing about this place is that there are hairless men with tails a span in length. In fact most of the inhabitants have tails. These men live in the mountains rather than the cities and their tails are like dogs' tails. There are also unicorns in Lambri and many birds.

We will now move on to Fansur.

CLXXI   THE KINGDOM OF FANSUR

Fansur is an independent kingdom. There is a king and the people are idolaters who pay allegiance to the Great Khan. This kingdom is also part of Lesser Java.

The best camphor in the world, called *fansurina*, is produced here and it is sold for its weight in gold. There is no corn so the people eat rice and milk, but they make flour from trees in these parts. The flour comes from inside a fine bark and is pounded to make a delicious paste. Marco Polo ate some himself and even took some back with him to Venice. Bread made from this flour tastes like barley bread.

Marco Polo did not go to the other three kingdoms on the island, so we will leave them and turn instead to the islands of Gauenispola* and Nicobar.

CLXXII   THE ISLAND OF NICOBAR

About 350 miles to the west of Lambri lie two islands, one of which is called Nicobar. There is no king and the people there live like animals, totally naked. They have a peculiar habit whereby they decorate their houses with long pieces of beautiful silk bought from passing merchants. They hang the silk from rods as a valuable ornament, regarding it rather as we would pearls, precious stones or gold and silver vases. They never use them for any purpose but decoration. They are considered a sign of wealth. The woods are full of the finest plants, including white and pink sandalwood, coconut trees, cloves, brazil and many valuable trees.

There is no more to add so we shall go on to Andaman.

CLXXIII   THE ISLAND OF ANDAMAN

Andaman is a very big island. There is no king and the people are idolaters who live like wild animals. All the men on this island have heads like a dog's head with dog's eyes and teeth so that they look like huge mastiffs. They are a very cruel people who eat human flesh whenever they catch a foreigner. Otherwise they eat rice, milk and all sorts of meat. They also have an abundance of spices and fruit quite unlike our own.

The sea around the island is very deep and the currents are so strong that ships cannot drop anchor, nor can they easily navigate the waters. Once they have entered the gulf, they have great difficulty in sailing out again. In fact the sea is so rough that trees have been uprooted from the shore and swept out into the bay where ships have become entangled in them. These ships are unable to free themselves and must stay there for good.

Now for the island of Ceylon.

---

*No description of Gauenispola is in fact given. It was either never written or has been lost.

An interpretation of Marco Polo's description of the
inhabitants of the Island of Andaman. He said they had heads like dogs,
but in fact they were oriental negroes

CLXXIV   THE ISLAND OF CEYLON

On leaving Andaman the traveller sails for nearly 1,000 miles to the south-west
before reaching the island of Ceylon, which is certainly the largest island in the
world with a perimeter of 2,400 miles. In ancient times it was even larger, having
a perimeter of 3,600 miles, according to maps made by sailors in those seas. But
the west wind blows so violently that part of the island has been submerged,
which is why it is now smaller. The island is completely flat so that it can only be
sighted by sailors when they are very close to it.

The King of the island is called Sendernam. The people are idolaters and pay
allegiance to no one. They wear nothing but a loincloth and have neither corn nor
wine, but they do have sesame seed from which they make oil. They live on meat,
milk and rice, and drink the juice from trees, as already described. They have a
large quantity of the best possible brazil.

Now we must change the subject and discuss a most precious thing. Wonderful rubies are to be found on this island, finer than in any other part of the world. There are also sapphires, topazes, amethysts, garnets and many other precious stones. The King owns the most beautiful ruby ever seen. It is nearly a palm in length and as thick as a man's arm. It is the brightest jewel in the world and has not the slightest flaw. It is deep red like fire and is quite priceless. The Great Khan has sent messengers asking to buy the ruby. He was prepared to give the equivalent of a whole city for it, but the King replied that he had inherited it from his ancestors and would exchange it for nothing in the world. So the Great Khan could not have it.

The inhabitants of the island are a miserable unwarlike people. If they need to be defended, they hire men from other countries, especially Saracens.

There is nothing else worthy of recording so now we will move to India and the province of Maabar.

43

44

VII

India

CLXXV THE GREAT PROVINCE OF MAABAR

About sixty miles to the west of Ceylon is the province of Maabar which is part of
Greater India. It is the most beautiful place in all India and is on the mainland.
Maabar is divided between five kings who are brothers and of whom we shall
speak later. The province is the noblest and richest in the world and we shall see
why.

Sender Bandi Devar is the King of the largest and most important of the five
kingdoms. Huge, fine pearls of excellent quality are found there, and they are
collected in the following way.

There is a gulf between the mainland and an island where the sea is only ten or
twelve paces deep, and in some places only two. And it is here that the pearls are
found. Groups of merchants form companies and hire large ships especially
designed for the purpose, in which everyone has his own cabin prepared with
everything he needs and a vat full of water. They start from a place called Bettala
on the mainland and sixty miles out from there, where pearls are most numerous,
they drop anchor and disembark into the little boats which have followed them.
The companies of merchants employ a large number of men whom they pay to
remain in their service throughout the fishing season, which runs from April until
the beginning of May.

The merchants are obliged to pay certain taxes. In the first place they must
give one-tenth of their catch to the King. Then they must give one-twentieth to the
men who during the daytime cast spells to protect the divers from predatory fish.
At night the spell is broken and the fish go where they want. These magicians are
Brahmins who can charm all kinds of animals and birds and living creatures.

When they have reached the desired spot, the men employed by the merchants
jump into the sea to a depth of four or five paces, some going down as far as twelve
paces. On the sea bed they find certain shells known as oysters. Inside the shells
are the pearls, some large and some small, all embedded in the oyster's flesh.
When they are short of breath, the divers come to the surface carrying the oysters
in a string bag tied to their waists, and then jump in again. And so they go on

153

throughout the day. The oysters are split open and put into the vats of water, where the flesh floats to the top, leaving the pearls at the bottom.

So many pearls are collected in this way that it would be impossible to count them. Round, smooth pearls from this sea are sent all over the world. The King's revenue from them is enormous.

As soon as May comes there are no more oysters to be found anywhere, although in September and October some can be found three miles further out.

Because of the temperate climate the natives wear nothing but a loincloth in winter and summer alike, and there are no tailors whatsoever throughout the whole country of Maabar. It is never too hot or too cold. The King is as naked as everyone else but his loincloth is made of rich material and he wears a necklace studded with rubies, sapphires, emeralds and other stones. The necklace is immensely valuable. But he also wears a narrow silk cord round his neck which hangs down over his chest and is threaded with 104 pearls alternating with rubies. There are 104 pearls because every day, morning and night, the King prays to his idols and repeats the prayer 'Pacauta, Pacauta, Pacauta' 104 times. This is a rule of his religion and his ancestors have always done it. Furthermore, the King wears round each arm, in three places, gold bracelets encrusted with precious stones and large rare pearls. He also wears three gold bands studded with jewels and pearls round each leg, and even more jewels on his feet. This King is an amazing sight since he wears precious stones worth as much as a city; in fact it is impossible to estimate the worth of his jewellery. It is not surprising that he has so much since his kingdom is filled with precious stones and pearls.

No one may take any precious stone or pearl weighing more than half a *saggio* out of the country. Every year the King issues a proclamation throughout the land to the effect that any subject bringing pearls or precious stones to the court will be paid twice their value for them. Because of this, merchants and others are only too glad to take them to court. This is why the King has so many jewels.

It is absolutely true that this King has 500 wives and as many concubines. He has only to see a beautiful woman or a pretty girl to want her for himself. Once he was very wicked and took his brother's extremely beautiful wife for himself. The brother was a wise man and decided to let the King have his way, but the two brothers have subsequently often come close to fighting.

There is another extraordinary thing about this King. He has a numerous following of so-called 'faithful'. They are faithful in a particular way because they believe that they serve the King not only in this world but in the next as well. The faithful wait on the King, ride with him and have a great deal of authority throughout the kingdom. When the King dies, his body is burnt and the faithful throw themselves on the funeral pyre and burn with him, so as to accompany him to the next world.

154

Also, when the King dies, leaving great riches, his son does not touch them, but says: 'I have inherited my father's land and his subjects, so, like him, I can amass my own wealth.' In this way the royal treasure is passed on intact to each king's heir, who then adds to it. As a result the royal riches are vast.

No horses are bred in this kingdom. Merchants from Hormuz, Kais, Dhofar, Shihr and Aden, provinces with every breed of horse, buy the best ones and export them by ship to the King and his four brothers, who are also kings. The King buys some 2,000 of these horses every year, and each of his brothers buys as many. By the end of the year only about 100 are left. They die because there are no farriers and no one knows how to manage them; they die, in fact, from neglect. The merchants who sell the horses take no farriers with them, and allow none to go there since they want the horses to die so that they can export more the following year.

Another custom in this country concerns men sentenced to death. A condemned man will announce that he wishes to take his own life in honour of a certain idol and the King gives his consent. Then all the man's relations put him on a seat, give him twelve knives and carry him through the town saying: 'This brave man is going to take his own life for the love of such and such an idol.'

When they have carried him through the town to the place of justice, the condemned man grasps a knife and shouts loudly: 'I am killing myself for the love of such and such a god.'

Then he takes two of the twelve knives and plunges them into his thighs. Then, two by two, he sticks the knives into his arms and his stomach until he finally dies of the wounds. When he is dead his relations bury him with festivity and joy.

Another custom in this country is for a woman to throw herself on her husband's funeral pyre and burn with him. The wives who do this are highly praised. And a great many of them do it.

The inhabitants of the kingdom worship idols and many of them worship oxen. Under no circumstances will they eat beef, nor will they ever kill an ox. Also all houses are smeared with cow dung. There are some men, however, called Gavi who do eat beef, but only when the animal has died a natural death.

The people who killed St Thomas the Apostle were the ancestors of the Gavi. So not one member of the Gavi tribe has the right to enter St Thomas's sepulchre. The saint's body emanates such holy power that even ten or twenty men would not succeed in getting one of the Gavi into the sepulchre.

In this kingdom everyone, including the King and his suite, sits on the ground and if they are asked why they do not sit in a more dignified manner, they reply that it is extremely dignified to sit on the ground since we ourselves are made of earth and destined to return to the earth, so the earth can never be too highly respected and should not be held in contempt.

There is rice but no corn in the kingdom. There is one other strange thing: if a beautiful warhorse mates with a magnificent mare of the same breed, the resulting foal will be undersized with crooked legs, unridable and worth nothing.

The men here go to war with lances and shields, but completely naked. They are not in the least brave but are a miserable and cowardly people. They do not kill animals, but when they want to eat them they ask Saracens or people of other religions to kill for them. Everyone, both men and women, washes their body in water twice a day. They would not dare to eat either in the morning or the evening without having washed first. Anyone who does not wash twice a day is regarded as a heretic. Furthermore, they only eat with the right hand and would never touch the food with their left hand. They do everything that requires purity and cleanliness with the right hand whereas with the left they do unclean things like washing their bottoms. They drink only out of their own personal cup which they never put to their lips but hold above their heads, pouring the wine down their throats.

Justice is very harsh in the kingdom. Murderers, thieves and all criminals are severely dealt with. If a debtor repeatedly puts off payment from one day to another, and if his creditor succeeds in drawing a circle around him, the debtor may not leave the circle until he has paid the debt or unless he has given solid proof that he will pay the same day. If he dares to leave the circle without having paid, or without having given some form of guarantee, he is punished.

Marco Polo saw this happen to the King himself. The King had to pay a foreign merchant for certain goods which he had received, and he had put off payment on several occasions. One day the merchant, who was inconvenienced by the perpetual delay, saw the King out riding in the town and managed to trace a circle on the ground round the King and his horse. When the King realized what had happened, he pulled up his horse and went no further until the merchant had been paid every penny owed to him. The people who witnessed this scene were amazed and said to each other: 'Look how the King has obeyed the law.'

The King replied: 'Since I made this law, how could I flout it just because it didn't suit me? In fact I should observe it even more strictly than anyone else.'

Few people drink wine and the word of a drinker, like the word of a sailor, has little value; on the other hand, no form of lechery or lasciviousness is sinful in their eyes.

The heat is unbearable and for this reason the people wear no clothes. It rains only in June, July and August. Without the rains, which alleviate the heat to some extent, the country would be uninhabitable.

There are a great many people versed in the art they call physiognomy, by which they can tell whether a man or woman is good or bad at first glance. They are also very clever at being able to tell the significance of an encounter with a particular bird or animal. No one pays more attention than these people do to omens, and they can distinguish between good and bad ones. If someone meets a person who sneezes and he feels the sign has no relevance to him, he will continue on his way. But if he sees it as an unfavourable omen he will stop and even turn back.

There is one unlucky hour in every day of the week, which is called the *choiach*. This hour is calculated by the length of a man's shadow. For instance, the unlucky hour in a certain day might be when a man's shadow measures seven feet; but as soon as the shadow has lengthened the unlucky hour will have passed. On another day the *choiach* might be when the shadow measures twelve feet – no more, no less. It is thought that no beneficial transaction can be carried out in that hour.

In the people's houses there are animals called tarantulas which run up the walls like lizards. They have a poisonous bite and it is an unlucky man who is bitten by them. They make a peculiar noise which sounds like 'chis'.

In this kingdom the parents of every newborn child write down the day, the hour and the month of the birth as well as the moon. They do this because their actions are governed by soothsayers. Their magicians are particularly skilled in spells, necromancy and astronomy.

As soon as a boy reaches the age of thirteen, his father sends him out of the house and no longer feeds him. He is thought to have reached an age where he can provide for himself as his father does. The boy is given the equivalent of twenty groats to set him on his way. This is done to encourage the boys to become sharp and clever traders. The boys then spend all day running from one place to another, buying and selling things.

During the pearl fishing season they buy five or six pearls which they take to merchants, who stand in the shade out of the sun, and say: 'Do you want them? I paid so much for them. Let me make a profit.'

The merchants pay a little extra for the pearls and the boys are off again. Or they may say to the merchants: 'Would you like me to go and buy something for you?'

In this way the boys become very clever in their dealings. They take their food home and their mothers cook it for them. They no longer eat anything at their father's expense.

In this kingdom – and indeed throughout India – the birds and animals are quite different from ours except for quail. Bats (birds which fly by night and have no feathers) are as big as goshawks there. And the goshawks themselves are black like crows and much bigger and swifter than ours, as well as better hunters. Another strange thing is that the horses are fed on meat cooked with rice and other cooked foods.

The monasteries are filled with idols, both male and female ones. Many young girls are dedicated to these idols, for their parents consecrate them to the idol they love most. Whenever the monks ask them to do so, these girls must go to the monastery to please the idol by singing and dancing. There are a lot of these girls and several times a week every month they take food to the idol. The girls prepare lavish meals with meat and other good things which they take to the monastery and leave on a table in front of the idol. Then they dance and sing and celebrate enthusiastically. They dance for as long as it would take a rich man to eat his meal. When they think that the idol's spirit has had time to absorb the substance of the food they remove it and eat it with great joy. The young girls continue this practice until they are married.

The pagoda at Tanjore (which Marco Polo described as a monastery)
where young girls entertained their gods by dancing

The reason why the girls go to entertain the idols in this way is, according to the monks, to appease the god, who is often angry with the goddess and will neither speak to her nor co-habit with her. If the god is not appeased, the people do not have his protection and things will go badly for them. So the girls go to the monastery and, naked but for the smallest loincloth, sing to their god and goddess. The god is alone on one altar and the goddess by herself on another, but the people believe that they often have sexual intercourse, but that when they are angry, they refrain. The girls come to the monastery to make peace between them. They sing happily, jump, play and joke in order to cheer up the gods and encourage their reconciliation. And they pray: 'O Lord, why are you angry with the goddess, and why do you not care for her? Isn't she beautiful? Of course she is beautiful. May you be reconciled to her and take your pleasure with her because she is very beautiful.' The girl who has spoken will then lift her leg above her shoulder and pirouette to delight the idol. When the festivities are over the girls return to their homes and the following morning the monks who guard the idols announce with great joy that they have witnessed the coupling of the god and goddess and that peace has at last returned. Everybody is then happy and grateful.

Until they are married these girls have such firm flesh that no one can succeed in pinching any part of their body, though they willingly allow men to try. Their flesh remains quite firm even after they are married, and their breasts never sag, but are always erect and high.

Having spoken a considerable amount about this kingdom, we will move on to Motupalli.

CLXXVI   THE KINGDOM OF MOTUPALLI

Motupalli is a kingdom which lies about 500 miles to the north of Maabar. It is ruled by a very wise queen. When Marco Polo was there, she had been widowed for forty years, and having loved her husband dearly, she announced that she would never marry again. For forty years she ruled her kingdom as justly as her husband would have. She is more loved by her subjects than any other ruler.

The people are idolaters and owe allegiance to no one. They eat rice, meat and milk and there are many mountains where diamonds are to be found. When it rains in winter, the water rushes down the mountainside, cascading through the rocks. When the rains stop and the water has run away the men go and look for diamonds in the watercourses. When the water has dried up completely, more can be found in the mountains, but it is so hot and there are so many snakes that people are frightened to roam around there. But some still go and find large and excellent diamonds. The snakes are poisonous and very dangerous so men dare not enter the caves where they live.

There is, however, another way of collecting diamonds. There are deep gorges whose sides are so steep that they are impossible to climb, so the men take succulent pieces of meat which they throw into the ravines. Quite a few diamonds get stuck in the meat as it rolls down. A breed of white eagle, which preys on snakes, lives in these mountains and when these eagles see the meat at the bottom of the ravines, they pick it up and carry it to the peaks. The men then watch where they land and while the eagles eat the meat, they quickly climb up to them. The eagles, afraid of the men, fly off, abandoning the meat embedded with diamonds.

There is yet another way of collecting the diamonds. The eagles often swallow some of the diamonds with the meat. Then at night they return to their eyrie where the diamonds are mixed with their droppings. Men then collect the droppings.

These are the three ways in which diamonds are collected and there is no other place in the whole world where these stones can be found. Here, however, they are plentiful and beautiful. The best ones are not exported to Christendom, but to Kublai Khan and other kings and barons. It is they who own the greatest riches and the most precious stones.

Now let us turn to other matters. In this country the best cotton, known as buckram, is woven. It is beautiful, very fine and extremely valuable. It is like Rheims linen and is so elegant that the greatest king and queen in the world could wear it.

There is no more to be said about this kingdom.

CLXXVII   THE BODY OF ST THOMAS THE APOSTLE

The body of St Thomas the Apostle is in the province of Maabar in a small, out of the way town where no merchants go, but which is a place of pilgrimage for many Christians and Saracens. The Saracens in those parts have faith in St Thomas and believe that he was a Saracen and a great prophet whom they call *avariun*, which means 'holy'.

There is a miraculous feature to this place. If someone has tertian fever or any other fever and a little of the earth from the place where the saint died is dissolved in water and given to the patient to drink, it will immediately cure him. Christian pilgrims come here to take home this earth. Marco Polo took some of the earth, which is red, back to Venice where he cured a large number of people.

A wonderful miracle occurred around the year 1288. The lord of the province had an extra large quantity of rice which he stored in the church and in the houses around the church. When the Christians guarding the church saw what was happening and realized that there would be nowhere for the pilgrims to spend the night, they politely asked him to store the rice elsewhere; but the ruler was so cruel and proud that he would not listen and continued to fill as many houses as he pleased with rice. When, much to the annoyance of the Christians, he had filled all the houses with rice, a great miracle happened. St Thomas appeared to the King at night, with a pitchfork in his hand. He held the pitchfork to the throat of the King and said: 'Either you empty my houses or you will die a dreadful death.'

While he said this, he squeezed the King's neck between the prongs of the pitchfork until the King was in such pain that he thought he was dying. After threatening the King, St Thomas disappeared. Next morning the King had all the houses emptied of rice and recounted the vision he had had. This was regarded as a great miracle and the Christians were overjoyed and thanked St Thomas and blessed his name.

An amazing number of miracles happen in this place throughout the year, in particular the curing of maimed and deformed Christians.

Now we must turn to the death of St Thomas. He was in the wood outside the hermitage, praying to God, and all around him were peacocks, of which there are more in that part of the world than anywhere else. While St Thomas was praying, an idolater of the Gavi tribe, who was unaware of the saint's presence, aimed an arrow at a peacock. He thought he had hit the peacock but the arrow had in fact pierced St Thomas in the side. The wounded saint continued praying to his maker but eventually died of the injury. Before coming to that place he had converted a great many Nubians, of which conversions we will speak later.

When a baby is born in these parts it is rubbed all over with sesame oil once a week to make its skin darker than it was at birth, because the darker a person is, the more he is respected. Furthermore, these people paint their idols black and their devils as white as snow. They believe that their god and their saints are black and that their devils are white, which is why they paint them in this way.

When the men from this country go to war they take with them some ox hair because, as we have said, they regard the ox as sacred and they have great faith in it. A horseman will tie the hair to his animal's mane and an infantryman will attach it to his shield. Some of them tie it to their own hair. They believe that the hair of the ox will protect them from danger in war and from all other danger. Ox hair, then, is very expensive because anyone going to war without it will feel unsafe.

Now it is time to move on to the province of the Brahmins.

CLXXVIII   THE PROVINCE OF LAR, THE LAND OF THE BRAHMINS

Lar is a province to the west of the place where St Thomas is buried. All the Brahmins in the world originate from this area. The Brahmins are the best traders in the world and the most truthful. Nothing would make them lie or elaborate on the truth. They neither eat meat nor drink wine. They lead an honourable life and have sexual relations only with their wives. They would never take another man's property; nor would they kill any living thing or do anything that they regarded as sinful.

Brahmins can be recognized by a cotton thread which they wear round their shoulders and under their arms in such a way that it crosses their backs and their chests. They have an enormously rich king who likes to buy pearls and precious stones. He has come to an agreement with all the merchants in his country whereby they bring him as many pearls as possible from the kingdom of Maabar, which they call Chola, which is the richest and most beautiful province in the whole of India, and the one where the best pearls come from. He pays the merchants twice what they pay for the pearls. So the Brahmins go to Maabar and buy the best pearls they can find for their King. They do not lie about the price they have paid and the King gives them double. This practice is always honoured so the merchants bring huge quantities of large and beautiful pearls.

Brahmins are idolaters and pay considerable attention to omens and the behaviour of birds and animals. If they are carrying out some business transaction, the buyer will stand in the sun for a moment and, looking at his shadow, will ask: 'What day is it today?'

When he knows the day of the week, he has his shadow measured. If the shadow is the right length for the day he will settle the affair, otherwise he will wait for his shadow to reach the proper length before reaching an agreement. There is a correct length of shadow for every day of the week.

If, on the other hand, the business is being conducted in a house where a tarantula (of which there are many) suddenly appears, and if the buyer sees it appearing from an auspicious direction, he will immediately agree to buy. But if the animal appears from the wrong direction, the deal will be called off. In addition, when someone is heard sneezing, the man who hears him will not go on his way if he thinks the sneeze is a bad sign. If a swallow flies across a man's path and if it is thought to have come from the wrong direction, the man will turn back.

Brahmins live longer than any other people in the world, and this is because of their diet and their abstinence. Their teeth are in excellent condition because they eat a herb which helps digestion and which is very good for the health. They never practise blood-letting.

There are some monks known as Yogi who live even longer than anyone else. Some of them are 150 or even 200 years old, and they are still able to serve their idols as well as they did when they were young. They eat only rice and milk, although the Yogi who live so long also eat an amazing mixture of sulphur and quicksilver which they believe prolongs life, and it is true that they survive longer than other people. They take it twice a month so as to live long and have been

162

accustomed to it since early infancy. Undoubtedly the people who live longest are used to this drink.

In the kingdom of Lar there is another religious sect also known as the Yogi who lead an unbelievably harsh life. These men go about completely naked, without even a loincloth. They worship oxen and most of them tie a small bronze ox with a cord to the middle of their heads. In addition they dry ox dung which they make into a powder and rub with great veneration all over various parts of their body, treating it as Christians would holy water. They do not use bowls or plates but eat their food off large leaves of various types. The leaves must be large and dry, as green leaves are thought to have a soul and it would be a sin to pick them. For the same reason they eat no herbs or roots until they have died.

These people kill no animals, not even fleas, flies or worms, all of which are thought to have a soul. To kill is to sin. They sleep naked on the bare ground with no covers at all. It is amazing how they survive; indeed they live to a great age. They are also extremely abstemious in their eating habits and can fast for a whole year, drinking nothing but water.

There are large numbers of priests or monks who sleep in the monasteries as custodians of the idols. These priests are first tested in the following way. The young girls dedicated to the idols are summoned to the monastery and are made to touch and caress various parts of the custodians' bodies. If a custodian's member remains as it was before it was touched, he is thought to be honorable; but if, on the other hand, it becomes erect, then he is expelled from the monastery for being lecherous. These idolaters are cruel and perfidious people.

The reason they give for burning their dead is that if they did not burn them, the bodies would produce worms which would die when they had eaten the body, having nothing more to eat. To allow these worms to be produced only to die of starvation would be a grave sin because the worms themselves are thought to have souls.

So much for the ways of these idolaters. But we must not forget an astounding thing which happened in Ceylon.

CLXXIX   THE ISLAND OF CEYLON AGAIN

As it has been pointed out, Ceylon is a large island. On it there is a very high mountain, the sides of which are so steep that they can only be climbed in one way. Iron chains are fixed to the top of the mountain and hang down to help men climb up. It is thought that Adam, the first man, is buried up there. This is what the Saracens believe, although the idolaters say it is Sakyamuni Burkhan's tomb.

Sakyamuni was the first man in whose name an idol was made, because, according to legend, he was the holiest man who had ever existed and the first man to be venerated as a saint. He was the son of a rich and powerful king and he led such a good life that he turned away from the things of the world and refused to be king. When the father saw that his son was not interested in worldly things and did not want to be king, he was furious and offered him many bribes. He was even prepared to abdicate all power in his son's favour, leaving him to reign as he wanted. The son replied that he wanted nothing. When the father was finally convinced, he was ready to die of sorrow, which was not altogether surprising as he had only one son and no one else to succeed him. He decided to do one thing which he was sure would turn the son's mind towards worldly things and persuade him to accept the kingdom and the crown. He housed his son in a beautiful palace with 30,000 beautiful serving maids. No other man was allowed inside the palace. The young girls put him to bed, prepared his meals and always kept him company. They sang and danced for him and in accordance with the King's orders, did everything possible to please him. But it was impossible to seduce the young man. On the contrary, he seemed determined to become more chaste every day, and led a very austere life.

It should be mentioned that the young prince had been so carefully brought up that he had never been outside the palace, had never seen a dead body or met anyone who was not completely healthy. His father would not allow him to see an old or unhappy man. But one day, the young man went out riding and came across a dead body. He had never seen such a thing and was amazed. He asked his attendants what it was and they told him it was a body.

'What,' exclaimed the prince, 'do all men die?'

He was told that of course they did.

The young man said no more, but rode on deep in thought. After a little while he met a toothless old man who could no longer walk. The King's son asked who this was and why he was unable to walk. He was told that the man had lost his teeth because of old age and that old age prevented him from walking. The young man was deeply moved by the dead man and the old man, and he returned to his palace saying that he no longer wished to remain in so sad a world, but wanted to go and find his creator who would never die. So he left his father's palace and went off into the steep mountains where he lived an abstemious, frugal and chaste life. And had he been a Christian, he would have been one of our Lord Jesus Christ's most holy saints.

When the King's son died, the body was returned to his old father who, needless to say, was very sad when he saw that his son whom he loved more than himself was dead. His misery was indescribable. He had a statue made of his son. It was gold and covered in precious stones, and his subjects worshipped it like a god. It was said that the prince had died eighty-four deaths and that each time he had been reincarnated as a different animal — first an ox, then a horse, then a dog, until finally, the eighty-fourth time, he became a god. He is not only the greatest of all the idolaters' gods, but the first idol, from which came all the others. This all happened in Ceylon in India.

It must be added that pilgrims come from very far to visit the tomb of this saint, just as Christians go to Santiago de Compostela in Spain. So thus it is that the idolaters claim that the mountain tomb is that of the King's son and that the teeth, hair and bowl which have all been preserved belonged to Sakyamuni Burkhan, which means Holy Sakyamuni. But the Saracens believe that it is our forefather Adam's tomb and that the hair, the teeth and the bowl are his. But only God knows who is buried there. Marco Polo did not think that Adam could be buried there because the scriptures say that his sepulchre is in a different part of the world.

When the Great Khan heard that Adam was said to be buried in the mountains in Ceylon and that his hair, his teeth and his bowl had been preserved, he decided that these precious things should belong to him and in the year 1284 he sent an embassy to Ceylon.

The Great Khan's envoys set out with a large suite and travelled across land and sea until they finally reached Ceylon. They went to the King and managed to persuade him to give them the two large, long molar teeth, the hair and the bowl. The bowl was very beautiful, made of green porphyry. The messengers then returned to the Great Khan and when they were near Khan-balik, where he lived, they sent word that they were bringing the things he had asked for. Kublai Khan immediately ordered all his people – priests and others – to form a procession and meet the supposed relics of our forefather Adam. The whole of Khan-balik turned out to welcome the relics, which the priests took into their care with much joy and veneration, and there were great celebrations. The priests found in their scriptures that the green porphyry bowl had a magic property. If food for one man were put into it, it would feed five. The Great Khan put this to the test and it was proved to be true.

So this is how these relics came into the hands of the Great Khan, and the cost to him in treasure was by no means insignificant.

Having given a true and orderly account of these events, let us move on to Kayal.

CLXXX   THE CITY OF KAYAL

Kayal is a large and important city ruled over by Ashar, the eldest of the five royal brothers. All the ships from the west – from Hormuz, Kais, Aden and other parts of Arabia – put in here laden with goods and horses. It is a great trading centre for merchants everywhere. The King is extremely rich and is magnificently adorned with many precious jewels. He rules with great justice, especially with regard to foreign merchants and their affairs. He protects them and treats them very fairly, so the merchants are more than willing to trade there; in addition they make huge profits in the city. The King has more than 300 wives. The more wives a man has, the more he is esteemed.

When a quarrel breaks out between any of the five brothers and it looks as though they are going to fight, their mother intervenes to prevent war and if they pay no attention to her prayers, she takes a knife and exclaims: 'If you do not stop fighting and make peace, I will kill myself, but first I will cut off my breasts which have suckled you.'

When the sons hear their mother's impassioned plea, and also realize that peace is better for them, they settle their disagreement. This has happened several times but it is obvious that when the mother dies, they will fight among themselves and destroy each other.

CLXXXI   THE KINGDOM OF QUILON

Quilon is a kingdom which lies about 500 miles to the south-west of Maabar. The people are mostly idolaters, but there are some Christians and some Jews. Their King pays tribute to no one and they have their own language. Quilon brazil, an excellent wood, grows here. Pepper trees are cultivated and vast amounts of pepper are harvested in May, June and July. Also, much indigo is extracted from a certain plant. The plant is cut off from its roots and put in buckets of water where it is left to rot. The water is then left to evaporate in the sun, which is extremely hot in these parts, and the indigo as we know it then appears, in small crystals. The sun here is so hot that it is almost unbearable. If an egg is hung over the edge of a boat into a river, it will be very quickly cooked.

Merchants reach here from Manzi, Arabia and the East and a great deal of trade takes place. The ships bring in foreign goods and sail out again laden with other products. Animals unlike those in any other part of the world are found here. There are black lions and many different kinds of parrots: some as white as snow with red beaks and claws; others are red and blue and very lovely. There are also some tiny and very graceful ones. There are peacocks which are much larger and more beautiful than our own. In fact everything here is different – more beautiful and larger. Because of the great heat the fruit, animals and birds are all unlike our own. There is no corn – only rice. Wine is made from dates and it is a much more highly-intoxicating drink than grape wine.

There is an abundance of everything and nothing is expensive. There are many clever astrologers and good physicians. The people are dark-skinned and neither men nor women wear anything other than loincloths made of the finest materials.

No form of love or carnal act is regarded as sinful. First cousins may marry and a man may marry his father's or his brother's widow. These customs are usual throughout India.

Let us now move on to Comorin.

CLXXXII COMORIN

Comorin is an area in India where the Pole Star, not visible since Java, can just be seen. It is visible from thirty miles out to sea. The area is not very civilized, in fact it is fairly wild. It is full of strange animals and many monkeys. Some of the monkeys look just like men. The leopards are unlike anything we know, and there are also large numbers of lions, lynxes and other big cats.

There is nothing else of interest here so we will now move on to the kingdom of Ely.

CLXXXIII THE KINGDOM OF ELY

Ely is a western kingdom about 300 miles from Comorin. There is a king and the people are idolaters with their own language. These parts are beginning to be more civilized. There are no ports in the province of Ely, but there is one vast navigable river with a fine estuary. Large quantities of pepper, ginger and other spices grow here. The King is very rich, but he has no army. The country has natural defences, however, and no unfriendly forces could invade it. So the King is afraid of no one.

If a ship comes close to the estuary by accident, it is captured and all its cargo confiscated by the people, who say: 'You were going one way, but God sent you here so that we could take all your possessions.'

Everything is taken away from the ship and people see no wrong in what they are doing. The same thing happens all over India. If a ship caught up in bad weather puts in at a port for which it was not heading, the natives take everything, always repeating: 'You wanted to go elsewhere, but good fortune has sent you here so we may have your things.'

Ships from Manzi come to these parts in summer; they take from three to eight days to load and then leave immediately because there is no port and because it is dangerous to stay. There are no ports at all, only sands and beaches. The Manzi ships are not afraid to drop anchor near the coast because they are built of such strong and heavy wood that they can withstand any storm.

There are lions and other wild beasts here, and plenty of game.

From Ely we will go on to the kingdom of Malabar.

CLXXXIV   THE KINGDOM OF MALABAR

Malabar is a huge western kingdom with a king and a language of its own. The people are idolaters and they pay tribute to no one. From here the Pole Star is more easily visible. It looks as though it is suspended about two cubits above the water.

Every year more than 100 pirate ships leave Malabar and the neighbouring province of Gujarat to rob the merchant ships. The pirates are real highwaymen of the seas. They take their women and little children with them and are a great danger to merchants throughout the summer. These unscrupulous pirates sail this way and that, looking for trading vessels. Twenty pirate ships will set sail with five miles between each of them, thus managing to dominate 100 miles of sea. As soon as one of them sights a cargo ship, the others are alerted by means of rockets and lights, so the cargo ship has no chance of getting past without falling into the hands of the pirates. But the merchants have learnt the pirates' ways, and they put to sea well armed and are not afraid when they come across the pirates. But nevertheless quite a few trading ships are still captured by the pirates. The pirates take the cargo but leave the merchants unharmed, saying to them: 'Go away and fetch more riches for us.'

Pepper, ginger and spices grow abundantly in Malabar. There are coconuts and large quantities of cinnamon. The very fine cloth known as buckram is woven in large amounts. It is the most delicate and beautiful cloth imaginable. There are other valuable goods too.

Foreign merchant ships ballasted with brass come laden with cloth of gold, silk, sendal, sandalwood, silver, cloves, spikenard and other spices. Ships come from everywhere, particularly from the great province of Manzi, and goods from Malabar are then exported around the world. Merchandise taken to Aden is carried on to Alexandria.

But enough of Malabar; let us move on to Gujarat. It would take too long to name all the different cities in turn. Each kingdom has many towns and villages.

CLXXXV   THE KINGDOM OF GUJARAT

Gujarat is also a large kingdom; the people are idolatrous, speak their own language and have a king. They pay tribute to no one. The kingdom lies to the west and the Pole Star is even more easily visible from here; it seems to be a good six cubits above the water.

This kingdom is also infested with the worst pirates in the world. They are so cruel that they force the merchants they capture to drink a mixture of tamarind and sea water until they are violently sick. The pirates examine the vomit to see if they can find any pearls or precious stones, as they know that when the merchants are captured they swallow the jewels so as not to be found with them.

There are vast amounts of pepper, ginger and indigo in Gujarat. A lot of cotton is collected from the cotton trees which grow six paces tall here, although they have to be twenty years old to reach that height. But when they are that old, the cotton is not so good for spinning and is used instead for padding and quilting. After the trees are twelve years old the quality of the cotton becomes less good.

The kingdom is rich in all kinds of leather; there are buffalo hides, deerskins, wild ox hides, unicorn hides, as well as the skins of various other animals. So much leather is made that whole ships are laden with it every year and it is taken to Arabia and many other places. Wonderful red and blue leather mats are made, all embroidered most finely in gold and silver thread with pictures of birds and animals. These mats are really beautiful and are used to sleep on by the Saracens. They are, in fact, very comfortable to sleep on. Beautiful cushions costing six silver marks are also embroidered with gold thread. The mats cost ten silver marks. The most delicate and precious leather work in the whole world is found here.

Now that everything has been said about Gujarat, we will move on to the kingdom of Thana.

CLXXXVI   THE KINGDOM OF THANA

Thana is a large and beautiful kingdom to the west. There is a king who pays tribute to no one; the people are idolaters and have a language of their own. There is less pepper and there are fewer spices than in the other kingdoms, but there is incense – not white, but brownish in colour.

A great deal of trade is carried on here and merchant vessels arrive in large numbers. Beautiful, strong leather worked in different ways is exported, as are spices, buckram and cotton. Traders arrive with cargoes of gold, silver, copper and other things, which they exchange for anything they can sell profitably elsewhere.

It is iniquitous that the King of Thana has come to an agreement with the pirates who put to sea robbing and plundering any cargo ship they find. The privateers must give the King all the horses they capture – and there are a lot of horses. The great horse trade with India has already been mentioned. Very few ships reach these shores without some horses. So the King has agreed that the pirates may keep all the gold, silver and precious stones, provided they hand over the horses. This is a disgraceful arrangement unworthy of a king.

From Thana we will go on to Cambay.

CLXXXVII   THE KINGDOM OF CAMBAY

Cambay is a western kingdom. It has a king and its own language. The King pays tribute to no one and the people are idolaters. The Pole Star is more clearly visible from here, for the further west a traveller moves, the easier it is to see.

A great deal of trade is carried on in this province. There is plentiful and excellent indigo. There are also large quantities of buckram and cotton which are exported to other kingdoms, and there is a busy trade in decorated leather. In fact the leather is more finely worked here than in any other country. There are many other goods which it would take too long to list. Trading ships arrive laden with merchandise, especially gold, silver and brass. The merchants bring the produce from their own countries and take away whatever they think will be most profitable. Here there are no pirates. The people are honest and live by trading and craft.

There being no more to say, we will move on to Somnath.

CLXXXVIII   SOMNATH

Somnath is a large western kingdom. The people are idolaters with a language of their own. They pay tribute to no one. There are no pirates and the natives live by working and trading like honest people. It is a very busy trading centre. Merchants arrive with ships laden with various goods and buy the local products. The inhabitants practise a harsh and cruel idolatry.

Now for Kech-Makran.

CLXXXIX   KECH-MAKRAN

Kech-Makran has its own king and its own language. There are idolaters but the majority of the people are Saracens. There is a great deal of rice and corn. The inhabitants eat rice, meat and milk. A great many merchants come here, either by land or sea, bringing a rich variety of goods, and buying the native produce. There is nothing much else to be said about Kech-Makran except that it is the extreme north-western province of India. All the kingdoms between Maabar and here are part of Greater India – the best part of the Indies. Only the coastal provinces and cities of Greater India have been mentioned as it would take far too long to describe the interior.

So let us now leave these provinces and discuss some of the Indian islands, beginning with the two known as the Male Island and the Female Island.

VIII

The Arabian Sea

CXC THE MALE ISLAND AND THE FEMALE ISLAND

The Male Island is a good 500 miles out to sea, to the south, off the coast of Kech-Makran. The inhabitants of the island are baptized Christians who live by the laws of the Old Testament.

When a woman is pregnant, her husband will not touch her again until forty days after the baby is born. When these forty days have passed, he will go back to her. The wives and other women do not live on this island, however, but on another one called the Female Island. The men leave their own island for the women's island where they live peacefully for the three months of March, April and May. At the end of this time they return to their own island and during the next nine months attend to their affairs.

A large amount of beautiful amber of very fine quality is to be found on the Male Island. The inhabitants are excellent fishermen, they catch enough large and good fish in the sea to be able to dry a great many so that they have something to eat throughout the year. They can even sell come of them. The island is ruled by a bishop who is subordinate to the Archbishop of Socotra.

There is a distance of about 300 miles between the Male Island and the Female Island. The men say that they do not stay with their wives all the year round because there would not be enough to eat. On the Female Island, the mother provides for the children; but as soon as the boys are fourteen, they are sent to their fathers on the Male Island.

These then are the ways of the people living on these islands. During the three months that the men spend with their wives, they sow the crops which are later harvested by the women. The women only bring up their children and gather the natural fruits of the island. The men supply them with everything else that they need.

There is no more to be said about these islands. So we will go on to the island of Socotra.

171

CXCI THE ISLAND OF SOCOTRA

The large and rich island of Socotra lies about 500 miles to the south of the Male and Female Islands. A great deal of amber is to be found there, some of it in the bellies of whales and sperm whales, the two largest creatures in the sea.

The sea is full of tunny fish which are caught for one reason only; they are very fat and the fishermen cut them up into big pieces which they then put into large vats with brine. Then fifteen or sixteen whalers take a boat which they load with the pickled tunny and put to sea. Before they are far out, they drench a bundle of rags in the oily brine which they tie to the boat with a rope and throw into the sea. Then they hoist the sails and cruise up and down all day, leaving in their wake a greasy, visible trail. A whale can smell the tunny from quite a distance and, greedy for it, will follow the boat for as much as 100 miles. When the men see it nearing the boat, they throw out two or three pieces of fish. As soon as the whale eats the tunny it becomes drunk like a man who has had too much wine. Then some of the fishermen jump onto its back with barbed iron harpoons which cannot be removed once they have been driven into the whale. One of the whalers holds the harpoon on the whale's head while another drives it right in with a wooden mallet. Because the whale is drunk it is barely aware of the men on its back so they are able to do what they want. At the top end of the harpoon is tied a rope at least 300 paces long, and at intervals of fifty paces along the rope a plank and a barrel are attached. A flag is fixed to each barrel with a counterweight underneath to prevent it from overturning – and to keep the flag upright. The end of the long rope is tied to a little boat which carries several whalers.

When the whale realizes it has been wounded, it turns to escape. The men standing on the whale's back swim quickly to the little boat. Then one of the flagged barrels is thrown into the sea with fifty paces of rope. When the animal dives it drags the boat behind it. If it dives too deep another barrel is thrown into the sea, and then another, so that the boat cannot be pulled under. The whale exhausts itself heaving and struggling, and because it is already weakened by the wound it soon dies. The men in the boat have meanwhile been able to follow the whale, guided by the flags. When they are sure it is dead, the whalers haul it close to the boat and drag it back to their island or another one nearby where they sell it. They make the equivalent of about 1,000 *livres*. Ambergris is extracted from the belly of the whale and large amounts of oil from the head.

The island of Socotra also produces beautiful cottons and other merchandise. There is an especially good trade in excellent, large, salted fish. The people live on rice, meat and milk; they have no corn. They go about naked like the other idolatrous Indians.

A great many ships put in at the island where they sell a variety of goods. The

172

merchants then sail away, their ships laden with the product of Socotra, which is very profitable. All ships come here on their way to Aden.

The Archbishop mentioned earlier has nothing whatsoever to do with the Church of Rome, but is responsible to the Archbishop of Baghdad, Catholicus. Catholicus sent the Archbishop to this island. Like the Pope in Rome, he has nominated many archbishops and priests to be sent to different places. None of these archbishops and priests obeys the Church of Rome; they regard Catholicus of Baghdad as their leader. When the Archbishop of Socotra dies another will be sent there from Baghdad.

Many pirates put in at Socotra with the boats they have captured. They set up camps here and sell all their stolen goods. The Christians are delighted to buy the goods, which they know to be stolen from idolaters and Saracens.

The Christians on this island are the most accomplished magicians imaginable. The Archbishop does not like them to work spells but he cannot dissuade them as they say that they wish to continue the tradition of their ancestors. Confronted by such obstinacy the Archbishop can do nothing and he is obliged to tolerate the magicians.

These magicians do strange things; it could almost be said that they can do anything they want. If a ship is sailing with a good wind, they can conjure up a contrary wind to send it in the wrong direction. They can unleash any wind or bring about a dead calm. They whip up great storms and gales at sea; indeed their spells are too amazing to be recorded in this book because people would be horrified to read about them.

There is nothing else to say about this island, so we will go on to Madagascar.

CXCII   THE ISLAND OF MADAGASCAR

Madagascar is an island which lies about 1,000 miles to the south of Socotra. The people are Saracens who worship Mohammed. They are ruled by four sheiks, or ancients, who govern the whole island. It is without doubt one of the largest and most beautiful islands in the world. It has a perimeter of about 4,000 miles. The people live by trading and craft, and there are more elephants here than anywhere else. It is certainly true that nowhere are there more ivory tusks than here and in Zanzibar. Only camel meat is eaten. An unbelievable number of camels are killed for their meat, which is eaten every day all the year round because it is thought to be the best and most wholesome meat in the world.

Red sandalwood trees grow here which are as tall as the trees in our country. The value of these trees would be enormous in any other country, but here they grow in forests like our own wild forests.

Because of all the whales and sperm whales there is no shortage of ambergris. There are leopards, lynxes and huge lions, and other animals like deer, roebuck and so forth. In addition, the bird life is rich and varied. There are huge ostriches and many other amazing and unusual birds. The island is full of riches. Ships arrive with different types of cloth of gold, amongst other things, all of which they sell or exchange for the island produce. The merchants are delighted by the trade they do here.

Ships cannot sail south to other islands beyond Zanzibar and Madagascar because the currents are so strong that it would be too difficult to turn back. It takes twenty days to come here from Maabar, and three months to return. The powerful current runs south without ever changing direction.

According to some people, gryphons are to be found on these southern islands which the ships are unwilling to visit because of the currents. Apparently these birds can only be seen at certain times of the year, but they are not, as people at home suppose, half bird and half lion. Those who have seen them say they look exactly like exceptionally large eagles. According to what Marco Polo heard and saw for himself, gryphons are large enough and strong enough to carry off an elephant and drop it to the ground from such a height that it will break into pieces. When the elephant has landed, the gryphon swoops down and feeds on its flesh. Those who have seen these birds say that they have a wing span of thirty paces and feathers at least twelve paces long. The width of the feathers is proportionate to their length. This, then, is how the gryphon is described by people who have seen it.

The Great Khan sent envoys to learn about these islands; he also sent them to free one of his men who had been taken prisoner. The envoys, including the one who had been captured, were able to tell wonderful things about these strange islands. They brought home enormous tusks of wild boars. The Great Khan found that one of these tusks weighed fourteen pounds, so you might well wonder how big the wild boar itself must have been. People say that there are boars the size of buffaloes. There are also giraffes and wild donkeys on these islands. The animals and birds are so unlike ours as to amaze anyone who hears about them, let alone sees them.

But to return to the gryphon, the envoy who had been taken prisoner finally brought a gryphon's feather back to the Great Khan and Marco Polo himself neasured it. It was nine palms long and a wonder to behold. Kublai Khan was delighted with the present.

The natives of the island call the gryphons *rukhs*. They have no other name for them and have never heard the word 'gryphon'. But their enormous size makes it almost certain that they are indeed what we call gryphons.

Enough has been said about these islands so we will turn to Zanzibar.

The *rukh*, from Lane's *Arabian Nights*, after a Persian drawing

CXCIII THE ISLAND OF ZANZIBAR

Zanzibar is a very large and important island. It has a 2,000-mile coastline. All the people are idolaters, they have a king and a language of their own and pay tribute to no one. The men are large and fat, although they are not tall in proportion to their bulk. They are strong limbed and as hefty as giants. They are so strong that they can carry as many as four ordinary men. This is not altogether surprising because while they can carry as many as four men, they eat enough for five. They are quite black and go about completely naked but for a loincloth. Their hair is so curly that they can only comb it when it is wet. They have wide mouths and turned-up noses. Their eyes and lips are so protuberant that they are a horrible sight. Anyone meeting them in another country would mistake them for devils.

There are a great many elephants, lions unlike ours, and plenty of lynxes and leopards. Their animals are different to others; for instance their sheep and rams are all the same colour, with white bodies and black faces. There are no other kinds of sheep on the island. But there are a lot of beautiful giraffes whose bodies are short, low at the back, with small hind legs. Their front legs and necks are so long that their heads, which are small, are at least three paces off the ground. These animals are not in the least bit fierce; they are reddish brown with round white spots, and are a most agreeable sight.

There is one thing to add about elephants: when they wish to mate, the bull makes a hollow in the ground in which the female lies on her back like a woman because her genitalia are below her stomach. The bull elephant then mounts her in a human fashion.

175

The women on this island are very ugly. They have wide mouths, bulging eyes and big noses. Their breasts are four times the size of other women's breasts; so much so that they can drape them over their shoulders. They really are ugly.

The natives live on dates, rice, meat and milk. They have grape wine but they also make an excellent wine from rice sugar and spices. There is a great deal of trade on the island and ships arrive laden with every kind of cargo to be sold. The merchants take away other goods, in particular ivory from the elephant tusks. Because of the whales there is a lot of ambergris.

The men on the island are excellent fighters and very courageous in battle. They are not afraid of death. Because there are no horses they use camels and elephants in war. They build little turrets on the elephants' backs which they cover carefully with the skins of wild animals. Between sixteen and twenty men get into these turrets from which they fight with lances, swords and pikes. Very bloody battles are fought on elephants. The only arms are leather shields, lances and swords, but the men can be cruelly killed. When the elephants have to charge, they are given as much wine and other drink as they want which makes them more aggressive and therefore more courageous in battle.

Apart from the men, the animals and the produce of Zanzibar, there is nothing more to discuss so we shall move on to the great province of Abyssinia.

But there is one last thing to be said about India. The Indian provinces, kingdoms and larger islands have only been touched on here because no one could give a complete account of the whole of India. The more interesting islands, the best of India, have been discussed. There are a great many lesser islands. According to the maps and writings of expert sailors and navigators, there are 12,700 islands in the Indian Ocean. Some are inhabited, others not. But now we will leave Greater India, which stretches from Maabar to Kech-Makran – thirteen large kingdoms in all, of which ten have been discussed. The mainland of Lesser India comprises eight kingdoms from Chamba to Motupalli, but there are also very many islands.

Now we will turn to the province of Abyssinia in Middle India.

CXCIV   THE PROVINCE OF ABYSSINIA IN MIDDLE INDIA

Abyssinia is a vast province which constitutes Middle India. The chief King of the province is Christian. All the other kings, three of them Christian and three of them Saracen, are his vassals.

Christians in this province bear three marks on their faces. One from the forehead to the middle of the nose, and one on each cheek. These marks are made at baptism with hot irons. After the baptism with water, the marks are made on the face as a sign of nobility and a proof of baptism. There are also some Jews here who have only two marks, one on each cheek. The Saracens have one mark, running from the forehead to the middle of the nose.

The chief King lives in the central part of the province. The Saracens live on the Aden side.

St Thomas the Apostle preached in these parts. He had already been preaching in Nubia, which he had converted to Christianity, when he came to the province of Maabar where he was killed and buried as we have heard.

The people of Abyssinia are excellent warriors and there are many ranks of cavalrymen. There are a great many horses here, which is just as well since the people frequently have to fight the Sultan of Aden, the Nubians and various other people.

One day, in 1288, the sovereign King of Abyssinia – a Christian as has been said – announced that he wanted to make a pilgrimage to the sepulchre of our Lord Jesus Christ in Jerusalem. His barons pointed out that it would be very dangerous to go there and advised him to send a bishop or some other important priest instead. The King took his barons' advice and summoned a very holy bishop and told him he was to go and worship at the Holy Selpulchre. The bishop relied that as a dutiful subject, he would obey, so the King told him to get ready to depart as soon as possible.

The bishop prepared everything necessary, took leave of the King, and set out as an honourable pilgrim with a large following. He travelled over land and sea until he reached Jerusalem, where he immediately went to the Holy Sepulchre to worship as a true Christian should in such a noble place. He also made a magnificent offering on behalf of the King who had sent him. When he had accomplished everything that he had come to do, like the good and wise man that he was, he started on his return journey which took him to Aden, a place where Christians are greatly hated and totally unwelcome, being regarded as mortal enemies.

As soon as the Sultan of Aden heard that a Christian bishop sent by the King of Abyssinia had arrived, he sent for him and asked him if he was a Christian. The bishop replied that he was. The Sultan said that if the bishop refused to convert to Mohammedanism he would be disgraced. The bishop answered that he would rather be killed than convert.

The Sultan was very annoyed by the bishop's reply and ordered him to be circumcised. So, held down by many hands, the bishop was circumcised after the fashion of the Saracens. When he had been abused in this way the Sultan told him that he had wanted to shame him, out of contempt for the King of Abyssinia. Then he let him go. The outraged bishop was very unhappy but he comforted himself by saying that he had suffered for the Christian faith and that the good Lord would reward him in the afterlife.

177

As soon as the bishop felt better and was able to ride, he set out with his retinue and travelled over land and sea until he reached Abyssinia. He was welcomed there with great joy by the King who asked him about the Holy Sepulchre. The bishop gave a faithful account of his pilgrimage, to which the King listened with veneration. When he had described the Holy Sepulchre, he told how the Sultan of Aden had had him circumcised in order to humiliate him. The King was siezed with fury and sorrow when he heard how the bishop had been violated. He shouted aloud, for all to hear, that he would renounce his crown and his lands if he could not take his revenge and make the whole world speak of it.

The King immediately mustered a great number of cavalrymen and infantrymen; he also prepared a great many elephants with armed turrets on their backs, each one big enough for twenty men. As soon as the army was ready it set out and finally reached Aden. The Sultan of Aden, having heard of the arrival of the King of Abyssinia, called neighbouring Saracen kings with large armies to his aid, which meant that a multitude of mounted Saracens and infantrymen were ready behind the fortifications to defend their country against the enemy invasion. A bitter encounter ensued. The cruel and dreadful battle began, but the three Saracen kings were not able to withstand the King of Abyssinia's vast army. It is well known that Christians are better soldiers than Saracens. So the Saracens were forced to flee and the Christian King penetrated further into the kingdom of Aden. Vast numbers of Saracens had been killed in the battle.

As the King of Abyssinia advanced through Aden, he came across further strongholds, but the Saracens were unable to defend themselves and further massacres took place. When the Christian King had been in Aden for a month, destroying and plundering everything and killing huge numbers of Saracens, he announced that the insult to the bishop had been avenged and he would return to his own country. There was indeed little damage left for him to do without crossing passes which were too dangerous for a worthwhile offensive. So the King turned towards home and, with his army, marched without stopping until he reached Abyssinia.

Abyssinia is a province rich in all the necessities of life. The people live on rice, meat, milk and sesame. There are elephants which are not born there but are imported from the Indian islands. Giraffes, however, are indigenous, and there are lions, leopards, lynxes and a great many animals unfamiliar to us. There are wild donkeys and every kind of bird, including many unlike our own. The chickens are the most beautiful in the world, the ostriches are as big as donkeys, and there are other strange animals which it would take too long to describe. Game is plentiful. The parrots are superb and the baboons are very strange, they look almost human.

Let us now leave Abyssinia for Aden. But first it should be mentioned that the province has a great many cities and towns with merchants living by trade. Beautiful cotton is woven here as well as the most delicate, transparent buckram and bombasine. There are other things which are not pertinent here, so we will move on to Aden.

CXCV THE PROVINCE OF ADEN

As we have seen, Aden is ruled by a sultan. The people are all Saracens, worshippers of Mohammed and mortal enemies of Christians. There are a great many cities, but Aden is the port where the ships put in from the Indies, laden with merchandise. At Aden, cargoes are transferred into smaller boats capable of sailing up-river for seven days. After seven days the goods are loaded on to camels which carry them on for a further thirty days until they reach the Nile, down which they sail to Alexandria. This is how the Saracens in Alexandria are supplied with pepper, spices and other rare goods, which cannot reach them more safely or more quickly by any other route.

A great many ships leave Aden with cargoes destined for India. From here beautiful and valuable Arab horses are exported to the Indian islands, to the great profit of the merchants. A horse can be sold in India for more than 100 silver marks. Undoubtedly the Sultan of Aden makes a great deal of money from taxes levied on the ships, which are constantly sailing in and out of the port. Because of the taxes imposed on ships, the Sultan of Aden is one of the richest rulers in the world.

This Sultan did something which was very harmful to Christians. When the Sultan of Babylon attacked Acre and so many Christians were massacred, the Sultan of Aden took 30,000 men on horseback and 40,000 camels to his aid, so the Saracens had the advantage and the Christians suffered severely. The Sultan of Aden acted more because of his hatred of the Christians than because of his friendship with the Sultan of Babylon.

But let us now move on to discuss the great city of Shihr, which has its own ruler although he is a vassal of the Sultan of Aden.

CXCVI THE CITY OF SHIHR

Shihr is a huge city situated 400 miles to the north-west of the port of Aden. The city and its surrounding towns and villages have a just ruler. This ruler is himself, however, a subject of the Sultan of Aden. The people here are Saracens and worshippers of Mohammed.

The city has a fine port where many heavily-laden ships arrive from India.

Other ships sail to India from here, many of them carrying chargers and saddle horses which the traders sell at a great profit.

Much fine-quality white incense is produced in Shihr and there are a lot of dates, but no corn, only some rice and millet. Grain is imported from elsewhere. There are a great many fish, especially huge tunny fish. There are so many of these that a Venetian groat will buy two large ones. The natives live on rice, meat, milk and fish. There is no grape wine but a delicious and delicate wine made from rice, sugar and dates. It seems incredible but the sheep here have neither ears nor an earhole. They have horns where their ears should be. These animals are small and very pretty. The livestock here – sheep, oxen, camels and horses – habitually eat fish because the entire province is without vegetation. Shihr is the most barren country in the world. The fish which are fed to the animals are very small and large amounts of them are caught in March, April and May. The people dry them to feed the animals throughout the winter, although they can be eaten alive, straight from the sea.

There are also big fish which are used to make a kind of biscuit. The fish are chopped up and put into a sort of flour, then some liquid is poured into the mixture to bind it. It is then dried in the sun until a hard substance is formed. The people eat it like biscuits.

As for the incense which is so plentiful, the ruler buys it for ten gold bezants a barrel and re-sells it for forty bezants on behalf of the Sultan of Aden. The Sultan has all the incense in the province bought for ten bezants and sold for forty. It is clear that he makes a very large profit from this.

There being no more to say about Shihr, let us move on to Dhofar.

CXCVII   THE CITY OF DHOFAR

Dhofar is a large and beautiful city 500 miles to the north-west of Shihr. The inhabitants are Saracens who worship Mohammed. Its ruler is subject to the Sultan of Aden.

The city is on the coast and has a fine port where many ships come and go with vast quantities of merchandise. Traders make large profits from the beautiful Arab horses brought here. Other towns and villages are dependent on Dhofar. Excellent incense is also found here. It is produced from trees which are like small firs. Slits are cut in various parts of the tree, out of which the incense drips. In fact, rubbery lumps of incense sometimes form on their own because of the great heat.

The incense, like the Arab horses which are taken to India, yield a large profit.

We will now leave Dhofar for Kalhat.

Harvesting incense in Arabia

CXCVIII THE CITY OF KALHAT

Kalhat is a large town situated on the gulf of the same name. It is 600 miles to the north-west of Dhofar. It is an imposing sea town inhabited by Saracens who

181

worship Mohammed. It depends on Hormuz and whenever the Malik* of Hormuz is at war with a more powerful neighbour, he takes refuge in Kalhat because it is well built in an impregnable position where there is no danger of being taken by surprise. There is no grain but it is imported by boat from other countries. The city has an excellent port where many cargo ships from India put in. It is easy to sell the merchandise here because it is an important trading centre from where spices and other goods are taken into the interior. Good horses are exported from here to India at great profit to the traders because, as we have seen, an unbelievable number of fine horses are sent to India from these countries.

The city stands at the mouth of the Gulf of Kalhat, so that no ship may arrive or leave if the inhabitants do not want it to. The Malik of Hormuz is therefore in a strong bargaining position with regard to the Sultan of Kerman, to whom he is subject. Sometimes the Sultan demands taxes from the Malik or one of his brothers which they do not wish to pay. The Sultan then sends in an army. At this point the Malik and his men leave Hormuz and sail to Kalhat, where they prevent any ship from passing. This is very harmful to the Sultan who is then forced to make peace and give up his claim to the tax. The Malik of Hormuz has, in addition, a castle above the city which dominates the sea and the gulf.

The natives of Kalhat live on dates and salted fish which they have in abundance. But there are a great many rich gentlemen who eat more refined food.

Three hundred miles to the north-west of Kalhat lies Hormuz. Kais is 500 miles to the north-west, but we will leave Kais and describe Hormuz.

CXCIX   THE CITY OF HORMUZ

Hormuz is a large and imposing city built on the coast. It is ruled by a malik and has many other towns and villages dependent on it. The people are Saracens who worship Mohammed. It is so hot in this place that ventilators are made to direct the wind into the people's houses. Otherwise the heat would be unbearable.

The city has been discussed earlier, together with Kerman and Kais, so we will say no more about it now. The path we took inevitably led us back here, but now we will move on to Turkestan.

*A malik is a ruler owing allegiance to a sultan

A Persian ventilator

IX

Northern Regions and
Tartar Wars

CC TURKESTAN

In Turkestan there is a king called Kaidu, the nephew of the Great Khan. He is a great lord and a Tartar; his subjects, who are also Tartars, are brave warriors and expert fighters. But Kaidu and the Great Khan have never been friendly; indeed, they have always been at war.

This part of Turkestan is to the north-west of Hormuz. It lies beyond the river Gihon and to the north borders on the Great Khan's territory.

Kaidu has already fought Kublai Khan's army many times for various reasons. Kaidu continually laid claim to Tartar conquests, especially parts of Cathay and of Manzi. The Great Khan told him that if he had come to his court and listened to his advice whenever he had been summoned, he would have been given his share, for the Great Khan wished to be obeyed by Kaidu as he was by his sons and barons. But Kaidu mistrusted his uncle and said that while he was willing to obey him from a distance he did not want to go to the court because he was frightened of being assassinated.

This is what divided Kaidu and Kublai Khan and led to so many battles. The Great Khan had armed men permanently stationed round Kaidu's land in order to contain Kaidu and his men. But despite the vigilance of Kublai Khan's men it was impossible to prevent Kaidu from invading his uncle's land several times and attacking the Great Khan's forces. Kaidu could, if he tried, muster an army of 100,000 cavalrymen, all courageous and versed in the art of war. Furthermore, he had at his court several barons of royal lineage, all descendants of Genghis Khan – Genghis Khan being, of course, the founder of the empire, the man who first conquered that part of the world.

When Tartars go to war each one carries sixty arrows with him in battle, thirty small ones with which to wound the enemy and thirty large ones with wide heads which are aimed at the faces and arms of the opponents, causing heavy losses, and cut through the enemies' bowstrings. When all the arrows have been shot, swords and clubs are used.

Some of Kaidu's battles against Kublai Khan are worth mentioning. In 1266

Kaidu, with some of his cousins, including a certain Yesudar, mustered a huge army and attacked two of Kublai Khan's barons who were also Kaidu's cousins, but loyal to Kublai Khan. One of these barons was called Chibai, or Chiban. They were both the sons of Chaghatai, the Great Khan's full brother and a baptized Christian. The two cousins also had a large army, and the total number of cavalrymen engaged in the battle was 100,000. The fighting was bloody and casualties were heavy. Finally Kaidu won the day, massacring the enemy. But the two brothers who were Kaidu's cousins escaped unhurt on their swift horses.

Kaidu, proud of his victory, grew more vain and more arrogant. He returned to his own country and stayed there peacefully for two years, during which time the Great Khan left him alone. But after two years, Kaidu mobilized a really large army. He knew that the Great Khan's son, Numughan, and Prester John's grandson, George, were at Karakorum with a very large army of cavalry. When Kaidu had prepared his men, he left his kingdom and rode throughout the day without adventure worthy of note until he reached Karakorum where the two barons were camping with their army. Neither the Great Khan's son nor Prester John's grandson showed any concern when they heard that Kaidu had arrived with so large a force. They displayed courage and daring, carefully deploying their army of 60,000 cavalrymen and preparing to confront the enemy. They advanced until they were within ten miles of Kaidu's army, where they camped in an orderly fashion. Kaidu's army were camping on the same plain, and both sides rested before the battle. There was no reason to wait too long. By the third day the two armies were ready. There was no great difference in strength, there being about 60,000 cavalrymen on each side, all armed with arrows, bows, swords, clubs and shields. Both sides divided themselves into six ranks of 10,000 cavalrymen each, commanded by capable captains. As soon as they heard the sound of the drums, which is the signal to attack, the battle began. While awaiting the order to attack it is the custom of the Tartars to sing and play a stringed instrument, which is a delight to hear. The singing and playing continued for some time and then the roll of the drums was heard on both sides.

Immediately the peace was shattered and soldiers hurled themselves against each other. Bows were drawn, arrows rained down, and men and horses fell, mortally wounded. The shouting and the clamour were so loud that the god of thunder himself could not have been heard. As long as there were arrows left, the remaining soldiers continued to shoot them. The number of dead and wounded was unimaginable; it was an ill hour that saw the battle begin, for the losses were great on both sides. When there were no more arrows, the men returned their bows to their quivers, took up their swords and fought a cruel and bitter battle, hand to hand. Terrible blows were dealt and received, hands and arms flew through the air and men fell to the ground. The battle had hardly begun before the plain was covered with the dead and wounded. Kaidu's daring knew no bounds. Had he not been there, his men would have fled, but he fought with such courage and inspired them with such fervour that they resisted valiantly. On the other side, the Great Khan's son and Prester John's grandson fought with equal courage.

This was one of the most dreadful battles ever fought between Tartars. The clangor of swords and clubs was tremendous, each side determined to overcome the other and every man fighting with all his strength. But neither side could triumph. The battle raged until the evening with neither side able to take the other's camp. It was horrible to see how many had fallen on both sides. That battle was fought under inauspicious signs, many men were killed, wives widowed and children orphaned. And the mothers and sisters of the fallen wept with the widows.

Despite the numbers of dead, the battle was still being fought as the sun began to set. Eventually everyone returned to his own camp, utterly exhausted. Worn out by battle the men slept soundly through the night. Next morning when Kaidu heard that the Great Khan was planning to send another vast army to attack and overcome him, he decided that the moment had come to go home. So at break of day he mounted his horse and, with his men, set out on his return journey. When the Great Khan's son and Prester John's grandson realized that Kaidu and his men were leaving, they did not follow but left them to go in peace. Kaidu and his army rode without stopping until they reached Samarkand, his kingdom in Turkestan. Here Kaidu remained without going to war for some time.

CCI   THE GREAT KHAN SPEAKS ABOUT HIS NEPHEW

The Great Khan was bitter and angry with Kaidu for perpetually raiding his land and harming his people. He said that if Kaidu were not his nephew he would have had him cruelly put to death. But the Great Khan's family feeling was so strong that he refrained from destroying Kaidu, and so the king was spared.

Now we will turn to the wonderful story of Kaidu's daughter.

CCII   KING KAIDU'S DAUGHTER

King Kaidu had a daughter called Aiyaruk which means 'shining moon'. This girl was so strong that no young man or boy could beat her in a trial of strength. Her father, the King, wished to find her a husband, but Aiyaruk did not want to marry and said that she would only accept a husband who was a nobleman and stronger than she. Her father agreed to her conditions. It should be explained that when a Tartar prince or nobleman marries, he does not insist on his wife being noble too;

he will marry a beautiful and attractive woman even if she is not of his rank. No family takes the name of the woman, only of the man. No one is referred to as the son of Bertha or Maria, but as the son of Peter or Paul, so the social position of the mother is unimportant.

When the King's daughter received her father's permission to marry whom she chose, she was delighted and let it be known in many parts of the world that if there was a young nobleman who could overcome her by force, she would marry him. Young noblemen arrived from many different places ready to try their strength against Aiyaruk's. The contest took place in the following manner. The King, with a great suite of men and women, took his place in the largest room of the palace. Aiyaruk then arrived dressed in a richly ornamented leather tunic. Then came the suitor, also dressed in a leather tunic. It was agreed that if the young man managed to make Aiyaruk's shoulders touch the ground, he could marry her; if, however, she won, the young man would forfeit 100 horses. In this way she collected some 10,000 horses, which is hardly surprising as she was not only beautiful but magnificently built, as tall and strong as a giantess.

In 1280 the handsome and rich young son of a king came with a large suite and 1,000 magnificent horses to try his strength against the young princess. Kaidu was delighted because this was the husband he wanted for his daughter, and he told his daughter in secret to allow herself to be beaten. She replied that she would not dream of doing any such thing.

The King and Queen, with a gathering of men and women, assembled in the largest room of the palace. Then came the King's daughter and the King's son, both of them so beautiful and attractive that they were a joy to behold. The young man was strong and robust; no one could equal him. When the two stood in the middle of the crowded room, the rules of the contest were read out. If the young man won, the girl would have to marry him; if he lost he would forfeit the 1,000 horses he had brought with him. The two then confronted each other. Everyone who was watching hoped the young man would win and marry Aiyaruk. The King and Queen hoped so too. The two young people began to fight, vigorously grappling with each other and pulling each other this way and that until finally the King's daughter floored the young man. So the prince was beaten. He lost his 1,000 horses and hurried back, humiliated, to his own country. Not one of those who witnessed the combat was glad.

After that Aiyaruk was often taken into battle by her father, and no cavalryman was ever more courageous than she. She often threw herself into the mêlée, captured one of the enemy by force and took him back to her army. This happened many times.

Enough of Kaidu's daughter. Let us now turn to the battle between Kaidu and Arghun, the son of Abaka, the Lord of the Levant.

CCIII   ABAKA SENDS HIS SON ARGHUN TO WAR

Abaka, the Lord of the Levant, ruled over many provinces. Some of them were in the vicinity of the Solitary Tree, which bordered on Kaidu's territory. To defend himself from Kaidu and to protect his people from raids, Abaka sent his son Arghun with a large cavalry escort to the region of the Solitary Tree, as far as the Gihon river, to guard the lands and the castles in the neighbourhood.

King Kaidu raised a fairly large force of cavalry which he put under the command of his brother, Barak, a brave and clever man, and sent them to fight Arghun. Barak pledged that he would obey his orders and do everything in his power to destroy Arghun and his army. They rode without adventure until they finally reached the Gihon river, some ten miles from where Arghun had pitched his camp.

On learning that Barak was on his way, Arghun carefully began to prepare his men. Within three days the two armies were in the field, armed and ready. When the ranks were well deployed, the drums rolled and, like lightning, the two armies fell on each other. Arrows darkened the sky. When they had all been shot and many men and horses killed, the soldiers resorted to swords and clubs and the most dreadful and bloody fighting began. Hands and arms were chopped off, horses and people killed with the utmost brutality. It was not long before the ground was littered with the dead and wounded. Barak and his men could hold out no longer against the violence of Arghun's attack, so they turned and fled to the other side of the river. Arghun's army chased them for a while, killing as many of them as they could.

Arghun, then, was the undoubted victor. Now we will turn to how he was captured and how he came by his kingdom after the death of his father.

CCIV   ARGHUN SETS OUT TO CLAIM HIS KINGDOM

Not long after his victory over Barak, Arghun heard that his father, Abaka, had died. He was very distressed and prepared all his men for the journey back to his father's court. But this was a journey of forty days. Meanwhile one of Abaka's brothers, Ahmed Sultan, who had become a Saracen, heard of his brother's death – although it was not known how. Ahmed decided that as Arghun was a long way off, he would claim the kingdom. So he raised a very large army and marched on the court, which he captured, and proclaimed himself king.

Ahmed found an immeasurable quantity of riches at the court. With amazing generosity he dispensed largesse to all the barons and knights. They, seeing his generosity, accepted him as king. Everyone loved him and said that they wanted no other head of state. He ruled justly and granted favours to everyone. He did, however, commit one grave offence which did him no good. He took all his brother Abaka's wives and kept them for himself.

Not long after Ahmed had conquered the kingdom he heard that Arghun was arriving at the head of a large army. Undaunted and with great daring, Ahmed summoned his barons and advisers and within a week he had raised a large force of horsemen who wanted nothing more than to kill Arghun or to capture him and torture him.

CCV AHMED AND HIS ARMY AGAINST ARGHUN

When Ahmed Sultan had raised 60,000 cavalrymen, he set out to confront Arghun. He rode for ten days without stopping and then learnt that Arghun was advancing with an army equal to his own, so he pitched camp in a wide and beautiful plain, suitable for battle, and awaited the arrival of Arghun.

When the camp was settled he called his men round him and made the following speech: 'Gentlemen, you all know that I should be lord of all my brother Abaka's possessions since I had the same father and have always played my part in conquering the lands which are now part of our kingdom. It is true that Arghun is my brother's son and some people say that the kingdom is his by right. But with respect to those who hold this opinion, it is neither right nor just. Since Abaka ruled for so long, it is only fair that I should rule for a while after his death. While he was still living, I should have had half of the kingdom, but in my generosity I let him have it all. Let us now, I pray you, defend our right against Arghun so that the entire kingdom remains in our hands. I want the honour and fame for myself alone and I want you all to benefit from the profits of the kingdom. I will say no more because I know how wise you are and how much you love justice, and I have no doubt that you will gladly undertake what will be to your own advantage and glory.'

He said no more. The barons and knights who heard him replied with one voice that they would not fail him so long as he lived, that they would help him against the whole world but especially against Arghun. They assured him that they would capture his enemy and hand him over.

When Ahmed had addressed his people and heard their answer he longed for nothing more than the arrival of Arghun and his army. But let us, for the moment, return to Arghun and his men.

CCVI ARGHUN SUMMONS A COUNCIL OF BARONS

When Arghun heard that Ahmed was waiting for him in the plain with a large army he was very angry. But he told himself that it would be wrong to show his anger since it might be mistaken for fear and thus lower his men's morale. It was essential to show decisiveness and courage. Arghun summoned his barons and wisest advisers to his tent – they were camping in very beautiful surroundings – and said to them:

'Brothers and friends, you must know how dearly my father loved you. So long as he lived he regarded you as his brothers and sons. You remember how many times you have fought beside him in battle and how you helped him conquer his various lands. You know that I am the son of the man who loved you so much and that I, too, love you with all my heart. And because this is the absolute truth you must help me against the man who without reason or right is taking away our lands.

'Furthermore, you should realize that Ahmed does not respect our laws but has ignored them to become a Saracen and worshipper of Mohammed. Does it seem right to you that Saracens should rule Tartars? There is right on our side, so take heart and do everything possible to overcome the enemy. I beg you, one and all, to be courageous in battle and to do your very best so that we may win and keep our kingdom from the hands of the Saracens. Every one of you must have faith in victory because we are in the right and the enemy in the wrong. I will say no more, but only beseech you to be brave.'

With this he was silent and said no more.

CCVII   THE BARONS REPLY TO ARGHUN

When the barons and knights heard Arghun's wise words, they made up their minds to die or to win. They were all silently considering the matter when one of the senior barons stood up and said:

'My lord Arghun, we know you have spoken the truth. So here is the answer in the name of all the men who will follow you into battle: each of us will fight to the death, and we would all rather die than be beaten. But we are sure of victory because right is on our side and wrong on the side of the enemy. We advise and beg you to advance on the enemy at the earliest possible opportunity. I pray that my companions will set such an example that the whole world will speak of us hereafter.'

When the brave man had finished speaking, no one had anything to add. Everyone was in agreement and all they wanted was to attack the enemy. The next morning Arghun and his men set out, eager for the fight. They rode as far as the plain where the enemy was and pitched their tents in an orderly fashion about ten miles from Ahmed's. When they were ready, Arghun chose two loyal men and sent them as envoys to his uncle.

CCVIII   ARGHUN SENDS MESSENGERS TO AHMED

The two ambassadors, both of them old men, took leave of Arghun, mounted their horses and immediately left for Ahmed's camp. They dismounted in front of his pavilion, where he was in council with a large number of barons. Ahmed and the messengers knew each other well and they greeted each other politely. Ahmed welcomed them in a friendly fashion and asked them to sit down. After a short silence, one of the messengers stood up and said:

'My lord Ahmed, your nephew Arghun is amazed by what you are doing. You have usurped his kingdom and now you are marching against him to fight a deadly battle. This is not right, and you have not behaved as a good uncle towards your nephew. He has sent us to you to beg you, a relation and uncle, to change your mind so as to avoid war and death. Arghun would like to make you the most important baron in his land and to look on you as a father. This is your nephew's message.'

Then he said no more.

CCIX   AHMED'S REPLY

Ahmed Sultan listened to his nephew's message and then replied: 'Ambassadors, my nephew is speaking like a madman. The kingdom is mine, not his. I, like his father, fought to win it. So tell your lord that I will make him a great baron, the first in the land after myself, and I will give him lands and treat him as a son. If he does not accept this I will do everything in my power to put him to death. This is how I wish to deal with him; do not expect me to change my mind.'

When the ambassadors heard what Ahmed had to say, they replied: 'Have you nothing to add to what you have said?'

'Not so long as I live,' Ahmed answered.

The ambassadors wasted no more time, but immediately returned to Arghun's camp where they dismounted in front of his tent and reported everything his uncle had said. When Arghun heard what they had to say he was extremely angry. He said in a loud voice, for all to hear: 'I do not wish to live or rule until I have taken such vengeance on my uncle for his wickedness and wrongdoing that all the world will speak of it!'

Then he turned to his barons and knights and said: 'There is now no reason to hesitate. We must kill this traitor to my father as soon as possible. Tomorrow morning we will attack and do everything we can to destroy him.'

They spent the night preparing for the battle. Ahmed Sultan, who had learnt through his spies that Arghun was going into battle the next day, was also making ready and exhorting his men to be brave and strong.

191

CCX   THE BATTLE BETWEEN AHMED AND ARGHUN

The next day Arghun's men armed themselves and were skilfully deployed. Arghun calmly encouraged his soldiers to fight and when everything was ready he began to advance on the enemy.

Ahmed Sultan had done the same and without waiting marched to meet the enemy. Soon the two great armies were face to face, eager to fight, and immediately fell on each other. Arrows flew thickly and a fierce and cruel battle began. Cavalrymen fell, there were cries and screams from the mortally wounded. When all the arrows were spent, the men attacked each other furiously with swords and clubs. Great blows were dealt with sharpened swords; hands, arms and heads flew through the air, and the uproar was thunderous. On that day many brave men died and many women began a life of weeping and lamenting.

Arghun himself was extremely courageous, setting his men a fine example, but it was useless; luck was not with him and he was defeated. When his men could no longer withstand the enemy attack they turned and fled, chased by Ahmed and his soldiers, who slaughtered them. During the chase Arghun was taken prisoner. Once Arghun had been captured, Ahmed's men stopped chasing the enemy and returned joyfully and triumphantly to their camp. Ahmed put his nephew in chains and had him carefully guarded.

Ahmed was an uncontrollably lecherous man and he decided to return swiftly to court to take pleasure with the women who awaited him there. He left the command of the army in the hands of a Malik whom he instructed to guard Arghun as he would his own life and to bring the battleworn army slowly back to court. The Malik said he would do his best to carry out the orders properly, and Ahmed left with a great retinue for the court. Arghun stayed in chains, feeling so miserable that he wanted to die.

CCXI   THE BARONS AGREE TO FREE ARGHUN

An important, elderly Tartar baron, called Boga, felt overcome with pity for Arghun and thought that it was treacherous to keep him prisoner. He decided to do everything in his power to have him freed and immediately went to the other barons and told them what a bad thing they were doing keeping Arghun prisoner; they should free him and give him back his rightful kingdom. The other barons knew that Boga was one of the wisest men in the kingdom and they decided to do what he said. Among those who agreed Elchidai, Togan, Tegana, Togachar, Ulatai and Samagar and they went together to the tent where Arghun was held prisoner. Boga, who was the most important among them, said: 'Lord Arghun, we recognize clearly that we have done wrong in taking you prisoner and we have come to say that we would like to turn back to the path of right and justice. We want to free you and acknowledge you as our rightful king.'

CCXII   THE FREEING OF ARGHUN

At first, when Arghun heard what Boga had to say, he thought he was joking, so he replied sadly and angrily: 'Gentlemen, you are wrong to mock me. You should be satisfied with having taken me prisoner and chained me up when you ought to regard me as your lawful ruler. You know what harm you have done me. I beg you to go away and to stop making fun of me.'

'My lord,' replied Boga, 'please believe that we are serious and have no intention of mocking you. We will swear by our religion that we mean what we say.'

All the barons then swore allegiance to Arghun, who in turn promised not to take revenge on them but to treat them all well and love them as his father had done. When these promises had been made, Arghun was freed and proclaimed king. Arghun then ordered arrows to be shot at the tent of the Malik who was in command of the army and who had kept him in chains. This was immediately done and the Malik was killed. Arghun then took command of the army and all his orders were obeyed. The Malik who was killed by the arrows was called Alinak Sultan and was the first lord in the land after Ahmed.

CCXIII   ARGHUN TAKES BACK THE KINGDOM

Now that Arghun was in command he did not hesitate to march back to the court.

Ahmed was feasting and enjoying himself in his palace when a messenger arrived and said: 'My lord, I have news for you which I would rather not bring. The barons have freed Arghun and recognized him as their king. They have killed Alinak Sultan and are marching here at full speed to capture and kill you. Do what you think best for your own safety.'

When Ahmed had heard the messenger, whom he knew to be one of his most loyal men, he was horrified and so frightened that he did not know what to do or say. But, being a bold man, he made the messenger swear not to repeat a word of what he had said to a living soul. Then Ahmed immediately mounted his horse and, with his most loyal men, set out to seek refuge with the Sultan of Babylon. No one but Ahmed's most trusted friends knew where he had gone.

When he had ridden for six days, he reached a pass through which he was obliged to go. The captain defending the pass recognized Ahmed and realised that he was running away. Ahmed had only a small group of followers, so the captain was able to take him prisoner. Ahmed begged for mercy, promising great riches to his captor if he freed him. But the captain was loyal to Arghun, whom he loved, and he told Ahmed that there was no point in shouting, not all the money in the world would save him from being handed over to Arghun. Then, without delay, the captain gathered a strong escort and began to march back to the court, watching over Ahmed so closely that he had no chance of escaping. After riding for a long time they reached the court to find that Arghun had arrived only three days before and was very angry about Ahmed's flight.

CCXIV THE DEATH OF AHMED

When the captain led Ahmed into Arghun's presence, Arghun was overjoyed. He told his uncle that he was not a welcome guest and that he would be dealt with as reason dictated. He then ordered him to be taken out of his sight, and without seeking anyone's advice he commanded him to be killed and his body destroyed. The man who received the order took Ahmed away and no one has ever seen him again. He was killed and his body totally disposed of.

CCXV THE BARONS PAY HOMAGE TO ARGHUN

After the conflict between Arghun and his uncle, Ahmed, Arghun established himself in his kingdom. Barons came to pay homage from all the territories that had been ruled by his father, and everyone obeyed Arghun, as they were bound to do.

When Arghun was well settled, he sent his son, Ghazan, with a force of 30,000 cavalrymen to the region of the Solitary Tree, there to defend his land and protect his people.

So in 1286 Arghun regained his kingdom. Ahmed Sultan had only ruled for two years and Arghun ruled for a further six until he died of an illness which some people said was caused by poison.

CCXVI KAIKHATU USURPS THE KINGDOM

As soon as Arghun died, one of his full brothers, Kaikhatu, seized the kingdom. He was able to do this because Arghun's son, Ghazan, was a long way off in the region of the Solitary Tree. Ghazan soon learnt that his father was dead and that Kaikhatu had taken control of the kingdom. He was very upset by his father's death and very angry with his uncle for snatching the kingdom, but he did not immediately set out for the court for fear of invasion by the enemy. But he said that when the moment was right he would take vengeance as his father had on

Ahmed. What more is there to say? Kaikhatu remained in control of the kingdom and everyone respected his rule except the men who were with Ghazan. Kaikhatu also took Arghun's wife. Being a very lecherous man he delighted in the company of women.

Kaikhatu died after having reigned for two years. He was almost certainly poisoned.

CCXVII BAIDU SEIZES THE KINGDOM

When Kaikhatu died, his cousin Baidu, who was a Christian, seized the kingdom. This was in 1294. Baidu's rule was accepted by everyone except Ghazan and his army. In fact Ghazan was very angry when he heard of Kaikhatu's death because he could no longer take vengeance on him. But he swore that he would take revenge on Baidu and that all the world would hear of it. Ghazan decided he would wait no longer. He would march against Baidu and kill him. So, with his whole army, Ghazan set out to recapture his kingdom. Baidu soon learnt that he was coming, so he raised a large army and marched for ten days to meet him. He pitched his tents and awaited Ghazan's arrival, exhorting his men to be brave.

Within two days of Baidu setting up camp, Ghazan arrived with his army and on the same day a terrible and bloody battle began. It was impossible for Baidu to hold out against Ghazan's massive attack partly because, as soon as the battle began, many of his men went over to Ghazan's side. Baidu was defeated and killed.

Ghazan returned to court and took power. All the barons paid homage to him and obeyed him as their legitimate king. This, then, was how Ghazan's reign began in the year 1294.

Historical developments from Abaka to Ghazan have been explained, but it should be remembered that the founder of this family was Hulagu, who conquered Baghdad and who was the Great Kublai Khan's brother. Hulagu was Abaka's father, Abaka was the father of Arghun, and Arghun was the father of Ghazan, the present King.

Having dealt with the Levantine Tartars let us now return to Turkestan, although there is not much to say as we have already discussed it and King Kaidu. But we must not forget the people in the northern provinces.

CCXVIII KING KAUNCHI WHO RULES IN THE NORTH

In the north there is a Tartar king called Kaunchi. His subjects are very wild Tartars but they live by Tartar laws which the King upholds just as they were instituted by Genghis Khan and as they are followed by Tartars elsewhere.

These people have made themselves a god of felt, who they call Natigai. They have also made a wife for him and they claim that Natigai and his wife watch over the land and care for the livestock, the crops and so forth. The people adore these idols and if they happen to eat good food they always anoint the mouths of their gods with it. In every other way they live like animals.

The King, Kaunchi, is nobody's vassal, but he is descended from Genghis Khan, which means he is of royal lineage and a close relation of Kublai Khan. This king rules over neither towns nor villages. His people live in wide plains, valleys or mountains; they eat meat and drink milk and have no grain.

The population is large but they neither fight nor make war and so there is continual peace. There is an enormous amount of livestock – camels, horses, sheep and other animals. There are huge white bears more than twenty paces long, great black foxes and wild donkeys, as well as many sables whose fur is so rich and wonderful that one alone costs 1,000 bezants. Also there are a great many gerbils. These are eaten in the summer when they are fat. The woods and more remote parts of the countryside are rich with wildlife of every kind.

There is one part of the kingdom through which no horse can travel. It is full of lakes and springs and so much slush, mud and ice that it is impossible for a horse to tread there. It takes thirteen days to cross this inaccessible part of the country. At every post house there are forty huge dogs, almost the size of donkeys, which are used to carry messages from one place to another over a distance of about one day's journey. Obviously carts cannot be used in this countryside for their wheels would get bogged down in the mud. Instead, a kind of sledge without wheels is used to slide across the ice and the sludge. These sledges are like those that exist in our countries for carrying straw and hay in winter when it rains and there is a lot of mud. A bearskin is put on the sledge and the messenger sits on that. Six of the large dogs pull each sledge. The dogs are not driven by anyone but go straight from one post house to the next, though a man guides the dogs along the best paths. When the post house is reached, other dogs and sledges take over and the first group returns to where it came from. The dogs have to be changed every day.

The men who live in these valleys and mountains are great hunters. They catch many animals which are valuable for their fur, like sables, ermines, squirrels, black foxes and other precious animals from which a great profit is made. They catch them in traps from which the animals cannot escape. Because of the extreme cold the people here build underground houses where they live all year.

There is nothing more of importance to add so we will move on to a place where it is always dark.

CCXIX THE DARK PROVINCE

Far beyond Kaunchi's province, to the north, lies a province called 'Darkness' for the simple reason that it is always dark. The sun, the moon and the stars are never seen there. It is always dusk. There is no ruler of any kind and the people live like animals. They pay taxes to no one. Occasionally a few Tartars go there. They travel on mares which have only just foaled, leaving the foals in the light, on the borders of the province. They do this because the mares will always return to their young and will find their way where men would get lost. So the Tartars ride in, rob the people of whatever they can find, and then let their mares bear them quickly and safely out of the province.

The people in this dark country have an unbelievable quantity of very valuable furs. They have sables, ermines, squirrels, black foxes and other valuable skins. They are all trappers and they kill an amazing number of animals. The people come from the dark province and sell their furs to the inhabitants of the lighter, neighbouring provinces, making a great profit from this trade. They are tall, well-built people but their faces are pale and colourless. Greater Russia borders on part of this region.

Let us now move on to the province of Russia.

CCXX RUSSIA AND ITS PEOPLE

Russia is an unending province to the north. The people are Greek Orthodox Christians. There are numerous kings and the inhabitants have their own language. They are very simple people and both men and women are very beautiful with white skins and fair hair. The country is defended by impregnable passes. Tribute is paid to no overlord, but some people pay tax to a western Tartar king called Toktai. They in fact pay him very little. This is not a country for merchants, although it has many of the finest and most valuable furs in the world – sable, ermine, squirrel, fox. Large quantities of silver are also mined here.

There is no more to be said about this place so we will move on towards the Black Sea and talk of the provinces and people around it, beginning with Constantinople.

But first of all let us turn to a nothern province called Lac which borders on Russia. It is ruled by a king and the people are both Christians and Saracens. They have many precious furs which merchants take all over the world. They live by trade.

There being not much else to say about Lac, let us return for a moment to Russia. Russia is the coldest place in the whole world; it is almost impossible to bear. Nowhere else is it so cold and, without their stoves, the people could not survive. But there are plenty of stove-houses because the rich and charitable have them built at their own expense, rather as people build hospitals in our countries. The stove-houses are always open and anyone may go into them whenever they want. Sometimes it is so cold that if a man leaves his house or a stove-house to go about some business he will be nearly frozen to death if he does not quickly find another stove. The stoves are very powerful and built no more than sixty paces apart. But if a man leaves a stove before he is thoroughly warm, he will be frozen before reaching the next one. When he reaches it he will quickly warm up before going on his way. He will continue like this until he reaches his destination. It is essential to hurry from one stove to the next in order not to freeze. Often someone who does not have enough clothes or who has far to go, or an old or weak person, will fall frozen to the ground where they would die if they were not helped to a stove-house by a passer-by, undressed and warmed up.

The stove-houses are rooms built with large beams of timber, laid one on top of the other. They are so well built that there is not the smallest gap between the timbers. They are then covered with lime or some other substance to keep out the cold and the wind. There is a vent in the roof for the smoke. There are huge piles of wood in the stove-houses so people can throw armfuls of it onto the fire and make a great blaze. While the wood is burning and producing a lot of smoke the vent is opened, but when the fire gives off less smoke it is closed with a thick piece of felt, and the glowing embers keep the room very hot. In the wall near the stove is a window, also covered with a heavy piece of felt. This is opened when light is needed or when there is no wind. But if light is wanted and the wind is blowing, the vent in the roof is opened. The door is also covered with felt.

The rich and noble have their own stoves and all the houses are tightly sealed as a protection against the cold.

They make, in these parts, excellent wine from honey and panic grass, called mead. Great drinking parties are held, mostly by the rich and noble, at which the mead is drunk. Sometimes as many as thirty, forty, or even fifty people gather together – husbands, wives and children. Between them they elect a chief who decides on the drinking rules and punishes anyone who breaks them. Innkeepers supply the mead and some people spend all day at the inn drinking it.

In the evening the innkeeper works out how much money is owed. He divides the total and everyone pays his share for himself, his wife and his children. In order to attend these drinking parties people will borrow money from merchants from Khazaria or Sudak and will even pawn their children; in other words, they sell their children so that they can drink.

Women who attend these drinking parties all day do not leave the inn when they wish to urinate. Instead their maids very carefully and discreetly put a sponge underneath the woman. Meanwhile another maid pretends to have a conversation with her mistress who, remaining seated, relieves herself into the sponge, which the first maid then removes.

One day a man and his wife were returning home from one of these parties and the woman, wishing to urinate, squatted down by the roadside. The excessive cold, however, caused her pubic hair to freeze to the grass in which she was squatting. The poor woman, in great pain and unable to move, cried out for help. Her husband, who was very drunk, leant eagerly over her, hoping to melt the ice with his hot breath. But instead the humidity from his breath froze and stuck his beard to his wife's pubic hair so that he too was unable to move and had to stay bent over his wife. Someone else was needed to free them.

For currency these people use gold rods a palm long, each worth five *gros sous*. They use martens' heads for small change.

The province is so large that it stretches right to the Ocean, in which there are many islands where gerfalcons and peregrine falcons nest. These falcons are exported all over the world.

It is not a very long journey from Russia to Norway. If it were not so cold it would take very little time, but the cold makes travelling difficult.

But now let us turn to the Black Sea, which is familiar to many merchants and others, but many more people know nothing at all about it so it is worth discussing. Let us begin at the mouth of the Black Sea, that is on the Constantinople strait.

CCXXI   THE ENTRANCE TO THE BLACK SEA

At the entrance to the Black Sea stands a mountain called the Faro. But before continuing with this subject, let us not forget the story of the western Tartars and their rulers.

CCXXII   THE RULERS OF THE WESTERN TARTARS

Sain, a great and powerful king, was the first ruler of the western Tartars. He conquered Russia, Comania, Alania, Lac, Menjar, Circassia, Gothia and Khazaria. Before Sain conquered these provinces they were all subject to the Comanians, although they were not united. This is how the people came to be dispossessed of their lands and scattered in many parts of the world. The natives who were not driven out became Sain's slaves. Sain was succeeded by Batu, Barka, Mongu-temur and Tuda-mongu. Toktai, the present king, came after Tuda-mongu.

A great battle took place between Hulagu, Lord of the Levantine Tartars, and

Barka, King of the western Tartars. We will now turn to the reasons for this war and its outcome.

CCXXIII   THE WAR BETWEEN HULAGU AND BARKA

In the year of our Lord 1261 a great quarrel broke out between Hulagu and Barka. The dispute was over a boundary province between the two kingdoms. Both rulers wanted it and both claimed that they had an absolute right to it. They challenged each other to battle, each saying he claimed the province and daring the other to oppose him. When the challenge had been made, two enormous armies were mobilized and preparations made for war. Both sides were determined to win. Just six months after the declaration of war the two rulers had raised 300,000 cavalrymen each; they were well armed and supplied with everything they needed. When they were ready, Hulagu, the Lord of the Levant, began to march with his men. They rode for several days and eventually reached a wide plain between the Iron Gates and the Sarai Sea, on the borders of the two countries. Here, in an orderly fashion, the army pitched their camp. They had some very elaborate pavilions and tents. It was clearly the camp of a powerful man. Hulagu decided to wait there for Barka's arrival. Let us now turn to Barka and his army.

CCXXIV   BARKA MOVES TOWARDS HULAGU

Barka had mustered his army and made all his preparations, so when he knew that Hulagu had set out with his men, he decided that there was no reason for delay and immediately began his march. He rode until he reached the plain and carefully pitched his camp ten miles from Hulagu's army. His camp was quite as rich and fine as his enemy's. Never had finer pavilions been seen, with their cloth of gold and luxurious hangings. Barka's army of 350,000 men outnumbered Hulagu's.

When the tents were pitched the soldiers rested for three days and then Barka summoned them and said: 'Gentlemen, you know that since I came to the throne I have loved you like brothers and sons; furthermore, a great many of you have already fought beside me in important battles and the lands we have conquered were conquered with your help. You know that everything which is mine is yours too, and each one of you must do everything in his power to protect our honour. Until now we have all done so, but here is Hulagu, a really great and powerful prince, who wrongly wishes to fight us. We are right and they are wrong, so we can be certain of victory. Let each of you think how much stronger we are than the enemy; they have no more than 300,000 cavalrymen, whereas we have 350,000 excellent soldiers as courageous as Hulagu's men or more so. Clearly, we are going to win. And since we have come from so far for the sake of this battle, we shall fight in three days' time. I beg every one of you to be as strong and brave as possible; let us fight, if we can, in such a way that the whole world will hear of our strength. I have no more to say except to urge you all to be ready for battle at the appointed hour. Have courage.'

Let us now go back to Hulagu and his men and consider their behaviour when they learnt that Barka's army was close at hand.

CCXXV   HULAGU ADDRESSES HIS SOLDIERS

It is said that when Hulagu heard that Barka had arrived with so large an army, he summoned a council of his wisest men and said to them: 'Brothers and friends, throughout my life you have always helped and supported me. You have seen me fight many battles and we have never been beaten. Now we have come to fight Barka, our great enemy. I know only too well that he has as many men and even more than we have, but their quality is not so good. I tell you that even if their number were doubled, we would be able to defeat them and put them to rout. We know from our spies that they are planning to attack in three days' time – which suits us well – so I beg you all to be ready for that day and to be as courageous as you have always been. I wish to remind you of only one thing: it is better to die honourably on the battlefield than to be defeated and humiliated. So let every one of you see that our honour is preserved and our enemy defeated and killed.'

Hulagu said no more. While awaiting the day of battle, both leaders did their best to ensure that everything was ready.

CCXXVI   THE GREAT BATTLE BETWEEN HULAGU AND BARKA

On the day of the battle, Hulagu rose early and ordered his men to arm. He was a clever man and he arrayed his army skilfully and to the best of his ability. He lined up thirty battalions, each of 10,000 cavalrymen with an expert commander in charge. Having taken great care over every detail, he ordered his army to march on the enemy. The order was obeyed and the men began to advance at a slow and steady pace. When they were half way between the two camps, they stopped and waited for the enemy.

That morning Barka had also risen early and, good and wise leader that he was, had carefully marshalled his men. He lined up thirty-five battalions, also with 10,000 men in each and commanded by courageous captains. When everything was ready, Barka ordered the lines to advance until they were within half a mile of the enemy.

The two armies then moved closer until they were two crossbow-shots apart.

Here the soldiers were deployed ready for the battle. It was a wide and beautiful plain, with room for a great many men to fight, as indeed it had to be, for two such large armies had rarely, if ever, encountered each other before. There were, all together, 650,000 mounted men led by the most powerful leaders in the world, Hulagu and Barka, who were close relations and both descendants of Genghis Khan.

CCXXVII   MORE OF THE BATTLE BETWEEN HULAGU AND BARKA

The two great kings stood opposite each other with their armies deployed, eager for the roll of the drums which would signal the start of the battle. The drums were heard and without delay the men charged, drawing their bowstrings and hurling arrows at the enemy. So many arrows flew through the air that the sky was darkened. Men and horses fell dead to the ground. The men continued to shoot until they ran out of arrows and the ground was covered with the dead and the mortally wounded. When they had no more arrows they took out their swords and clubs and began to fight a harsh and cruel battle which was horrible to see. Hands and arms were amputated, men and horses collapsed; not for a long time had so many people been killed in one battle. The screams and the wailing were loud enough to drown the god of thunder himself and it is true to say that the soldiers had to walk on the dead bodies which covered the ground. The earth itself was red with blood. The harsh cries and the prayers of the dying were terrible to hear and the battlefield was a dreadful sight. The battle was begun under inauspicious signs for both sides. The losses were enormous and many women were widowed that day. Clearly a deadly hatred existed between the two sides.

King Hulagu, who was a great hero and powerful ruler, fought valiantly and proved himself worthy of his crown and kingdom. He was brave and ceaselessly encouraged his men. His behaviour so heartened his soldiers that each one wished to be a hero. The battle was undoubtedly a marvellous trial of arms which amazed friends and enemies alike. Hulagu seemed more like a thunderbolt than a man.

CCXXVIII   BARKA'S BEHAVIOUR

Barka, too, behaved with immense courage and he deserves great praise. But his bravery did him no good. Too many of his men were killed or wounded, and he was unable to resist the onslaught. The battle wore on until evening but in the end King Barka and his men were obliged to abandon the battlefield. When they were certain that they could hold out no longer, they turned and fled as fast as their horses could carry them. As soon as Hulagu realized they were in flight he chased them and killed many more. The slaughter was a dreadful sight to see. When Hulagu's men had chased the fleeing army for a while they returned to their tents. Here they laid down their arms, and bathed and bandaged their wounds. They were all so tired that they wanted nothing more than to sleep. So that night they rested their tired and aching limbs.

In the morning Hulagu ordered all the dead, of both sides, to be burnt. When this was done he returned to his own country with those of his men who had survived. They had won the day but they had suffered great losses, although more of the enemy had been killed.

This then was the story of the Lord of the Levantine Tartars' great victory. Let us now move on to discuss in detail another war with the western Tartars.

CCXXIX   TUDA-MONGU, LORD OF THE WESTERN TARTARS

When Mongu-temur, the Lord of the western Tartars, died his kingdom should have passed to Tulabugha, who was only very young. But Tuda-mongu, an extremely powerful man, murdered him with the help of another Tartar king called Noghai, and seized the kingdom. He ruled for some time and when he died the wise and courageous Toktai was elected to the throne.

However, the two sons of Tulabugha, the young murdered king, were by now old enough to fight. They were wise and brave and they mustered a large army with which to march on Toktai's court. When they arrived they presented themselves to him, and greeted him politely, kneeling motionless in front of him. Toktai welcomed them warmly and asked them to stand up. When he had a chance to speak the eldest son said: 'Dear lord, we will explain the reason for our visit as best we can. We are the sons of Tulabugha who was murdered by Tuda-mongu and Noghai. We can do nothing to punish Tuda-mongu because he is dead, but we ask for justice to be done to Noghai. We beg that you, being a fair ruler, avenge our father's death. Please summon Noghai to your presence and make him give a reason for the death of our father. This is why we have come to court and this is what we ask.'

The young man said no more.

CCXXX   TOKTAI SUMMONS NOGHAI

Toktai, listening to the young man, knew that he was telling the truth, and replied: 'Dear friend, I will gladly summon Noghai to court and treat him as he deserves.'

So Toktai sent messengers to Noghai asking him to come to court and justify himself in front of Tulabugha's sons. But Noghai made a joke of the affair and refused to obey the summons. The ambassadors returned to tell the King that nothing in the world would make Noghai come. When Toktai heard this, he was very angry and shouted, for all to hear: 'With God's help we will attack Noghai with our whole army and destroy him unless he comes here to explain himself to Tulabugha's sons.'

Then, without hesitation, he sent two more ambassadors to Noghai with another message.

CCXXXI   THE SECOND MISSION FROM TOKTAI TO NOGHAI

The two ambassadors hurried to Noghai's court. They presented themselves to him and greeted him politely. Then one of them spoke: 'Sir, Toktai says that unless you come to his court to explain yourself to Tulabugha's sons he will attack you with his entire army and do as much harm as he possibly can to you and to your kingdom.'

Noghai acted as though offended and said: 'Ambassadors, go back to your king and tell him from me that his threat of war means nothing to me. If he should attack me, I shall not wait for him to invade, but will meet him half way. This is my reply to your king.'

The ambassadors left without delay and delivered Noghai's message to their king. Toktai realized that war was inevitable and hastened to prepare his army. He sent messengers throughout his kingdom warning his people to get ready for war against Noghai. He then made all the preparations possible.

Meanwhile, Noghai knew without doubt that Toktai would attack, and himself began to make preparations, although on a less grand scale, for Toktai was stronger and more powerful.

CCXXXII   TOKTAI AGAINST NOGHAI

As soon as his army was ready, Toktai and his men marched. There were no fewer than 200,000 cavalrymen. They rode for days without adventure until they reached the beautiful wide plain of Nerghi where they pitched their camp and awaited Noghai. Tulabugha's two sons were with Toktai, eager to avenge their father.

As soon as Noghai learnt that Toktai's army was on the move, he began to march towards his enemy. He had no fewer than 150,000 able and valiant cavalrymen, who were better soldiers than Toktai's. Noghai reached the plain of Nerghi only two days after Toktai and camped there, ten miles from the enemy. The tents were pitched and among them were many pavilions of cloth of gold with the richest possible hangings. These were indeed the tents of a great king. But

Toktai's camp was, if anything, even more splendid. The pavilions and their sumptuous hangings were a wonderful sight.

When both armies had reached the plain they rested so as to be fresh for the battle.

CCXXXIII   TOKTAI ADDRESSES HIS SOLDIERS

Toktai summoned his men and said: 'Gentlemen, we have come this far to fight King Noghai and his army. We are right to do so. You know that the hatred and bitterness between him and me arose because Noghai refused to come to my court and explain himself to Tulabugha's sons. Since he has put himself in the wrong we are bound to win the battle and he will be destroyed and die. Each of you must be calm and endeavour to beat the enemy. I urge you to be brave and to do your utmost. The enemy must be defeated and killed.'

Toktai said no more.

Contemporary Asian warriors in combat, from a Persian miniature

Meanwhile, Noghai had also summoned his men, to whom he said: 'Friends and brothers, you know how many great battles and serious engagements we have won; we have fought better armies than Toktai's and we have always prevailed. You well know that you can win this battle. We have right on our side. The enemy are in the wrong. Toktai has no right to summon me to his presence to account for myself in front of other people. I beg each one of you to be resolute and to fight in such a way that the whole world will hear of us and generations to come will fear our name.'

Noghai had nothing more to add.

When the two leaders had addressed their men, they delayed no longer. The next morning the armies were carefully marshalled and armed. Toktai divided his army into twenty battalions, all of them led by competent captains. Noghai divided his men into fifteen battalions of 10,000 cavalrymen each. He put excellent captains in charge of them. When everything was ready the two armies began to march towards each other. When they were only a crossbow-shot apart, they halted and waited a while. After a few moments the roll of the drums was heard and, at great speed, the armies charged, shooting arrows from their bows. Men and horses could be seen falling dead or mortally wounded to the ground. Cries and shouts were heard from all sides. When all the arrows had been used, swords and clubs were drawn and the two sides fought each other bitterly, dealing the most dreadful blows. There was terrible confusion. Hands, heads, arms and bodies all flew through the air. The din was tremendous and dead and wounded fell to the ground in huge numbers. Undoubtedly more of Toktai's men fell than Noghai's because Noghai's men were the better soldiers. Tulabugha's sons proved very valiant and did everything in their power to avenge their father's death. But it was useless. They were unable to kill Noghai. What more can be said? So many hale and hearty men rose that morning only to be killed in battle, and so many wives were widowed by evening. The battle was horrible.

Toktai did everything possible to support his men and his honour, and he fought with great bravery. He deserved the whole world's admiration. He attacked as though he had no fear for his own life, striking the enemy to left and to right; he sowed disorder in their ranks and broke through their lines. His courage on that day put fear into friend and foe alike. He killed many of the enemy with his own hand. As for his men, they were so inspired by his example that they threw themselves on the enemy with great courage, in many cases only to be killed.

CCXXXIV   NOGHAI'S COURAGE

The same can be said of Noghai. No one was braver than he. He threw himself on the enemy like a lion hurling itself at wild beasts, felling and killing them. He charged into the thick of the battle, disrupting the enemy ranks. His men, seeing his example, fought with all their might, wreaking destruction among the enemy. In short, Toktai's army did all they could to preserve their honour but the enemy was too good for them and more experienced than they. They were so exhausted that they knew they would all die if they went on fighting. When they could hold out no longer, they fled as fast as they could, with Noghai and his men giving chase and killing as many of them as possible.

Noghai had won but there were more than 60,000 casualties, and Toktai and

Tulabugha's two sons managed to escape. Toktai, having been certain of victory and sure that his army was larger than Noghai's, had not mustered as many men for the battle as he could have. In addition, Noghai's men were better trained. Toktai had been obliged to surrender and accept defeat.

Later, however, Toktai gathered his whole army and once again marched on the enemy. This time Noghai was defeated and killed, as were four of his most courageous sons. So Tulabugha's death was at last avenged.

And so ends the tale of all the marvellous things seen and heard by Marco Polo while he served at the court of the Great Khan.

Medallions of Marco Polo and Kublai Khan

Index

Page numbers in italics refer to illustrations.